ISRAEL,

THE
CHURCH
& THE
JEWS

JAMES JACOB PRASCH

21ST CENTURY
PRESS
PUBLISHING WITH PURPOSE
WWW.21STCENTURYPRESS.COM

ISRAEL, THE CHURCH AND THE JEWS

First published in Great Britain in 2007 by
St Matthew Publishing Ltd
St Matthew Publishing Ltd, 24 Geldart St, Cambridge CB1 2LX UK
Email: PF.SMP@dial.pipex.com
Copyright © James Jacob Prasch 2008

Published in the United States by 21st Century Press

Requests for permissions should be addressed to:
21st Century Press
2131 W. Republic Rd.
PMB 41
Springfield, MO 65807

ISBN 978-0-9779535-6-1

Cover: Keith Locke
Book Design: Philip Foster

Visit our website at: www.21stcenturypress.com

21st Century Press
2131 W. Republic Rd., PMB 41
Springfield, MO 65807

21ST CENTURY PRESS
PUBLISHING WITH A PURPOSE
WWW.21STCENTURYPRESS.COM

Israel,
the Church
and the Jews

Taken from sermons of

James Jacob Prasch

Edited by Tania Fenwick

Foreword
by former Rabbi Michael Guberman

CONTENTS

FOREWORD

Michael Guberman (Orthodox Rabbi turned believer in Yeshua).

As an Ultra Orthodox rabbi who has come to a saving faith in Yeshua (Jesus), I am troubled by those in the extreme axis fringe of the contemporary Messianic Movement who are neo-Galatian legalists.

In direct defiance of Jesus in Matthew 23:8, some actually call themselves 'rabbi' when they are not rabbis and never have been. Few of these 'rabbis' know anything about rabbinics or the massive body of literature that constitutes modern rabbinic Judaism. Nor does it seem to bother them to identify with modern Judaism, which lies under the deception of Satan not recognizing its own Messiah.

Many of these so called 'messianic rabbis' cannot speak the Hebrew language, yet attempt to place others (including non-Jews) into bondage under, not only the Mosaic Law, but the rabbinic interpretations of it.

Indeed, in several articles such as 'The New Galatians,' 'Why I do not Accept the Jerusalem School of Synoptic Research,' and 'Satan's Seduction of the Hebrew Root Movement' Jacob Prasch (like Arnold Fruchtenbaum, Andrew Gould, and *Jews for Jesus* founder Moishe Rosen) warns of these fringe movements. These movements discredit and misrepresent the movement and its true beliefs; whereas the Word of God defines them.

Having studied for many years in the Ultra Orthodox Yeshiva tradition in Bnai Braq, Israel, I became a rabbi. It is therefore with considerable caution that I sanction or endorse anything broadly defined as 'Messianic.'
What sets Jacob Prasch apart, is that in warning of this hyper-messianic extremism on the one hand, (as he rightly warns of the

errors of supercessionist replacement theology on the other), Jacob actually does speak Hebrew, and his knowledge of Talmud, Midrash, Tannaim, Amorim, the Tractates, and Mishna are impressive, even to me as a rabbi. Jacob could successfully debate any rabbi I have known and his knowledge of Scripture would surpass any one of them, including my own teachers.

I first met Jacob before entering yeshiva when I was an Israeli soldier who was recovering from the injury of having had a hole blown through my hand during the first Lebanon war in the early 1980s. My own testimony is a long and complex one, and I thank the Lord, as a Jew and also as a rabbi, for the instrumental role Jacob Prasch played in my own coming to faith in my Messiah Jesus. I thank God for the many other Jews and non-Jews saved under his ministry.

I do not want to praise a mere man, but when fitting and appropriate I will praise God for a man that God uses. In an age of gimmicky Christian books based on paraphrased bibles and marketing psychology, I also thank the Lord for books that are solidly based on Scripture that the Lord uses to edify the true church and reach the lost.

I believe James Jacob Prasch to be such man, and this to be such a book.

After coming to a personal saving faith in the risen Messiah, I attended Bible College hoping to learn Christian theology from an Evangelical perspective. It was equally frustrating to discover the same lack of understanding of Scripture in the church as I had seen with the rabbis.

The rabbis dismiss and misunderstand the New Testament as 'gentile' (which it is not) and as a result they do not understand how the Old Testament points to Yeshua. They read Torah through the prism of ancient and medieval rabbinic tradition.

Likewise, so much of the church is influenced by Hellenistic perspectives of both the Old and New Testaments that they do not understand its true depth. The church also perceives the Scriptures through the lenses provided by the patristic traditions of the church fathers and the Reformers, which like the rabbinic literature, consists of things both true and false.

Like me, Jacob Prasch is one who has studied both Jewish and Christian approaches to holy writ. He recognizes the apologetic value in understanding the rabbinic literature, knowing both its errors and its truths, in evangelizing Jews.

I am a Messianic Jew, formally trained and qualified as a rabbi in the Ultra Orthodox tradition. My prayer as a Jew and as a Christian is that many Christians will read and be blessed by this book and that many Jews, both believers in Yeshua and those who are as yet non-believers, will read it also.

Michael Guberman

PROLOGUE

We live in a time of rapid social, cultural and political change. Unfortunately, too much of the Evangelical Church, too many Bible believing Christians, as well as too many Jews have forgotten that God does not change and that His Word endures forever.

Among Evangelicals, we have seen much confusion, disparity and contradictory opinion, written and preached concerning the prophetic purposes of God for Israel and the Jews relative to the Church. The Messianic Movement has become so fragmented that it can be no longer considered a movement in any monolithic sense but rather a series of multiple expressions of Jewish belief in Jesus with nothing more in common than a joint conviction that He is the Messiah.

From a Jewish Roman Catholic Cardinal in Paris, holding sacramentalist beliefs of pagan origin that are completely alien to the New Testament to the neo-Ebionites who believe Jesus is Messiah but not God, we have seen a doctrinal undermining of the historical and Biblical Messianic movement. This has included everything from Messianic Jewish involvement in the leadership of the lunatic fringe of the Charismatic movement and the hyper-Pentecostalism scene in the counterfeit revival of Pensacola, Florida and in the laughing and drunken phenomena, that saw Michael Evans, Dick Rubin and Michael Brown among the cheerleaders, to the hyper Messianic legalism of extremist groups virtually seeking to place non-Jewish believers under Mosaic and in same cases Rabbinic law. It has seen the publication of a paraphrased Bible by David Stern whose New Testament is so far from the original that it cannot be considered a translation in any normal sense of the term.

On the other extreme, we have seen a trend towards replacement theology and supersessionism pioneered by deceived Calvinists who deceive others such as Y2K guru, D James Kennedy and John Piper as well as their Charismatic equivalent in Rick Godwin and in the UK Restorationists such as Roger Forster.

Even at Dallas Seminary we see a trend away from the dispensational mainstay of that institution under the unfortunate leadership of Mark Bailey and the progressive dispensational influences of Daryl Boch. On top of this, there is an avalanche of hypocrisy that is difficult to define as anything other than anti-Semitism in the anti-Zionist biases of England's Stephen Sizer, a British Calvinist, who aligns himself with non-evangelicals in his cause to brand Israel as an apartheid state, while at the same time, remaining silent about the genocide extermination of Christians in Islamic countries. Similar hypocrisy has prevailed in the Presbyterian church of America, much of Methodism and in the World Council of Churches as Calvinism and liberal Protestantism alike gravitates further from the teaching of the Word of God concerning his ancient covenant people. Somehow, their solution to the widespread persecution of Christians in Muslim countries is to gang up on Israel, the one nation in the Middle East genuinely protecting the religious freedom and human rights of Arab Christians.

Finally, in reaction to Christian anti-Semitism, anti-Zionism and irrational biases, ignorance and prejudices that fuel it, multiple Christian Zionist organizations misrepresent themselves as Christian ministries to Israel, but do so in flagrant rejection of the teaching of Jesus and the Apostles that Jews be evangelized with the good news of their own Messiah Yeshua.

Not least of all, the cacophony of near madness has been exasperated and amplified by one form of bogus scholarship after another including the Jerusalem School of Synoptic Research and the pathetic idiocy of rabbis who are not rabbis, attempting to teach that which they do not know themselves in the name of 'Hebrew roots' (too ignorant to realize that in the Greek text of Romans 11, the term *reza* is the singular 'root" not 'roots"). Meanwhile the wild antics of

Joseph Good, Israel Hawks and other non-Jews dressing up like Orthodox Rabbis is too ridiculous a spectacle to deserve serious comment. The cultic beliefs of the 'Two House" theorists and the sacred name movement have managed to delude significant numbers of sincere people, much the same as the debunked folly of British Israelism deluded so many sincere Christians in decades past.

Tragically, this collection of pseudo-academics, bogus rabbis, hype artists and just plain religious kooks of almost every conceivable description has managed to obfuscate the genuine Messianic Jewish scholarship carried out by both Jewish and non-Jewish regenerate theologians dating back to John Lightfoot, followed by Alfred Edershein, R.N.Longenecker, to the more contemporary Arnold Fruchtenbaum. Indeed, the entire atmosphere of Messianic pandemonium has not only clouded our authentically Biblical understanding of the issues involved but has eclipsed a Scriptually based recognition of what is really happening as God, in His providence, works out His promised prophetic agenda for both Israel and the Church in these last days.

The world hears the rhetoric of Desmond Tutu, who wants to ordain lesbian priestesses into the Anglican community and rants against Israeli policies towards Muslims but remains all but silent in the face of the Islamic genocide of black African Christians in Sudan, Eritrea in the Horn of Africa, and the church hears the convoluted misrepresentation of the facts, of the Sabeel movement. We see the hyper Messianic lunacy of the fringe access of the Messianic movement and the replacement theology that stems from the abject doctrinal premise of reformed theology. Conversely, we witness the unbiblical antics of so much of mainstream Christian Zionism that withholds the gospel and in the name of some perverse definition of love for the Jews allows them to continue to eternal perdition without their messiah who died for their sin and arose from the dead to give them eternal life.

Lastly, unbelieving Jews generally and Israelis specifically look upon all of this chaos with an understandable sense of confusion. The multiple strata of complexity is largely not biblical in origin but rather man-made. It is the hope and indeed the prayer of the author that the compilation of teachings in the book will encourage Jew and Christian alike not to look at what Christians are saying, but at what the Jew, Jesus Christ has done and that instead of being preoccupied with what people have said and written they will instead focus on what the God of Israel, the one true God has said and ordained to be written in his eternal Word.

James Jacob Prasch

"I am a Jew, and nothing but a Jew. Yet as a Jew I am intrigued and indeed totally fascinated with the Jew, Jesus of Nazareth. I have absolutely no doubt whatsoever as to the historicity of Jesus and the New Testament!"

Albert Einstein, *The World As I See It*

Editor's note:

As these chapters have been taken from taped sermons, some themes and examples will repeat and overlap but all are crucial to each individual chapter.

Thank you to David, Jackie, Carol, Virginia, Chris, Oxana, Celia, Thea, Melissa and Brian for all your help with transcribing and proof reading.

American spelling has been retained throughout.

THE PEOPLE

Chapter 1

Who are the Jews?

There is a controversy in the church today regarding the true identity of the Jews. Who are the physical descendants of the twelve tribes of Israel, and where does the church fit in? Has God given up on Israel forever in favor of a Gentile church? Are the secular citizens of modern-day Israel God's chosen people? These are just some questions that come up frequently among Christians when talking about Israel.

Let's begin our study by looking at two passages of Scripture that speak of the time of the Gentiles. One is in Romans 11:25 where Paul dealt with it from a salvation aspect when he said, *"the time of the Gentiles will come to an end."* Jesus dealt with the national prophetic aspect when He said in Luke 21:24, *"Jerusalem will be trampled down by the feet of the Gentiles until the time of the Gentiles comes in."*

God's purposes for the Jews were put on the backburner partially and temporarily, although there have always been individual Jews who have believed. It didn't just end one day. God didn't say, "That's it - I'm going to the Gentiles." It began in Acts 10 when the first Gentiles came to believe in the house of Cornelius. Then there was the ministry of Paul and Barnabas in the 13th chapter of the book of Acts.

It was progressive. It wasn't one day, now the Jews then the Gentiles – there was a period of transition, as it is when the time of the

Gentiles comes to a close. There is a period of transition when God turns His grace from the Gentiles back to the Jews.

Isaiah prophesied the <u>Millennial</u> return of the Messiah. The early church was all pre-millennial and the New Testament prophesied the return of Christ in a time when God would again restore his grace to Israel.

God said to Israel, "I called you but you broke my covenant, so I sent you Jeremiah and you put him in prison. I sent you Isaiah but you sawed him in half; I sent you preachers of righteousness who brought revival; I sent you King Josiah, King Hezekiah; I sent you Ezra and Nehemiah but you have forgotten those revivals. You have broken my covenant and now you have rejected My Son, the Messiah. I am going to the Gentiles."

But Paul told us a time would come when the boot would go on the other foot. So we have the Gentiles and we have the Jews. But who are these Jews?

There are five promises to Abraham in Genesis 12 and Paul's description of what a true Jew is in Romans 2:29. Paul wrote using wordplay:

> *But he is a Jew that is one inwardly; and circumcision is of heart, in spirit, not in letter; of whom the praise is not from men, but from God.*

That word praise is the key; it is wordplay. The word "Jew" comes from the tribe of Judah – Yehudah. Its root meaning is "praiser of God." He is doing a word play here. He is saying his praise is not from men. It is a play on the word of what a "Jew" means: praisers of God from the tribe of Judah.

Gentiles Redefined "Jews"

The popular definition of what we call a "Jew" today largely emerged from the Babylonian captivity. Originally, they were called Israelites. Now it is interesting that the term "Jew" was first applied to all the descendants of Abraham, Isaac and Jacob, mainly by Gentiles and not by Jews themselves. This is even evident in the gospels. In Mark 15:32, Jesus is called "King of Israel" by the Jews, but in the same chapter in verse 2 He is called "King of the Jews" by the Romans. For the Jews, it was "Israelites." This idea of the popular term "Jew" was something that largely developed during and after the Babylonian captivity. We have the geographical definition of the inhabitants of the southern kingdom of Judea, according to 2 Kings 16. The only thing a "Jew" was, was being a descendant of the Judeans who returned from the Babylonian captivity. Originally, they were called "Israelites" which came from the Hebrews. An "Israelite" was a descendant of Jacob, wrestlers with God - this embodies the Jewish character. The Jewish people wrestle with God. Jacob wrestled with the Angel of the Lord. The Rabbis call this the "Metatron." We know it to be a Christophany - an Old Testament manifestation of Christ.

Now remember, Jacob wrestled all night with the Angel of the Lord until he saw his face. The night is the most common metaphor in biblical typology for the Great Tribulation. "Watchmen, watchmen, how far is the night?" Is He coming in the second watch of the night, or the third? He is coming life a thief in the night. "Work while you have the light; night will come when no man will work." Jacob wrestled till the end of the night. Unbelieving Israel goes through the entire tribulation and then it recognizes Jesus at the end of the tribulation. When you see Jacob in the Bible, it is ethno-specific to the Jews. They are wrestling with God. But before they became a nation, after the Exodus, they were called the "Hebrews."

The New Testament develops this further. In the New Testament, a Jew was a descendant of the Southern Israelites, of the Judeans who returned from the Babylonian captivity and came through the Hasmonean period after the Maccabees. John, however, put a particular slant on it. He used the term, the "Jews," in a unique way from the other gospels and it has led to much misunderstanding and even suggestions of Christian anti-Semitism inherent in John's gospel, but not when we understand the context. We have a translation problem from the Greek word *iudeos*. John mainly used the term "Jew," except in John 4 when he used the term "Jew" to mean "a member of the religious establishment dominated by the Sanhedrin who lived in and around Jerusalem." So when you see it saying "because of the Jews," or "any of the Jews who believed" (they were all Jewish), it is pointing to those who were party to the religious establishment, usually Pharisees, sometimes from other sects, but all of them under the dominion of the Sanhedrin. The epistles and Acts use the term "Jew" in a more general sense. One who is not a Gentile; one who is not a *gaer;* or one who is not a Samaritan.

Judaism

There are three main kinds of Judaism: Mosaic, Talmudic, and Israeli Juridical. Two are valid; one is not. The first, Mosaic Judaism, is what you read in the Pentateuch, the first five books of the Tanach, the Old Testament. That was a Judaism that has not existed since 70 AD. The prophet Daniel said the Messiah would come and die before the second temple would be destroyed. Whoever the Messiah was, He had to come and die before the second temple was destroyed, according to Sanhedrin 96b - the Mishnah. In fact, people call Isaiah 53 the forbidden chapter. The Talmud actually says there's a curse in reading Daniel 9. Why? The time of the Messiah's coming is foretold in it. The Messiah had to come and die. Many Jewish people will ask, "If Jesus was the Messiah, why are there still wars?" They don't understand. Daniel said when the Messiah comes and dies, wars are determined to the end with desolations. He brings worldwide peace at His second coming.

In Judaism, we have two pictures of the Messiah: HaMashiach ben-Yoseph and HaMashiach ben-David - the son of Joseph; the son of David. In His first coming, He comes in the character of Joseph, the one who was betrayed by his Jewish brothers into the hands of the Gentiles. His brothers didn't recognize Him at His first coming - they recognize Him at the second. And then they wept bitterly with Joseph and so they will do likewise with the son of Joseph. In His second coming, He's the son of David who will set up the Messianic kingdom. Yes, Jesus will bring peace, but His first coming was to bring salvation. And so we have Mosaic Judaism, the Judaism of Moses which has not existed since 70 AD.

Nobody picking up a Bible and reading it would arrive at some of the conclusions people would have you to believe. There are thousands of people who became born again just by reading the New Testament. Nobody just picking up a New Testament would ever become a Jehovah's Witness. Nobody just picking up a New Testament would ever become a Mormon and nobody just picking up a New Testament would ever become a Roman Catholic. Likewise, no Jew ever picking up the Torah would believe Talmudic Judaism is the Judaism of Moses and the prophets. They call Moses Moshe "Rabeinu." The word "rabbi" is not even found in the Tanach.

That is the second Judaism - it is Talmudic. And it was founded by Rabbi Yochanan Ben Zakai at the Council of Yavne in 90 AD. He was the classmate of St. Paul, from the school of Gamaliel. He was in the same group of rabbis that was trained by Gamaliel, the grandson of Rabbi Hillel, from the Pharisaic school of Hillel. It is a tale of two Rabbis. There were two classmates: Rabbi Saul of Tarsus and Rabbi Ben Zakai. (a comprehensive account of these two Rabbis is presented in "A Tale of Two Rabbis" in "Jesus in the Talmud" - Chapter four of this book)

When the temple was destroyed in 70 AD Rabbi Yochanan Ben Zakai was smuggled out of Jerusalem in a box, in a casket, and he convened a council where the Hebrew Canon was agreed upon - the Old Testament. He said, well instead of a temple, now we will have a synagogue; instead of a high priest, we will have a rabbi; and instead of the sacrifices we will have more Mitsvot - good works.

Every Jew will follow one of these two classmates, either Yochanan Ben ZaKai who had no assurance of salvation, or Rabbi Saul of Tarsus who had the assurance because Yeshua was his Messiah.

Talmudic Judaism is not the Judaism of Moses and the prophets. It is a hybrid - the same as nominal Christianity. It comes in various forms - Hassidic (Cabalistic believers in Jewish Mysticism), Orthodox, Conservative and then the Liberal Reformed who are basically humanists. The religion has more to do with culture and ethics than with real belief - That's Talmudic Judaism! Then there is a third kind of Judaism, also valid. It is what Paul and the Apostles observed. It's that Judaism which says Jesus it the Messiah who fulfilled the Torah - Messianic Judaism. However, within the Messianic movement today there is the good, the bad and the ugly, discussed in more detail in later chapters.

Let's talk about a definition of status - what a Jew is not. Paul wrote in Romans 2: 28-29:

> *For he is not a Jew who is one outwardly; neither is circumcision that which is outward in the flesh, but he is a Jew that is one inwardly; and circumcision is of the heart, in spirit, not in letter; of whom the praise is not from men, but from God.*

By the spirit, not by the letter!

Now, he is a Jew who is one inwardly. A misinterpretation of these two verses is one of the things that has bolstered the belief in Replacement Theology. "Oh, we are Jews inwardly, our heart is circumcised." However, if you were to receive a letter, you cannot take an excerpt from the letter and read it in isolation from everything else in the letter. Romans is a letter, and that interpretation is directly contrary to what you read further on in the letter. In chapter 11 alone, the writer of the letter, Paul, writing under the direct inspiration of the *Ruach Ha Kodesh*, the Holy Spirit, draws a distinction between the natural and the engrafted branches.

In Jeremiah 31:31 we read, "I will make", literally, "I will cut a new covenant with the house of Israel and the house of Judah, not like the one I made with their fathers." I will make a new covenant with whom? The church? Jesus never made a covenant with the church. He made a covenant with Israel and the Jews. If God is finished with the Jews, He's finished with this place. If He is finished with the Jews, He's finished with all of us. Fortunately, the validity of a covenant never depends on the faithfulness of man, but the faithfulness of God. God knew from the beginning that His people would be unfaithful. Anything I can say about the infidelity of Israel, I can say as much or more so about the infidelity of the backslidden church.

It is true that Gentiles, non-Jews who believe, replace Jews who don't. That is true. Believing Gentiles replace unbelieving Jews who are cut off from their own tree. **But it's not a new tree; it's the same tree.** You don't see the root, but if that root was dead, the tree would be dead. If God is finished with Israel, He is automatically finished with the church.

What about the ten lost tribes of the north? The Scriptures tell us what happened to them. The faithful people from the northern kingdom of Israel came south in the days of King Asa and kept their tribal identity. That is why the epistle of James is addressed to the "twelve tribes." Anna, in the nativity narrative in the book of Luke, was from the tribe of Asher. The Mishnah has all kinds of records of people's tribal identity all the way to the 3rd and 4th centuries. They were never lost according to Scripture. Others stayed and intermarried with the Assyrian invaders and became the Samaritans, and then others disappeared into the Assyrian empire and became the Jewish communities of central Asia or just assimilated.

Look at Romans 2:28-29:

> *He is not a Jew who is one outwardly, circumcision is that of the heart.*

Jeremiah 9:25-26 uses the term:

> *Those who are circumcised yet not yet circumcised.*

He says of them:

> *I will punish those who are circumcised yet uncircumcised, Egypt and Judah and Edom and the sons of Amon.*

Notice he puts Judah in there right with the Gentile nations. Why? If you behave like pagans, you're no better than they are. You've forsaken your Jewish heritage. The Jewish people who rejected their Messiah have forsaken their Jewish heritage. As Paul says, they can be grafted in again to their own tree. God can make Jews believe quite easily because He has already done something more difficult. He has made Eskimos believe in the Jewish God. He has made Venezuelans believe in the Jewish God. He has made Chinese people believe in the Jewish God. He has made Europeans believe in the Jewish God. If He can take all the nations in fulfillment of Isaiah 11:1 that the *goyim* will come to the root of Jesse; if He can make non-Jews believe in the God of this despised little nation, how much more easily can He make Jews believe in their own Messiah.

Circumcision is a metaphor for conversion. What is the status of non-Jews who are born again believers? We read about it in Isaiah 56:3 and in Ephesians 2:12. Isaiah tells us:

> *Let not the foreigner, the non-Jew who has joined himself to the Lord say, the Lord will surely separate me from his people.*

God will not separate you from the Jewish people if you have faith in the Jewish Messiah. Remember, Abraham is the father of all who believe; that is because he was a Jew who was converted from being a Gentile. Abraham ethnically was both a Jew and a Gentile. That is why he is the father of all who believe. That is why we see Gentiles in the genealogy of Jesus. He would be the Savior of all. Paul used a political term for citizenship in the Greek language in Ephesians 2:12-13:

> *Remember that at that time you were without Christ, alienated from the commonwealth of Israel and strangers of the covenants of promise, having no hope and without God in the world. But now in Christ Jesus you who then were far off came to be near by the blood of Christ.*

Gentiles are grafted in through faith in Jesus by adoption and patriarchal inclusion. In adoption, the father becomes legally the baby's father; the mother legally his mother. And of course with this in Scripture goes patriarchal inclusion. In 1 Corinthians 10, Paul writes to a mainly Gentile church:

> *Our fathers were all under the cloud and all passed through the sea.*

By faith in the seed of Abraham, Abraham becomes the father of all, irrespective of race.

Secondly, by conversion - a change of belief. There are two kinds of conversion. When a Buddhist gets saved, he stops being a Buddhist. When a Hindu gets saved, he stops being a Hindu. When a Jew gets saved, it's a different word for conversion – it's *teshuva*. He turns from sin toward God and his Jewish identity becomes complete. Only a Gentile can convert, a Jew completes. Jewish completion is *teshuva*. This is shown in the case of the adoption of a black African infant of pagan origin who gets adopted by a Christian Polish family. He becomes Polish by legal adoption, he learns how to speak Polish and he also converts to Christianity. After he grows up he marries a Polish girl and is also Polish through matrimony. He becomes a Pole by culture, but his skin is still black. So it is when a non-Jew becomes a believer in Jesus. Through a patriarchal inclusion he becomes, not a Jew, but a son, by adoption - by conversion - religious conversion. As well as by matrimony, because Christ is the bridegroom of the predominantly Gentile church. In 1 Corinthians 9 we read about acculturation when Gentiles take the Lord's supper they are celebrating the natural successor and meaning of the Pesach, the Passover, that is the status of a Gentile Christian.

Just think of this kid from Africa who's adopted by a European family out of poverty. For all intents and purposes, for any legal, matrimonial or cultural reasons he becomes as a Pole, but he still remains a black African; he keeps his own identity. Yet, he is just as good as any other Pole. He's loved as much as any other child. It takes no less love to adopt a child then it does to procreate one. He has the same legal rights; the same legal status.

Then there's the legal definition. The first is the Israeli law of return. The fathers of the Zionist movement argued about this - not for years but for decades. Finally Ben Gurion said, "let our enemies decide who is a Jew." So that's what they did. Because the Nazis said if you have one Jewish grandparent, you go to a concentration camp, the

Israeli government said if you have one Jewish grandparent you have the right to make *Aliya* and emigrate to Israel. That was the original law of return.

Second it was the Chalachic one, set up by Jewish religious law. According to Chalachic law it would be by matriarchal descent. If your mother was Jewish or if you underwent a *Chalachic* conversion to Judaism, in other words circumcision, then you would get patriarchal inclusion if your mother was Jewish.

The third was the Israeli Rabbinic definition of the status of a Jew that should be the same as the Chalachic, except the quagmire of Israeli politics complicates things. Of the approximately 55 nations of the world that are democracies, there's only one where a Jew does not have freedom of religion - that is Israel. That is the Israeli rabbinic definition of what is the status of a Jew. They say you must be in acceptance of the Shulchan Aruch, a codification of the *Mitsvot* by Rabbi Yosef Karo centuries ago and if you do not accept the *Shulchan Aruch*, you are not officially a Jew. This created a dilemma for the black African Jews, the *Falashe*, it created a dilemma for the Jews who came from India, and it creates a dilemma for any Jew who is not Orthodox. An anti-Zionist Rabbi has no problem being a rabbi but a reformed or liberal rabbi can't be licensed. Again, we talk about how people deny freedom of religion to Jews, I agree it's an historical tragedy, a disgrace, but Israel denies freedom of religion to Jews, especially to Messianic Jews.

That brings us to the Israeli Juridical position. Several years ago they decided that you are not a Jew if you had a conversion to another faith, especially if you had *mikve-brit*, if you were baptized. Even then it was a politically charged decision. Now when you look at those four legal definitions of what constitutes a Jew in terms of legal status you realize that there's no consensus. There is no legal consensus and no religious consensus. They make arbitrary decisions based on political expediency to define Jewish identity.

Scriptural Classifications

But what does Scripture say? The *Tanach*, the Old Testament, is mainly paternal, but has a maternal genealogy in Chronicles and then there's the story of Ruth. This is very important. Orthodox Rabbis will attempt to discredit the Messiah-ship of Jesus and the voracity of the New Testament on the basis of the genealogies. What they don't like to tell you is that the rabbinic literature itself (Sanhedrin 25C) tells us that Luke's genealogy is through Mary. "Oh but Jewish identity had to be through the father!" "You Rabbis say that it has to be through the mother." The Rabbis contradict themselves. But there is a precedent for matriarchal genealogies in Chronicles and in Ruth.

The New Testament is more generous. It could be either maternal or paternal. Paul circumcised Timothy. Remember, circumcision was not part of the Law of Moses originally; it was given way before that to Abraham. Circumcision, *brit-mila*, preceded the giving of the law on Mt Sinai.

If God wanted a great nation to be His messengers of salvation; if God was going to give His word and His salvation to a great nation, He could have chosen Babylon; He could have chosen Assyria. If He wanted people who were smart, He could have chosen the Greeks in the ancient world. If He wanted to choose clever business people, He could have chosen the Phoenicians. Remember even in the days of David and Solomon when Israel was at its peak, it was never a super power and Israel will never be a super power until the Millennial reign of Christ. It will never be a predominant world power until the Millennial reign of Christ. Why does God choose a little nation instead of a great one? The same reason He chooses us. Why is it easier for a poor person to get saved than a wealthy one? Why is it easier for an uneducated person to be saved than an educated one? So no man should boast. Less ground for pride, less grounds for "look at me!" So we'll know we're nothing other than the unmerited, undeserved beneficiaries of unmerited grace. That's why He chose me.

Don't misunderstand the nature of election. It is not for status. It's for service! Secondly, privilege comes with liability. Blessings always have a counterpart. Romans 1:16:

> *The gospel is the power of salvation to all who believe.*

To the Jew first, that is true, as are the consequences for rejecting it. It is available to the Jew first. That's right. To them belong the oracles of God. The New Testament says so. Salvation is available to them first and so are the results of rejecting that salvation. Why the Inquisition? Why the holocaust? Why the pogroms? Why anti-Semitism? Why even in their own land, the Jews have no peace? Read Leviticus 26, Deuteronomy 28, and not least of all read Deuteronomy 18:18,

> *I will raise up a prophet like Moses and if you don't pay attention to him, that's the Messiah, I will require of you.*

Yes, salvation is available to the Jew first, but so are the ramifications for rejecting it.

A believing Gentile is grafted in; an unbelieving Jew is cut off, from his own tree. What a tragedy!

Catholics and Reformed Protestants alike have made infant baptism the equivalent of circumcision. That was a national covenant - the state church. People thought they were in a relationship with God simply because they were born into a Jewish family and circumcised. This is directly contrary to what it was supposed to be – "it's not like the covenant made with your fathers".

The Transition

Jeremiah said that when the Messiah comes it wouldn't be like that. When John the Baptist came, using Jewish Midrash to explain it, he said God could raise Abraham's children out of the stones. Remember what Yeshua said on Palm Sunday, referring to the stones of the temple? If you don't accept me the stones will cry out. What He was saying in Jewish metaphor was that if you don't accept me and proclaim me as *Mashiach*, the Gentiles will - the stones will cry out. 1 Peter 2:5 states, "we are the stones of the temple."

So what makes this time different from the other times in history when believers thought it was the last days? This is not the first time that Middle East events have been at the center of the world's focus. I have no doubt that what is happening in the Middle East is of prophetic significance, but it's not the first time.

After all, the Plymouth Brethren thought that Napoleon was the antichrist. Why is this time different? Believers in England thought Mussolini was the antichrist. Believers in England thought that Napoleon was the antichrist. He invaded the Middle East. He tried to re-confederate the Roman Empire. He put the crown on his head. He made himself emperor. They thought that was him. In the first century, the Messianic Jews thought it was the end, when they escaped from Jerusalem under Simeon, the cousin of Jesus. They thought that was going to be the rapture. When Mount Vesuvius blew up, it put volcanic ash into the atmosphere. The sun and moon didn't give its light. The temple was destroyed. They thought Nero was an antichrist figure. The Roman Emperors were numbering people, counting people's heads to gain financial control. They thought that was the end. Why is this time different? There has been no less than seven major times and at least a dozen less notable times when Christians thought it was the last days.

What makes this time different than the other times in history when true saved born again Christians thought it was the last days? What was missing then that's not missing now? My Israeli son Eli was missing a hundred years ago, my friend Kev was missing five hundred years ago; my brother Larry was missing 1000 years ago; my brother David was missing 1500 years ago, but they're not missing now.

The time of the Gentiles is coming to a close. Some years ago, the American college of Rabbis issued a statement saying that more Jews have come to believe in Jesus as their Messiah in the last eighteen years than in the last eighteen centuries. That was then! We will come to a time when whole synagogues will be won over His Messiahship. I have friends who are rabbis - Orthodox rabbis - who got saved and believe.

What did God say to Israel when the time of the Gentiles began? "I held my hands out to you for centuries, oh Israel. I pleaded with you to keep my covenant, to prepare for my Messiah but you rebelled. I sent you Jeremiah, but you put him in prison. I sent you Isaiah, but you sawed him in half. I sent you one prophet after another, but you stoned them between the porch and the altar. I sent you my messengers, I sent you preachers of righteousness Israel, but you rejected them. I sent you men who brought revival; I sent you Hezekiah and Josiah, Ezra and Nehemiah, but you've forgotten those revivals. Alas, you have rejected My Son. Now I am going to the Gentiles."

But now the time of the Gentiles comes to a close. "I called you Gentile church; I called you English speaking nations; I called you Protestant democracies; I called you America; I called you Britain; I gave you my covenant. I sent you John Bunyan, but you put him in prison. I sent you William Tyndale, but you burned him at the stake. I sent you John Hus but you burned him as well. I sent you preachers of righteousness who brought revival to America; I sent you Jonathan

Edwards; I sent you DL Moody and Billy Sunday. You have forgotten those revivals, America. You have rejected My Son. I have taken all I am going to take. Now I am turning my grace back toward My ancient people, Israel."

Am I saying that is what is going to happen? I tell you by the Spirit of Jesus, no - that is what is happening. Before God turned his grace to the Gentiles, the second greatest harvest of Jewish souls took place in the second century. Even the secular Jewish historian Max Dimont said that at least 25% of the Jews in Jerusalem accepted Jesus as their Messiah before Bar Kochba's rebellion around 120 -132 AD. The most we can believe God for is the same. All I want before God turns his grace back to the Jews is to give America and Britain one more chance to repent. Israel did not deserve it and we do not deserve it either, but He is turning his grace back to the Jews. The time of the Gentiles is coming to a close. The time will not come again. The time is now.

Chapter 2

Who are the Palestinians?

Moriel and the author wish to preface this article by stating categorically that the purpose of addressing current political issues in this article is not to misrepresent the gospel or the Christian church as aligned with any political party or ideology. We purely address these matters from the point of view of biblical prophecy as an expression of faith and not of political activism. We are not opposed to "Palestinian" Muslims as people and we distinguish between philosophical and fundamentalist Islam, even though our own beliefs are Judeo-Christian and the convictions mandated by our own faith cause us to fundamentally reject Islam as being incompatible with the Judeo-Christian Scriptures. To the highest degree possible, we also believe in the human rights and religious freedom of moderate Muslims (irrespective of our own disagreement with the teachings of Islam in the Koran and Hadith) and we do so despite the fact that most of the Islamic world demonstrably refuses to reciprocate by according the same level of tolerance to Christians and Jews – a cruel and inhuman injustice and inequality which as advocates of religious freedom we firmly oppose.

> *The burden of the **Word of the Lord** concerning Israel.*
>
> - Zechariah 12:1

HaDavar Adonai - HaDavar Adonai translated to Greek would be the *Logos*, the word that identifies divinity taking on human flesh in the first chapter of the book of John. We are talking here of something Christological; it points to the Lord Jesus Himself. It is His burden concerning Israel and it points to Him as Creator.

> *The burden of the Word of the Lord concerning Israel. Thus declares the Lord who stretches out the heavens, lays the foundation of the earth, and forms the spirit of man within him. "Behold, I am going to make Jerusalem a cup that causes reeling to all the peoples around; and when the siege is against Jerusalem, it will also be against Judah. And it will come about in that day that I will make Jerusalem a heavy stone for all the peoples and all who lift it will be severely injured and all the nations of the earth will be gathered against it."*
>
> -Zechariah 12:1-3

What is the source of the conflict in the Middle East? Is it Satan? In a manner of speaking, yes. Is it Islam? In a manner of speaking, yes. But, ultimately, it is God. He makes Jerusalem a heavy stone. Jerusalem is where Satan got his biggest defeat and it is where he will get his final defeat. A spiritual battle wages over the Middle East and, as we can see from this passage, this is the burden of Jesus Himself.

This spiritual battle is evident as we observe the irrational attitudes of the nations regarding the state of Israel, even as they turn a blind eye to atrocities committed by governments around the world. We read the statistics of how many UN Security Council and General Assembly resolutions were passed against Israel. At Tienamen Square, from between seven and eight thousand students were murdered by the Red Chinese army; over one billion people saw it on television. How many UN resolutions or boycotts were passed against China? - None, absolutely none!

Look at the open genocide taking place in black Africa at the hand of Islamic regimes funded by the Saudis. How many academic boycotts against Saudi professors have there been? - None, absolutely none! The Lord sees this injustice - but we have to remember, it is something that He has stirred up.

God does not love Jews or Arabs more than He loves anyone else as individuals. But as nations He has a special love for the Jews because of His promise to Abraham. He also has a prophetic agenda for the Arab nations, but in the character of their forefathers they still despise their birthright.

Israel has regathered for what Jeremiah referred to as "the time of Jacob's trouble." Will there be peace and blessing in the Middle East? Yes, there will be, but only when the Messiah returns. It is Jesus who is stirring up this trouble and will bring it to its prophetic conclusion.

Not long ago, I was in Jerusalem driving down the street when a bus that was a few blocks ahead of me blew up killing nearly twenty people. Had I been there just two or three minutes earlier, I would have been one of the casualties. Those couple of minutes separated me and the grave. This was not the first time I had come very close to terrorism. I had seen some very serious things in Ireland, though nothing nearly as bad as I had seen in the Middle East. Tragically, my sister's husband was killed in the World Trade Centre in New York City on 9/11. Ironically, I had to cut my visit to the Middle East short in order to attend my brother-in-law's memorial service in the United States. There was no actual funeral because they could not find any of his remains to bury. How strange it was for me. This wasn't in Belfast; this wasn't in Jerusalem; this was where I grew up. I always knew terrorism would come to America - now it is here!

But we read how it will be in the land:

> *I will pour out on the house of David and on the inhabitants of Jerusalem, the Spirit of grace and supplication, so that they will look on Me whom they have pierced; and they will mourn for Him, as one mourns for an only son, and they will weep bitterly over Him like the bitter weeping over a first-born.*
>
> -Zechariah 12:10

The Talmud continually reiterates this about the Messiah, as does Rashi who taught that this is referring to the Moshiach, "he would be pierced and the Jews would look upon him."

In Judaism there are two pictures of the Messiah, HaMashiach Ben Yosef and HaMashiach Ben David - the son of Joseph and the son of David - the suffering servant and the conquering king. Joseph's brothers did not recognize him at the first coming, but at the second they wept bitterly. This prefigures Jesus' brothers who will be in the same character. Joseph's brothers came the first time and thought he was a Gentile. Since he represented the Egyptian Pharaoh, he was for the Gentiles. Similarly, most Jewish people believe that Jesus is for the Gentile Christians, not recognizing he is one of their own.

(A comprehensive comparison of Yeshua and Joseph is presented in *One Messiah, Two Comings* - Chapter two of this book)

The parallels are endless: Joseph was betrayed by his brother Yehuda into the hands of Gentiles for 20 pieces of silver; after inflation Jesus was betrayed for 30 pieces of silver by Yehuda, Judas, into the hands of Gentiles. But God takes that betrayal and turns it around in both cases and makes a way for all Israel and all the world to be saved. They bring Joseph's coat to prove that he's not in the pit and Jesus' shroud to prove that he's not in the tomb. Joseph was condemned with two criminals and he prophesied one would live and one would die. Jesus is condemned with two criminals and he prophesied one would live and one would die. Joseph goes from a place of condemnation to a place of exultation in one day. To him, every knee had to bow, and so with Jesus who goes from a place of condemnation to a place of exaltation in a single day, every knee shall bow. Upon exaltation Joseph marries a shixa; he takes a Gentile bride and upon exaltation Jesus in figure takes a Gentile bride, the church.

Messiah, son of Joseph, is the suffering servant. When He comes back, it is in the character of David, the conquering King. That is why most Jewish people rejected Jesus in his first coming. They wanted a political Messiah in the character of David, who would get rid of the Romans the way that the Maccabees got rid of the Greeks. That is his purpose in his second coming. His first coming was for salvation, to the Jew first (all of his apostles were Jews) and then to the Gentiles. His second coming is to save Israel - to bring God's judgment on the kingdom of Satan and the Antichrist.

The kingdom of Satan is obviously entrenched in the world today. When I look at the way the world is going - when teachers in San Francisco read books to children like "Daddy's Roommate" and "Heather Has Two Mommies" - I just want Jesus to come back. There's no end to evil being called good and there's no stopping it. It will only get worse before it gets better. Yet for us, I've read the end of the book; and in the end, we win.

A History Lesson

And so we have the issue of the Palestinians, a term used by the President of the United States, the Prime Minister of Great Britain and even the Prime Minister of Israel. Who are the Palestinians?

The first definition of a Palestinian is the anthropological one. It is simply the Latinization of the word Philistine. However, the Philistines were an Indo-Hellenistic people from the area of the Aegean around Crete, and they worshipped the fish-god Dagon.

The Romans Latinized the word Philistine to Palestine (Syria Palaestina) in 135AD as an insult to the Jewish people. In reality the Philistines disappeared from history after the reign of King David. As a distinct anthropological identity, a Palestinian has not existed on the face of the earth in three thousand years. No use talking about Palestinian rights when they have not existed in nearly three thousand years.

The second definition of the word Palestinian is the academic one used by scholars in a theological discipline. The pre-eminent proponent of this concept or this school of theology today would be E.P. Sanders who wrote books like "Christ in Palestinian Judaism." It simply refers to the theology that came from that area between the Jordon and the Mediterranean. However, only Jewish and Christian theology originated in that area. Islamic theology began in Saudi Arabia and developed in Egypt in the Middle Ages. So as a theological term, Palestinian is something Jewish and something Christian - not Islamic. The Arabic term for Jerusalem is only found four times in the Koran, but in the Bible there are close to 1000 times when Zion and Jerusalem are mentioned.

Then there is the historical and geographic definition of Palestine and a Palestinian. For centuries it referred to anybody of any race or origin who lived between the Jordan and the Mediterranean descent. They could have been a Jew, a Christian, or a Muslim. They could have been Arabs, Greek Orthodox, Syrian Catholic, or they could even have been Armenian. All these ethnic groups and ethno-religious groups still exist in that area. The only thing a Palestinian meant was somebody who lived in this region that the Romans called Palestine. There were 30,000 Jewish soldiers who fought in the British army under Montgomery in World War II. On their patch it said they were the Palestinian legion.

The popular definition of a Palestinian was largely developed during the Cold War. Palestinian nationalism was simply engendered, under the advice of Soviet military and political advisors, as a propaganda tool to attack Israel. The fledgling state of Israel was seen as an outpost of pro-western democracy in the Middle East. The United States had foolishly handed Egypt and Syria over to the Soviets' sphere of influence after 1956, due to an unfortunate intrusion of the Eisenhower administration. This was a big mistake - one the West is still paying for.

So the Soviets supported the Palestinian Liberation Organization that was founded in 1964. The PLO was committed to destroying Israel, long before the Israeli capture of Samaria, Gaza and East Jerusalem in the 1967 Six-Day War.

This myth you have today of a Palestinian people was an invented term. Most ethnic Arabs living in Israel today are the children and grandchildren of Arabs who entered the land illegally after World War I under the British Mandate.

Under the British Mandate, the British built a system of roads and railroads in Haifa and Jews began draining the swamps, planting moshavs and kibbutz's. As a result, the standard of living increased and that drew the Arabs to leave Arab countries to come to where the grass was greener. Some of the land was owned by absentee feudalistic Arab landlords like the Husseini family of which Yasser Arafat was a member. Yet Yasser Arafat was not a "Palestinian", but an Arab, born in Cairo, Egypt. Most of his deputies were Tunisian Arabs.

Arabs talk about the occupation of Palestine, but fail to mention Arab incursions into North Africa, Egypt, Libya, Tunisia, Algeria, or Morocco. They won't tell you about the occupation of Coptic land by Arab Muslims. They won't tell you about the occupation of Berber lands by Arab Muslims. Those are not Arab Muslim countries, they were stolen. The Berbers were Christian people who were slaughtered. The Muslims took their children and forced people to convert to Islam by the sword. To this day, Berbers have their own culture and identity suppressed throughout North Africa. Nobody complains about their rights. Not much is said about the Syrian occupation of Lebanon. In 1991 President George Bush Senior effectively gave Lebanon into the hands of Syrian dictators.

Who are the Indigenous People?

The archaeological records bears out historically that the Jews are in fact the indigenous people of the land of Israel. Apart from the biblical record, a strong legal argument could be made, simply based on the archaeological record that the Jews are the indigenous, historical inhabitants of the land. Islam can make no such claim. Islam can only argue for propriety of the land based on religion. They don't tell you that. They believe in the doctrine of Jihad - that if Muslims ever conquer a land, it is then holy land and must be theirs forever. Islam divides the whole world into two camps - the world of Islam and the world of the sword. Mohammed said Allah commanded him to make war against all nations and peoples until everyone says "there is no God but Allah and Mohammed is his prophet."

Once a Muslim conquers the land, according to them, it is theirs forever; their claim is based solely on religion. I believe what both the Tenach - the Old Testament - and the New Testament say about the land belonging to the Jews, but even if that was not the case, both history and archaeology verify that the Jews are the indigenous people.

Going back to the time of Abraham and the patriarchs, there were another people in the land - the Canaanites. Because of the abominations carried out by the Canaanites, God's judgment fell upon them. They practised child sacrifice, ritual bestiality - all the prohibitions of moral conduct prescribed in the Torah for Israel to

24

avoid. "You shall not do these things like the nations I drive out before you." The Canaanites existed pre-thirteenth century, and then the Hebrews arrived in the 13th century BC. They stayed there for centuries but due to the sin of the people, as the prophets like Hosea predicted, the Northern kingdom went into the Assyrian captivity. Some Jews remained and intermarried with the Assyrian captives becoming the Samaritans in approximately 720 BC.

Later on as Isaiah and Joel had prophesied, the Babylonians similarly conquered Judah as a judgment for their sin and in fulfillment of the warnings of the Torah. The Jews were then sent back as Jeremiah prophesied, that captivity would be approximately 70 years in duration, and again the Hebrews returned. They remained there for some centuries until the days of Antiochus and the Seleucids.

Then, as Daniel prophesied, God raised up the Maccabees and the land was liberated and was once again in the hands of the Hebrews. There was a period of Jewish expansion, taking over much of Jordon and the area of Nabatieh. Herod the Great was of Nabatien descent and was only a Jew by the fact that the Hebrews converted the Nabatiens to Judaism.

Once again due to the sin of the people as Daniel prophesied, the Romans controlled the land until the second century BC. There were two Jewish revolts against Roman occupation, one in 70 AD and one that went on from approximately 120 to 132 AD under Simon Bar Kochba. The Jews got the land back temporarily but then the Romans recovered it again.

The Roman Empire was divided between the Latin west and the Greek speaking east. The natural successor became the Byzantines. They remained in control until the Muslim invasion, but Muslim civilization in the Middle East was not Arab. It was quickly taken over by the Turks. The Turks, although they were Muslims, did not like the Arabs - a strange situation, given the fact that Islam came from the Arabs. Why would the Turks, adopting that religion, oppress the Arabs? It had its western equivalent, in the fact that every writer of the New Testament was a Jew, except for Luke who was a proselyte to Judaism and yet you have so-called Christians who are anti-Semitic. How could Christians be anti-Semitic? It should be a logical contradiction given the fact that Jesus was Jewish and all of his disciples were Jewish. It is a logical contradiction for a Christian to be an anti-Semite. And it is a logical contradiction for a Turk to be anti-Arab but that's the way people are.

Then came the crusades. The economy of the western world today depends on oil from the Middle East, as the economy of the western world once depended on the spice trade in an agricultural economy. The banking families of Italy were always in rivalry to get their man in the papacy, plus the papacy was the brokerage house of international banking. The popes, on behalf of the banking families they represented, wanted to control the spice trade to the east. That was a major underlying economic reason for the Crusades - to use religion as propaganda - but it all boils down to money.

Crusaders invaded, although religious freedom issues were involved, and they established the holy Latin kingdom. Finally at the Battle of the Horns of Hattin, Saladin and 12,000 of his knights defeated the crusaders in Galilee on the fourth of July in the year 1187. Now at that time the barbarians were not the Muslims; the barbarians were the crusaders, particularly the Knight's Templar.

Islam then had its golden age, although it was different than it is today. Today Islam is dominated by Saudi Arabia and the Arabs who have the economic influence. During its golden age, it was dominated by the Turks, and it was westernized. They adopted platonic and then Aristotelian philosophies. Egypt became a learning centre, but it was a Hellenistic, westernized Islam. When Europe was under the clutches of medieval Catholicism, Islam was having its golden age.

You could write a check in Baghdad and cash it in Morocco; such was their advanced banking system. They were at the forefront in architecture, mathematics, astronomy, medicine, philosophy and literature. When the Crusades brought these influences, together with the influences of the Byzantine Empire, back to Western Europe, the Renaissance began and Europe slowly climbed out of the Dark Ages.

Today, Islam seeks to revive itself as a world class empire, as a world economic power, and as a cultural force in civilization. However, they are going in the wrong direction. In order to attain that goal they would have to westernize themselves and put their empire into the hands of Wahabist Saudis. When Islam was at its peak, it was an entirely different essence than the Islam they have now. It has always been a false religion. It was never a libertarian religion, but even medieval Roman Catholicism was more barbaric than Islam in those days. Saladin was relatively benevolent compared to the Knights Templar or St. Bernard who led Children's Crusades. No wonder they named a dog after him. In the same way that Muslims today send children in to be suicide bombers, the Roman Catholic Church did that in the Middle Ages at a time when Islam was culturally superior.

God's Purpose for Islam

We need to put this in perspective. Why did God allow Islam to grow? It was a judgment upon the idolatry of the Byzantine church, with their icons. They believed that an icon, an image, was a window, with a metaphysical property, to enter the spiritual realm. The original Christianity of the New Testament came from Judaism, "you shall not make a graven image; you shall not bow down to them and serve them." The idolatry that became incipient in the Byzantine and the Roman Catholic worlds brought the judgment of God. The same as the judgment came on backslidden Israel and Judah, it came on a backslidden Christendom. Islam was a judgment.

September 11th was a judgment from God and it is with great pain that I say that, having lost family in the World Trade Centre. One month before that calamity, Paul Crouch, the founder and president of the Trinity Broadcasting Network, the largest "Christian" television network in the world, held up the Koran and announced that he wanted his Muslim brothers to help him understand this book. A month later they did.

And at the same time a book was making the rounds in evangelical circles by Roman Catholic author Peter Kreeft called "Ecumenical Jihad." It was calling for ecumenical union with Islam in an effort to morally redeem society. It won the endorsement of Evangelical leaders such as Chuck Colson and J. I. Packer.

Almost exactly one year before the towers fell, on September 10, 2000, the pastor of the Crystal Cathedral in Garden Grove, California, the "Reverend" Robert Schuller introduced a special speaker, during his church services that are televised around the world, on his program "The Hour of Power." His guest was Sheik Salah Kuftaro, Chief Director of the Abu Anour Islamic Foundation and the son of Sheik Ahmad Kuftaro, the Grand Mufti of Syria who appeared on both the 9:30 and 11:00 services and told the 6,000 Christian/Muslim/Jewish congregation, with many religious leaders:

Islam is a judgment on the backslidden Protestant democracies. It is God's judgment on us, the same as it was God's judgment on the medieval Roman and Byzantine churches. What do you suppose a Muslim thinks when he sees churches ordaining homosexuals? To him "we're morally superior to you, we'll take care of your homosexual problem. You have feminists; you know what we do to feminists? In Islamic countries, we flog them. We'll solve your feminism problem. We'll morally redeem you; we're morally superior to the Christians." That's the way they think. It is a judgment on a nation that has turned its back on its Christian heritage.

By family, by birth and by citizenship, I have allegiances to three nations, Israel, the United States and Great Britain. There are no three nations in the history of the world that have had more Biblical influences, in their heritages, as societies and nations - three backslidden nations. Israel has aborted 1.6 million Jewish children; they are killing more Jews than Adolf Hitler. They are heading for the time of Jacob's Trouble. There are only two kinds of people that God calls God's chosen - Jews and Born Again Christians. And although there is a faithful remnant of both, the rest are apostate and backslidden and the judgment of God is falling.

Turkey foolishly backed the wrong side in WW I, and Imperial Britain took the land in 1917. After the terrible defeat at Gallipoli, the Australians and Kiwis from New Zealand were very angry. At a dramatic cavalry charge at Beersheva, Muslim forces were thrown back so much that the defense at Jerusalem was abandoned. They saw airplanes for the first time and ran away. Israeli ambassador Gabby Levy, speaking to a gathering of Jewish Victorian former servicemen in November 2001, recalled: "Who can forget the celebrated Battle of Beersheva in late October 1917, where the 4th regiment of Victoria, as part of the infamous 4th Light Horse Brigade, succeeded in breaking the Turkish defense line between Gaza and Beersheva. It was this victory, coupled with many more like it, which ultimately contributed to the Allies winning the war. It was also within this environment that the British government issued the Balfour Declaration in 1917, "pledging support for the creation of a Jewish national homeland in Palestine."* General Allenby entered and it became a territory of Britain. Then in 1948, the land was returned to the Jews. Look at that. No matter who had the land, it always reverted to the Jews. No matter who had it and for how long, it always went back to those to whom God promised it.

There was a madman on the Banks of the Tigris and Euphrates River who was determined to destroy the Jews. He hated everybody. He was a demigod, virtually had himself deified, but he particularly hated the Jews and was determined to destroy them. He was defeated on the 14th of Adar. I am speaking of Haman, from where we get the Hebrew feast of Purim, the feast of Esther. There was another mad man on the banks of those same rivers with the same agenda more recently. On what day did Saddam Hussein surrender to the Americans and British in 1991? The 14th of Adar - What day did "shock and awe" commence? The 14th of Adar. Is that a mere coincidence? Today Saddam is in chains, seen on television sitting in a cage. Now he has received the judgment and is awaiting his execution.

There have been multiple opportunities to create an Arab Palestinian Muslim state. However, the Turks, the Ottoman Empire, and even Muslims themselves, saw no need to create an Arab Muslim state in the area called Palestine by some people. They saw no need. On the contrary, get a copy of "Lawrence of Arabia," read how the Turks enslaved the Muslims.

Muslim Against Muslim

Islam has a problem. You'll see Muslims in Los Angeles; you will see them in London, trying to get into the western world. They know the Islam world is unable to deliver the freedom, affluence, and justice of the Western world. They know they could not get the standard of living, or the standard of personal freedom under an Islamic government, so they come to the West.

Although 90% of the victims of the Tsunami were Muslim, the vast majority of the assistance came from the Western Judeo-Christian World. Despite a doubling of oil revenues, most oil rich Arab states donated peanuts in comparison, proving the moral superiority in terms of humanitarian values of The Christianized world over the Islamic world. Even in most of the Gulf states the majority of petro-wealth is kept by Islamic feudalism in the hands of royalty and their cronies. Many Muslims therefore resent and hate the West for giving what the Islamic world cannot.

Israel is a fairly poor country by western standards but the moment you go from Eilat to Jordan, you've stepped in a puddle of urine, and you know it. It even smells like camel urine. When you cross the border the other way, into the Sinai, when you're into Egypt, it gets even worse. If you think going to Tijuana from San Diego is a shocker, all you have to do is drive across the causeway from Singapore to Malaysia. The moment you come on to Muslim land, you feel an oppressive spirit.

They forget that they're under a curse since the time of the book of Genesis. Mohammed assumed that because during his time Jews didn't fight Jews and Christians didn't fight Christians that by having a monotheistic religion he could stop Arabs from killing Arabs. But he forgot what it says in Genesis. Ishmael's seed will always be divided and Esau's sword would be against his brother. Unless the Arabs turn to Christ, they will never have peace.

There is the Surah in the Koran called Umma, "Unity." However, 1.5 million Muslims were killed by other Muslims in the war between Iran and Iraq. When Iraq invaded Kuwait, the king of Saudi Arabia begged America and Britain to protect him from Muslim brothers. Then there was Black September in Jordan, Northern Yemen fights Southern Yemen. There is no Umma. Their religion doesn't work. The reason they must wage Jihad desperately is because it is the only basis for unity in their religion. Unless the Muslim can kill the Christian and the Jew, they will inevitably kill each other and they don't even know why.

The Turks saw no need to make a state, although they were Muslim themselves. In fact, after the Inquisition, the Turks invited the Jews to come from Spain and return to "Palestine" and settle there. How did the Jews first begin returning to the land? The Muslims brought them, they asked them to come! "Save us from the throngs of Arab civilization." Then the British passed the Balfour Declaration promising much more than the present land of Israel, inclusive of Judea and Samaria. They even promised the East Bank of the Jordan and the Gaza. That was cut back until they wound up with about 16 percent at most, of what they were supposed to get originally.

Now at that time after WWI, the only power in the world that would have rivaled Britain was America. Britain could have done anything it wanted. In that area of the world, no one would have objected. But the British Empire saw no need to create a Palestinian-Arab-Muslim state. The League of Nations who supported the British Mandate saw no need to create a Palestinian-Arab-Muslim state. And in 1948 with the partition, the United Nations saw no need. The United Nations did see a need to establish a Jewish State, but if the UN wanted a Palestinian state, why didn't they do it when they had the chance? If Tony Blair, the British Government supports the Palestinian state, why didn't he do it? But in addition to the Turks, the British, the League of Nations and the UN, there is one other power that had the opportunity to create a Palestinian-Arab-Muslim state. The Arab Muslims themselves.

From May of 1948 to June of 1967, for nearly 20 years, the control of the West Bank, the Gaza Strip, the Golan Heights, Judea, Samaria, was in the hands of Arab, Muslims. If they wanted a Palestinian-Arab-Muslim state why didn't they make one when they had 20 years to do so? It wasn't until September of 1970 that the idea emerged. Approximately 70% of the Arabs who lived in Jordan would identify themselves as Palestinians. Only 30% of the Hashemite Bedouin minority. The real natural leaders of the Arab world are actually the Jordanian Bedouins, the *Hashemites*, the descendants of Mohammed, according to the Sunni tradition, not the Wahabist, House of Saud. They're only in power with Western backing and collaboration of the corrupt and barbaric Wahabist clergy whom they bribe. And so when Arafat tried on King Hussein and the Jordanians what the PLO tried on Sharon and now on Olmert in Israel, the Jordanians had a simple solution. King Hussein massacred between 15 to 18 thousand of Arafat's followers in twelve days - Black September. Many in the West believe that Western democracies have much to learn from the way The Jordanians handled thugs like Arafat and his ilk. No one understands the nature of militant Islam and how to respond to it better than other Muslims.

We do not endorse the genocide perpetrated against *Shia* fundamentalists in Iraq by Saddam Hussein, or the extermination of 30,000 *Shia's* by the Syrian air force, but the hypocrisy of the Islamic world in condemning Israeli, British, and American reactions to radical Islam is noteworthy, when Western responses are very moderate in contrast to what Muslims consistently do to each other. This proves their doctrine of Umma is a fallacy. Even now most of the victims of Islamic terror are Muslims. The only way the Islamic world can forge an artificial unity is to form an alliance to murder non-Muslims, otherwise they will always butcher each other as they always have done.

Unlike the West, for all of their brutality other Muslims have been effective in dealing with the militancy of other Muslims. It was the Turks who ransacked Mecca and once destroyed the *Kabba*. It can be argued that the west must learn how to deal with militant Islam from the Turks as well as from the Jordanians. Western values of tolerance are seen by radical Islam as a weakness to be exploited.

At the time of independence, the Israelis were asking the Arabs not to flee. It was the United Arab Command that demanded them to withdraw and "we'll push them into the sea" and then go back. The UN said there were about 600 thousand. Now all of a sudden, there's somewhere between 3-5 million people depending on whose lies you believe. They only left at the behest of their own leaders, by and large. Where do the Palestinian refugees and those in Sabra and Shatilla refugee camps in Lebanon come from? Where do the poor

Palestinian refugees come from? They came from Black September when the Jordanians drove them out of Jordan into Lebanon. How dare those Jews do that? Whose fault is it that the Jordanians kicked them out? "Well, it's the Jews fault!" This is revisionism to the point of absurdity, a rewriting of history. It is so mind boggling, we would wonder how an intelligent person could entertain such things.

"Palestinian Confusion"

But as Voltaire said "history is the lie everybody agrees on!" He was no Christian, but he was right about that. Arafat had another chance to make a Palestinian Arab Muslim state. Several years ago, Barak offered it to him. He was offered 97% of the land captured in the Six Day War in total and in exchange for the 3% the Jews were to keep. He was offered a proportional amount of Israeli territory adjacent to it. So they wouldn't have lost a square inch. "Here's your state, a compromise on Jerusalem. You take 97% back of what we captured in self-defense, we'll keep 3% and in exchange for that 3% we will give you an equivalent amount of good land." What was Arafat's response? He called for a million martyrs and put bombs on Egged buses. How do you make peace with someone like that?

In 1968 Yasser Arafat said that Palestine was Jordan. In 1970 King Hussein of Jordan said Jordan was Palestine. After two years of Oslo 2 when the Israelis made the deal where King Hussein of Jordan was shaking hands with Yitzhak Rabin, Arafat failed to stop terrorism. He talked peace, but he was using a duel strategy of allowing terrorist groups like Hamas, Hezbollah, Islamic Jihad, Al-Aqsa Brigade to continue. Arafat couldn't make peace, it would have been his undoing. That was his problem. When King Abdullah of Jordan, the grandfather of King Hussein, tried to make peace with the Jews, you can still see the bullet holes in the pillar at the Al Aqsa mosque. "Bang - dead!" Bashir Gemayel another Arab who tried to make peace with the Jews – the result: "bang - dead!" When Anwar Sadat, who was only half Arab and half black African, tried to make peace with the Jews: "bang – dead!" What can we expect would have happened to Arafat had he tried to make peace? What do you think would happen to Mahmoud Abbas if he really tried to make peace? The same outcome as them all.

There is a need to understand the doctrine of Hudna in Islam. Islam teaches permissible lying for expediency and that the whole world is divided into two - the world of the Islam and the world of the sword. When Mohammed was surrounded in Mecca, he declared a temporary truce and said "let's make peace" and he used the time to reorganize and rearm. When a militant Muslim says "peace" it is Hudna, a period of reorganization and preparation for renewed attacks when your enemy doesn't expect it. It is not seen as a lie in their religion, it is seen as a military disinformation strategy in the Jihad.

I've spoken to people in the CIA, the State Department, and the American defense department. There are plenty of academics educated at Princeton, Columbia University and Harvard, who speak fluent Arabic and work for the CIA and the State Department. They work with the think tanks to advise the American government. Don't think for one moment that President Bush's White House doesn't know what's going on. They know it's not peace - its Hudna. Islam doesn't allow peace. The mentality of Islam is to misinterpret kindness as weakness. You show kindness to a militant Muslim, you are weak. He's trying to get something out of you. If you go to Morocco, go anywhere, they will be nice to you as long as they can get money out of you. Kindness equals weakness.

Perhaps you saw the 1991 film "Not Without My Daughter" starring Sally Field. It is a true story about an American woman named Betty Mahmoody. In 1984 her Iranian husband took her and their daughter to meet his family in Iran. He swore they would be safe and happy and would be free to leave. He lied! She became trapped in the Islamic county and her husband's true brutish nature came out, and the rest of the movie shows her trying to flee her subjugation and get back home to America with her daughter.

Even highly westernized, highly educated Arabs, who are educated in America and Europe, become like that. There's something demonic about it. Do I sound tough in my talking? The London July 7th bombers were western born and educated. I haven't led a lot of Muslims to Christ but I have led some Muslims to Christ including Shia Muslims. Everyone that I've led to Christ from Islam, I've led to Christ by hitting them right between the eyes with God's truth. I'll introduce you to families of former Muslims who today follow Jesus and are so grateful that somebody told them the truth.

Mohammed, according to the Hadith, married Aisha the daughter of Abu Bakur when she was six years old and took her virginity when she was nine. You expect me to believe a 54-year-old man that had sex with a little girl is God's greatest prophet? Even Islamic countries would arrest him for pedophilia. Several years ago, a major American documentary, showed footage of wealthy Saudi Sheiks in private jets going to India to buy girls from impoverished families for $200 USD. Some of the men were as old as eighty; some of the girls were as young as eight. When asked how could you do this, they said "what's wrong with it? Our prophet did it."

Any Muslim can verify that Mohammed married Aisha, a little girl and took her virginity at the age of nine. In the Western World, liberal scholars are free to express their views, no matter how wrong and biased they can be. Evidence in the Dead Sea scrolls debunk higher criticism time and time again, but at least we allow open and critical scholarship in the West. The only place for this in the Islamic world, for open scholarship, is in the West. Real Muslim scholars are called Orientalists. There are no Orientalists in the Muslim world. If they dealt with the real history of Islam and the Koran in an Islamic country, they would get beheaded.

Our numbers are Arabic numbers - our digits. The Hebrews, the Greeks, and the Romans all used letters for numbers, but the Arabs invented numbered digits. Arabs invented numbers and pioneered advanced mathematics in the Middle Ages while Europe was backward. However, the Koran says that every night the sun sets into a miry pit of mud when it gets tired and rises the next day. If God created the universe and Allah is God, why doesn't he know what happens to the sun? Arabs do not lack intelligence, yet they accept Islamic superstition as fact. Islam confuses Miriam, Mary, the mother of Jesus, with Miriam, the sister of Moses? They can't deal with open scholarship, so they pick up the sword. They are afraid, they know it doesn't work. They see the prosperity and affluence and freedom in the West and it is an indictment of the current stinking misery of Islamic civilization.

War as a Way of Life

Professor Samuel Huntington told the truth when as a professor at Harvard University, he wrote "clash of civilizations." There are three times as many conflicts in today's world involving Islam than all of the other religio-people groups put together. No two Judeo-Christian democracies have ever had a war. The politically correct say Islam is a religion of peace and tolerance. But find me one Muslim country that will give Christians and Jews the rights Islam demands and receives in the Western World. Find me one Islamic country that is a genuine democracy.

Most Islamic wars are Muslims fighting other Muslims. It just doesn't work and they know it. Again when they had their golden age, it was Turkish, not Arab. It was philosophical, not fundamentalist and it was based in Egypt, not Saudi Arabia. The schism in Islam, the war between Iran and Iraq dates back to the battle of Kaballah. When Mohammed died, there was a contention between the followers of Ali, his relative and his theocrats. Memories run very long in the Middle East. They are still fighting over the battle of Kaballah. They go back and mutilate themselves, beat themselves and flog themselves.

The Crusaders saw this when they went to trade spices in Bombay and went through Iraq and Iran and viewed the flagellation rituals which the Muslims were practising in Kaballah. They brought this back to Europe, where the monks and nuns began flagellating themselves in Roman Catholicism. (Counting prayers from beads was brought from the Hindus and became rosary beads for the Catholics.) As well as flagellation rituals being copied from Islam, so was the mutilating of children. The practice of hacking the children's heads off with hatchets was simply the Islamization of the old Molech worship mentioned in the Bible.

This Islamic assault against the West has been ongoing from the 8th century to the 21st century. In the 16th century at the second battle of Vienna, they were turned back. This is not the first time they tried to take over the West but this time when they were turned back from Geneva in the 16th century, the Islamic power went into decline. This is what they're trying to revive and using oil money to do it.

Muslims interpret what is happening now, Jihad against the infidel, as fighting the Crusaders and Jews. They relate this back to the Crusades in the Middle Ages. To them it is the same struggle. The closest thing I've seen to it in the West is Northern Ireland, where Catholics and Protestants speak of William of Orange and the battle of the Boyne as if happened last Tuesday, but it was in 1690. The battle between Jew and Arab goes back to the struggle in the womb of Rebecca.

Islam has another problem. The Koran says that Allah will give them victory in the Jihad against the Infidel. But how come after six Jihads, 150 million Muslims can't beat 4, 5, 6 million Jews? It is an indictment of their religion; it undermines the credibility of their belief system. So they will say, "Oh it's because of America!" Is Allah afraid of America? America did not begin to support Israel in a major way until 1973. The Jews captured that land in 1948, 1956 and 1967 when the Soviets were backing the Arabs. Israel was getting a minimal amount of support from America and the West. In fact at one point they were getting as much support from France as they were getting from the USA. American support didn't begin until the act in Athens, until the aftermath of 1967. It didn't really become what it is today, about three billion a year, until 1973. Israel wasn't counting on American support, they weren't dependants, they were outnumbered something like 80 to 1. Why didn't Allah give them victory in the Jihad? Well, it's the God of the Jews that must be right. Habub, the Bible must be right, the Koran must be wrong.

Let's pretend Israel didn't exist. If there was no such nation as Israel there would still be 55 thousand dead Christians in the south of the Philippines. There would still be between 10 and 20 thousand dead Christians in the Mollucan Islands. If Israel didn't exist, there would be nearly 30 thousand dead Christians in Nigeria. Churches are burned down almost every day of the year. In Sudan in ten years, Muslims have killed 2.1 million black African Christians. Why no UN resolutions? Why no condemnations of Saudi Arabia for funding the Islamic regimes in Africa? Is it because they are black? Is it because they're Christian? Or, is it because they don't have any oil?

If Israel didn't exist, you would still have the Balkans. In complete violation of the NATO treaty, Clinton and Blair bombed Serbia. I am no admirer of Milosevic, by any means, but the problem was provoked by the Kosovo Liberation Army, aligned with Al Qaeda and trained in Afghanistan. The NATO charter says that NATO can only attack a country which attacks a NATO country.

Many would argue, "Well, Islam is a religion of peace and tolerance, you're just an Islamaphobe!"

Well, what about the 55 thousand dead Christians in the Philippines?
"Oh, that's nothing to do with Islam, you're an Islamaphobe!"
What about the 20 thousand dead Christians in the Mollucans?
"Oh, that's nothing to do with Islam, you're an Islamaphobe!"
What about the 30 thousand dead Christians and the church burnings in Nigeria?
"Oh, that's nothing to do with Islam, you're an Islamaphobe!"
What about the 2.1 million dead Christians in Sudan?
"Oh, that's nothing to do with Islam, you're an Islamaphobe!"
Well, what about the Balkans?
"Oh, that's nothing to do with Islam, you're an Islamaphobe!"
Well, who bombed India's Parliament?
"Oh, that's nothing to do with Islam, you're an Islamaphobe!"
Well, what about the Bradford riots in England?
"Oh, that's nothing to do with Islam, you're an Islamaphobe!"
What about Locherby in Scotland?
"Oh, that's nothing to do with Islam, you're an Islamaphobe!"
What about the apartheid government in Malaysia, Islamic apartheid?
"Oh, that's nothing to do with Islam, you're an Islamaphobe!"
What about the Bali bombing?
"Oh, that's nothing to do with Islam, you're an Islamaphobe!"
What about the theatre in Moscow?
"Oh, that's nothing to do with Islam, you're an Islamaphobe!"
What about thousands of barbarians rioting in the streets of London, demanding the murder of British citizen Salman Rushdie for writing a book?
"Oh, that's nothing to do with Islam, you're an Islamaphobe!"
What about the Kenya bombings?
"Oh, that's nothing to do with Islam, you're an Islamaphobe!"
What about the Jakarta bombings?
"Oh, that's nothing to do with Islam, you're an Islamaphobe!"
Who's doing it? The Quakers?

If Israel did not exist you would have the same problem. The only thing Israel is guilty of is something that every thinking civilized person on the planet and every civilized nation should be guilty of, standing up to them.

Hypocrisy and Dual Standards

To this we can add the Islamic murder of Theo Van Gough for making a film about human rights in the savage Muslim world, the Washington Sniper, the Malmo Muslim gang crises, and the tragedy of Denmark.

Denmark has a 4% Muslim population, yet 40% of those on the dole are Muslims, some of whom admit they see the Danish tax payer funded welfare, to Muslims as the Dhimmi – the Islamic penalty tax on non-Muslims. The overwhelming majority of convicted rapists in Danish prisons are Muslims while most of the victims are Danish.

The Islamic community and world were up in arms over the Mohammed cartoons published in a Danish newspaper which was supposed to be some kind of outrage. We are proud of a free press that published those cartoons and we do not find them blasphemous or unfair. Only God can be blasphemed, not a man, and portraits of Mohammed as a terrorist only echoed and reflected what was being published in pro jihad fundamentalist literature. Persian miniatures of Mohammed can be viewed on the internet are on display in Islamic museums.

The notion that their religion forbids icons or images of Mohammed is itself a lie, and even if it was not, no violent fundamentalist barbarian has the right to come to a civilized country and demand that others bow the knee to his beliefs.

These cartoons were published months before the Islamic riots. It was only when Denmark was about to preside over a UN committee addressing Iran's nuclear ambitions that Iran and Syria launched and orchestrated the campaign. These cartoons moreover were light compared to the hate mongering found in the newspapers in Islamic countries. We salute those who wear the T-shirts of those cartoons proudly and defy those who would seek to deprive us of our right of free expression. If the BBC can broadcast the Jerry Springer "The Opera" which portrays Jesus as "a little bit gay" (which is blasphemy), why are Muslim sensitivities to be protected and Christian ones not? Why is the world not up in arms at the cartoon portraying Islamists murdering Jews in the Muslim world?

While the Bush White House eager to please the Saudi Arabians at the behest of the oil lobby spoke against the cartoons, Bush uttered not a word at the Saudi and Kuwaiti anti Christian *fatwahs* or new anti-Christianity laws in Algeria. Bush has increased the numbers of Wahabist Saudi students entering the USA bringing their Islamic fundamentalism with them and allows the Council for American Islamic Relations to continue unhindered while he allows the Saudis to build a ring of mosques around Washington DC. The shameful antics of Britain's Prince Charles are even worse, as patron of various Islamic propagation institutions, while not a single church can be built in Saudi Arabia.

Meanwhile, the pro Saudi policies of Condolezza Rice and President Bush pressuring Israel into a unilateral withdrawal from Gaza without security guarantees have created a new Iranian funded and Iranian armed terrorist state in Gaza while Bush and Rice simultaneously warn of Iranian nuclear ambitions and terror. In the war on terror, one can only wonder if Islamic terror does not have a valuable ally bought for the price of a barrel of Saudi oil who resides in the white House. The lies, corruption, and hypocrisy of politicians know no bounds and are eclipsed only by the lies, corruption, and hypocrisy of tele-evangelists.

These are facts that the White House, the State Department, the oil interests, 10 Downing Street, the EU, the Arab League, Republican Party Leadership and most of the media want us to ignore. Now, I'm treading here on thin ice, I'll tell you why. Jesus lived in a politically charged environment and wouldn't get political. He did however deal with prophecy. When you deal with prophecy, you are in a grey area. Secondly, we are told in the book of Timothy to pray for those who are in authority. I am not trying to condemn our government. I am trying to encourage Christians to do two things. One - pray for them and two - "appeal to Caesar." Both have a Biblical precedent.

Much has happened since the death of Arafat and now we see a continual power struggle between Hamas and Fatah. The election of Hamas and the pressure for the world and Israel to accept the leadership is nothing new. We have seen this before with Abu Masen. Abu Masen was a kingpin in the terrorist assassination of the Israeli Olympic team in 1972. Can you imagine, the American Olympic team getting murdered by terrorists? and the person who organized it and helped finance it being accepted as a partner for peace? Would America be bullied into accepting somebody who killed our Olympic team in cold blood? Killed the whole team!

President Bush thought they should. We see a long history of double talk. The Palestinian authority talks of peace to the western media in English and French, but simultaneously when leaders like Arafat talked to his own people, in Arabic, he would say the diametric opposite.

I've listened to chants, do you know what they say? When Arafat spoke, when they cheered him? "First the Saturday people, then the Sunday people." First we will murder the Jew, then we will murder the Christian. What is said to the western media, and what is said to the people are two different things, and it's proven, it's indisputable, that's why the State Department is trying to read out certain statements in Arabic. As stated before, when Arafat was offered a state by Barak, he turned it down and he called for Jihad. He was offered a state with much better terms than the UN offered Israel in 1948, yet he called for a million martyrs.

A Sell-Out

The axis of evil is not Iraq, Iran and North Korea as Mr. Bush asserted. Iraq became a problem for only one reason; George Bush Sr. left Saddam Hussein in power. The real axis of evil is not that. A Republican government left North Korea in power only to have to face them another day. The same as a Republican government left Saddam Hussein in power only to have to face him later.

A Republican government handed Egypt to the Soviets on a silver platter, and Eisenhower bullied Britain, France and Israel to go along. The real axis of evil is Saudi Arabia, Iran and North Korea, in that order. The Wahabi of Saudi Arabia remain the number one dynamo of Islamic terror while falsely claiming to be fighting terror. The White House plays up to the Saudis instead of standing up to them to please the oil interests. They won't stand up to Saudi Arabia, instead they will twist Israel's arm. The Bush White House is owned and operated by international oil interests first and foremost and yet he won the White House on the Evangelical vote. While America condemns Israel for erecting a defense on their God given land, America puts up a similar fence along the Mexican border.

The Israelis are trying to save lives. The U.S.A. is only trying to save jobs. When we do it, it's one thing, when they do it; it's something else – this is a double standard. Saudi Arabians, a nation under American protection, hanged a 15-year-old boy for accepting Christ. The President welcomed Saudi Arabia's Crown Prince Abdullah to his ranch in Crawford, Texas and led him around holding hands after greeting him with a kiss. "These are our friends" said Mr. Bush. You are telling me that a regime that arrests, flogs, hangs and decapitates people for accepting Jesus Christ are our friends? Well, they may be a friend of Bush, but they are no friend of America. The CIA and the State Department knows full well that it is not peace, it is Hudna!

The Nixon/Ford administration said under détent we'll dialogue with the Soviets to try and stop this. We lost Vietnam. Now they are dialoguing with the Saudis to try and stop it but we are going to lose the war on terror. Unless you stand up to Saudi Arabia, the war on terror is lost. Recently, Bush was sequestering sections of the congressional investigation, divulging the involvement of Saudi Intelligence apparatus of September 11. They don't want you to know. "We'll dialogue with the Saudis." That's what you did in Vietnam! Every time a Republican wins the presidency, the economy goes down the tubes, and you wind up losing a war. And I'm not Democrat, believe me. I am pro-life, independent, conservative, but I'm not a Democrat or a Republican.

The State Department knows the PLO's true agenda. They know that the only real Islamic claims to the land are based on religion, not based on history or legality. The legal department of the State Department has assessed Palestinian claims to the land as baseless. But members of the Council on Foreign Relations control the State Department. George Bush Sr. who coined the phrase "New World Order," was a member of David Rockefellers Trilateral Commission and two recent presidents were a member of the Skull and Bones Society when he was a student at Yale. I do not flow with the conspiracy theorist notions about The Illuminati (even though such beliefs exist and are absorbed in a free masonry that no saved Christian should be part of as Jesus forbad such oaths) but American and British foreign policy is clearly made by an entrenched elite.

Claims by the former and the latter President Bush that Islam is a religion of peace and tolerance is just a strategy to try to get moderate Muslim states on their side. No Islamic country is a true democracy. The Saudi Arabian government funds militant Islam in America and the construction of mosques all over the free world but will not allow one church to be built in Saudi Arabia. We respect their rights and they trample all over ours.

The Wahabist regime funded by the Saudi government and royal family financed the culture of terror that engendered Al Qaeda and continued to fund terror after September 11th and still continue to fund Hamas. Today, the Saudi Arabian government at the behest of the Wahabi is funding anti-American terror and anti-Israel terror and the White House knows it.

Most of the suicide bombers who crashed hijacked commercial jets into the World Trade Center were Saudi Arabian. Yet for one year after September 11, Bush refused to stop the express visa program for Saudi Arabians that gave them an automatic visa to come to America. They blew up the Twin Towers and the Pentagon and he is importing them. Even European countries wouldn't give them express visas. If the same standards that we applied to Spain when the battleship Maine was sunk were applied to September 11, we would have declared war on Saudi Arabia on September 12.

We can't victimize Arab Americans, yet they must show the same loyalty that German, Japanese and Italians showed during WWII. You had an Arab American throwing hand grenades at his comrades in arms. In World War II, Japanese Americans, Italian Americans and German Americans, proved their loyalty. Why shouldn't Arab Americans prove their loyalty? Why should you pay $15 extra to go on an airplane and have to get to an airport an hour early? The common sense thing to do is to imitate El Al and security profile Muslims. "Oh no we can't offend the Saudi Arabians." Pay up Christian, pay up Jew, we have to placate the Muslims, they have rights and we don't! And if they get their shoes searched "you're discriminating against me because I'm a Muslim."

Bush knows that the committee for Arab Islamic relations is a front for militant Islam financed by the Saudi Arabians. "Oh, only some Muslims are like this, just the extremists." The most comprehensive poll taken six months after September 11 determined that 60% of Muslims in 18 countries agree with the September 11 attack as being morally justified. That is six out of ten Muslims! After the first Islamic attack on the Twin Towers that damaged the parking garage,

Clinton was offered Osama Bin Laden in an exchange deal to improve relations by the Sudanese. Clinton turned it down. We could have had Bin Laden and Clinton turned the deal down.

Any time Americans train and arm Muslims they end up having those weapons used against them - the Taliban in Afghanistan, Iraq, the war with Iran, Muammar Gaddafi in Libya. Now in total disregard of the record of history, Bush is using the CIA to train Palestinian para-militants. Bush has pulled away from conservatives and pro-Israel Evangelicals. His advisors have told him to distance himself from men like Franklin Graham, Hal Lindsay, Pat Robertson and Jerry Falwell. Some of these men have gone done the ecumenical road, but they are right about Israel. Bush has been told, "pull away from those guys" but he has embraced interfaith proponents such as Ted Haggard and Chuck Colson who think that Islam is acceptable and compatible with Christianity.

Evangelicals proclaimed Ronald Reagan a "Christian president," but he was a Freemason who supplied a terrorist Islamic regime in Iran with weapons. He was highly reliant on his wife for advice and she conferred with psychics and fortune-teller to get advice to tell him how to run the country. Most Evangelicals are naïve and too trusting.

No wonder the national deficit quadrupled. There is this myth that the Republicans are the Christian party. I wish that was true. Recently, four of the six Republican appointments on the Supreme Court voted to outlaw Texas anti-sodomy laws. Most of the conservative justices on the Supreme Court voted not to reconsider Rowe v. Wade. It is a total misconception that the Republican Party is the one for Christians.

In conclusion, I want to look at the 'dirty dozen.' Those who are most biased against Israel, who fabricate, distort, and engage in an outrageous standard of revisionism. The BBC, CNN, (partly owned by Arabs, Muslims), Reuters, the news service, wire service and

Associated Press, The Guardian Newspaper in England, the Independent Newspaper in England, ITV in England, the Washington Post, MSN, Al Jazeera, Channel 4 UK and the German De Spiegel. Now there are more but these are the worst twelve that I know from my continual travels around the globe. Less than twenty interest groups control approximately 75-80% of the world's media? If it weren't for the Internet they would control 90%.

The second chapter of the book of Daniel says, "God establishes kings and removes them." Because America twists Israel's arm to bow the knee to Islamic terror, Americans are coming back from Iraq in body bags. God's promise that "I will bless them that bless you and curse them that curse you" is a reality. Bush is bringing God's judgment on America. He is selling us out for the price of a barrel of oil.

I pray that God will remove any government that will bring His judgment on the UK & USA. The day after Israelis were forced from their homes in Gaza without a treaty or security guarantee by the bullying of Bush anxious to please the oil interests, American's were forced out of their homes in New Orleans and the Gulf Coast with one third of America's oil refining capacity in ruins. As Obadiah 15 warns, nations will reap consequences of their foreign policies concerning Israel. If Bush and Blair do not stop bullying Israel and turning their backs on the persecuted church in the oil producing Islamic states that fund and breed support for terror with their fundamentalism, God's judgment will come on America and on Britain.

Following the Israeli withdrawal from Gaza under pressure from Condoleezza Rice, as always acting in the perceived interests of international oil and their Saudi partners, Hamas and the Al Aqsa Brigade both simply used Gaza as a new platform to continue rocket attacks on Israel and to threaten renewed campaigns of suicide bombings. This is precisely what the Muslims did following the

Israeli withdrawal from Lebanon when Syrian and Iranian backed Hizbollah, used southern Lebanon to again attack Israel in 2006. As in Iraq, when America and the West tried to impose democracy on Muslims, they simply voted for terror and elected Jihadists. Democratic values such as democratic institutions, pluralism, tolerance and democracy itself are only for the non-Islamic world. Even in Britain and Europe up to 40% of Muslims want an end to democracy and Islamized Europe ruled as a Muslim Calipath.

The stupidity of the Bush Government and other western powers to believe Islamic countries can be democratized is the result of a naïve misunderstanding of both Islam and history. When MacArthur democratized Imperial Japan, he first needed to castrate Shintoism and publicly humiliate the Emperor. Thus demythologizing the religious philosophy upon which the Japanese warlords based their conquests; a tradition dating back to the medieval Shoguns.

Unless the West was willing to castrate Islam and totally humiliate it in its own eyes, such a MacArthurization of Islamic countries is a futile and stupid pursuit, but far from doing what needs to be done as MacArthur did, or as General Pershing did with the Muslims in the Philippines insurrection, Bush and other American administrations pander to Saudi funded Wahid fundamentalism that inherantly breeds support for terror.

A "corporate among corporates" is Saudi Vassal James Baker, secretary of State under George Bush senior. Baker, is the attorney acting on behalf of the Saudis against the families of September 11th victims in a class action suit. It was Baker in the first Bush government who left Saddam Hussein in power in 1991 to begin with when the Saudis did not want the precedent of regime change in the region. Now it is Baker who wants to link new demands for Israel to forfeit more of its ancient Biblical homeland to Islam, to the quest for peace in Iraq. Baker is also the legal counsel for the Carlyle investment group in which the Bush family, the Saudi Royal family and allegedly the Bin Laden family are investors.

It is not only the oil owned religious rites government of George Bush or a democratic administration, but even elements of the evangelical church who are now demanding acquiesence to Islamic terror. In November 2006 "Purpose Driven" author Rick Warren paid homage to terrorist Syria, the very week Syrian intelligence murdered the Christian political leader of Lebanon, Pierre Jemalyel, and as Syria and Iran continue their partnership with Hizbollah to destroy Israel and persecute Lebanese Evangelicals.

The Inevitable Future

There has never been a Palestinian state other than the Hashemite ruled one that exists already demographically and geographically in Jordan. As Arafat admitted in 1970 as did King Hussein – Jordan is Palestine. There is no anthropological distinction between Palestinian Arabs and other Arabs and up until 1967 West bank Arabs were called Jordanians. As Voltaire said 'history is the lie everyone agrees on' and as Hess said 'Tell a lie enough times and people will believe it is the truth.' The real truth is that "Palestine" is an invented historical and anthropological myth.

There will be the battle of Gog and Magog when God's judgment will fall mercilessly on much of the Islamic world and there will be a false peace that will be a covenant with death initiated by the anti Christ. While perverted liberal theocrats and bias driven left wing journalists denounce pre-millennial Christians as dangerous and compare them to Islamic terrorists despite them being non-violent (except for a few lunatic fringe abortion clinic bombers outside and Northern Irish extremists disowned by biblical Evangelicals) , there will also be a Battle of Armageddon.

Directly or indirectly, Israel's calamities derive from rejection of the true Messiah in accordance with Deuteronomy 18:18-19, and God's wrath on the Islamic nations is prophetically inevitable. Hence it is vital to proclaim Jesus as the way of salvation.

May God's hand stop Western governments from continuing their betrayal of us to Islamic fundamentalism, and may both Jews and Muslims come to know the saving power of Jesus. As a matter of extreme urgency, we beseech prayer for the governments of the USA, the UK, and Israel and for the persecuted church in Muslim countries whose desperate plight the Western media and oil thirsty politicians are too happy to ignore.

The even more important truth however is that Israel is losing its land and being driven into a corner under both the permissive will of God and the hand of Satan as divine judgment looms over the Islamic world in order to set the stage for the return of Yeshua - the Jewish Messiah. Ultimately, it is Jesus - He and He alone who can and will save Israel.

Annapolis Summit – November 2007

The first Bush administration of President George Bush, along with his Secretary of State James Baker, handed Lebanon to Iranian-aligned and terror-sponsoring Syria on a silver platter in 1991. In the tradition of his father, George W. Bush and Secretary of State Condoleezza Rice, have pursued a foreign policy creating Iranian-controlled Islamic terror enclaves in southern Iraq and in Gaza. They continue the policy of the Clinton administration in Kosovo who, in league with Britain's Tony Blair, EU High Representative Javier Solana and retired U.S. General Wesley Clark, bombed the Serbians. That was a total violation of the NATO Treaty that only allows an invasion of a nation that attacks a NATO country. Clinton intervened in the three way blood bath (in which there was no totally innocent faction) on the side of the Islamic Kosovo Liberation Army, which is allied with Al Qaeda, alienating pro-western opinion in Russia and helped to pave the way for Putin's incipient neo-Stalinism to gain momentum. Bush and Rice oppose the Christian population of Kosovo siding with Islam, while trying to create an Islamic state in Europe.

Not content with this, Bush and Rice have teamed up with the most unpopular and scandal-ridden Prime Minister in Israeli history, the left wing Ehud Olmert. They are desperate to reconstruct their legacy as a failed administration before the end of Bush's term in office and need a foreign policy success, so they turn against an easy target: Israel.

It was against this backdrop that the Annapolis summit was staged and the pro-Islamic foreign policy advanced that would create another Iranian backed terrorist enclave in the West Bank as they did in Lebanon, Gaza, and southern Iraq. It is again, Daniel chapter 10 that warns us that the demonic principality over Iran (Persia) would rise up to attempt to destroy Israel in the Last Days. George W. Bush has given that demon a guestroom at the White House. While claiming to build a buttress against Iran, Bush in practice continues to bolster Iran.

Bush, Rice, and 'Road Map to Peace' ambassador Tony Blair pushed the myth that Fatah, the heirs of Yasser Arafat under President Abbas, are moderates and only Hamas is bad.

Blair, with probable presidential ambitions within the European Union (his style of governance as UK Prime Minister was in fact 'presidential', not 'parliamentarian'), has an agenda that is personally political.

Second term US presidents are generally consumed with preserving their legacy for posterity. While Jimmy Carter is usually regarded by presidential historians, the press, and the academic world as the weakest and most failed president in modern American history, history will still acclaim him for the Camp David Treaty he arbitrated with Menachem Begin and Anwar Sadat.

George W. Bush however has no feather in his cap, and will eclipse Carter as the president remembered as "the President of Failure".

Condoleezza Rice is often estimated, even by many Republicans, as the most incompetent Secretary of State in American history and has a lot to live down. Bush must find a feather.

The Bush administration and its Republican Congress at the dawn of 2008 is frantic in its efforts to salvage a legacy after one diplomatic failure after another, a massive expansion of the federal debt and a serious decline in the value of the US dollar. Former Federal Reserve Chairman Alan Greenspan, who is not without his own culpabilities but is himself a Republican, holds Bush and the first term Republican Congress directly responsible for hyper deficit spending which makes the record quadrupling of the deficit under Ronald Reagan almost insignificant in comparison. Reagan indeed took America from being the world's biggest lender to its biggest borrower and destroyed the balance of trade in favor of Asia with his Reaganomics that the senior George Bush, his Vice President, had termed "voodoo economics". But the economic decline of America under George W. Bush went well beyond this.

Bush failed to significantly correct the record trade deficits that cheaper dollar based exports normally would, while his beloved oil cartel profited. Bush made the USA more and more dependent on Saudi Arabia and Persian Gulf's support of the dollar to retain it as the currency of world oil reserves by keeping Arabian crude priced in petro-dollars.

Bush's abysmal economic record of mega-fiscal deficit, combined with mega-trade deficit and Saudi-sweetened record oil prices, will haunt his legacy. It can only be managed as a facet of Middle East foreign policy with Israel being the sacrificial lamb. This was magnified by the Bush imbroglio in Iraq that dates back to his father and James Baker leaving Sadam Hussein in power in 1991 because the Saudis did not want a regime change in the Persian Gulf. This was characteristic of the Reagan Administration supplying arms to the vehemently anti-American regime of Ayatollah Khomeini in Iran and covering it up in the Reagan Contra scandal.

If Sadam Hussein was to be deposed, the US could have done it with world approval, including most Arab and Islamic approval in 1991, but their Saudi masters said no amidst fears of an Iranian Shia regime in Southern Iraq. The most desperate factor in the failed Bush legacy remains Iraq. The senior Bush failed to finish the job, so his son just botched it up.

Bush, Iraq, and the Vietnam Ghost

A Republican administration under Richard Nixon, with a hostile Democratic Congress and a fed-up public saw the loss of Vietnam. Today, a Republican with a hostile Democratic Congress and a fed-up public is losing the 'War on Terror'. The Republicans moreover are doing so for the same reasons. As Americans died in Vietnam, ships of American allies visited the North Vietnamese Port of Haiphong. As the Soviets and Chinese supplied the North Vietnamese with the wherewithal to kill Americans, Richard Nixon and Henry Kissinger pursued détente with the Soviets and an open door to China, increasing trade with those funding the war effort to kill Americans. Some non-partisan conservatives saw this as a diplomacy of treason.

As a Vietnam style imbroglio has taken root in Iraq and the terror threat looms, Bush has pushed America more and more into economic league with the Saudi and Emirate Wahhabist financiers of radical Islam that inherently generates support for terror. Again, a Republican Party diplomacy of treason places the West in bed with the enemy, whom we are not allowed to identify as the enemy, in the name of 'oil détente'. We can be certain that the imbroglio taking place in Iraq has the Democratic Congress and Senate as its co-architects and that any Democratic president will be just as beholden to oil industry interests and Moslem oil interests as any Republican one.

Indeed, as the American presidential race took shape in 2007, Al Qaeda toned down its activities in Iraq and elsewhere to prevent a conservative from being elected, which the White House exploits as evidence that its strategy against terror is working. The strategy of either party, in fact, does as much to work in favor of terror as it does to oppose it.

Once the plight of persecuted Christians is ignored and God's covenant land of Israel is divided, judgment becomes inevitable and the stage is further set for Joel chapter 3 and Zechariah chapter 12.

Putin and Bush, Gog and Magog

There also appears to be a political insanity to policies of Russian President Vladamir Putin. After the Moscow theater and stadium ordeals and the Beslan slaughter of little children in front of their parents by Islamic terrorists in the Chechnya dispute, common sense would demand a recognition that a fundamentalist Iran on the doorstep is not desirable. In fact, Iran constitutes a serious militant Islamic threat to Russia, potentially more serious than the one faced by the West.

Russia has a 70% abortion rate with only Moslems growing as a demographic sector of the society. The Islamization of Russia is more pronounced than similar trends in Holland, France, and Britain (China also faces a rising Islamic threat in its extreme west). Yet, in a policy that makes no strategic or logical sense, Putin repeatedly aligns himself with Iran against the West. And he does so for the sake of short term political gain in his quest to revive a defeated and humiliated Russia that lost the Cold War and saw its Soviet Empire collapse as a major player once again on the global stage.

The irrationality of Putin's policies cannot be explained pragmatically or politically. It is indeed conspicuous in its resemblance to the Hebrew Prophet Ezekiel's warning to Gog and

Magog that God would put a hook in their jaws and draw them into a Middle East conflict to destroy them in chapters 38 & 39 of that amazing prophetic book.

In Putin's world, the short term gain of alignment with heathen Shia Iran is attained at the expense of long term security of Mother Russia. In the world of Bush, it is precisely the same. Short term gain is attained from alignment with no less barbarian Saudi Arabian Wahhabists is attained at the expense of long term security of America and the West.

Many conservatives wonder what kind of president refuses to define the enemy, protect the nation's borders during a time of war, and hands out express visas to Saudi Wahhabists after September 11th; (as irrational as handing out visas to Japanese kamikaze pilots after Pearl Harbor). Bush and Putin are two of a kind. It is most unlikely that the successors of either Bush or Putin will have any more integrity than their predecessors or that either of them would ever read the Book of Ezekiel.

ANNAPOLIS – The Feather Came from a Vulture

The Bush Administration knows that George W. Bush is the Jimmy Carter of the Republican Party. The Republican president who lost Vietnam, Richard Nixon, will be remembered as a liar and a thief, but he saw Apollo 11 land on the moon, a highlighting moment for his administration. Reagan was half-senile and may have run the most corrupt and sleaze ridden administration in American history, but he saw the collapse of the Iron Curtain. So Bush must have his place in history. He needs a publicity ploy that will be remembered as his crowning achievement in what is otherwise a legacy of failure. He needs a feather in his cap. But the only place he can get it is from a bird of prey.

The following are items Bush and Rice do not want addressed in setting the agenda for the Annapolis conference:

1. Abbas and Fatah have a Palestinian constitution that is Islamic and inherently supportive of future jihadist terror and suppression of women, non-Moslems, and enshrines hatred of Jews and Christians in its Sharia laws.

2. Fatah and Abu Abbas have a militant terrorist faction as bad as Hamas also supported by Iran.

3. In the weeks prior to the summit Fatah TV, radio, and media continued as usual broadcasting its anti-American, anti-western, anti-Judeo Christian, and anti-Israel hatred and promulgation of jihadist violence implicitly endorsing terror. Yet Bush demanded further concessions to those openly wanting to destroy you.

4. Abbas has no electoral mandate from his own people. Bush and Rice claim to be in pursuit of their fantasy endeavor to democratize Moslems, yet Abbas has no democratic or electoral mandate. In any free election, Hamas would likely win.

5. Fatah stole most of the international assistance provided for the development of an infrastructure. Blair and Bush want to give them even more American and Western money without the misallocated hundreds of millions being accounted for. Of course, it is the over-taxed European and deficit strapped American taxpayers that Bush, Blair, and Rice expect to pay for this, not the oil wealthy Saudi Wahhabists with escalating oil revenues they use to propagate the intolerance of Wahhabism globally.

6. The Palestinian delegation claims it will never accept as a condition the existence of Israel as a Jewish state, maintaining no nation can mix its religious and national identity; except of course their own Islamic Palestinian constitution and more than thirty

Islamic nations, including Saudi Arabia. Bush uttered not a word. Israel is supposed to negotiate away its land to those not prepared to recognize its existence as a Jewish homeland to those who have a fundamentalist Islamic one.

7. The "National Intelligence Estimate" that Bush was aware of since August, 2007, (although not released until after the Annapolis summit in early December, 2007), stated that active Iranian pursuit of nuclear arms has been dormant since 2003, even though the supposedly peaceful technology could be converted to enrichment of weapons grade plutonium in the future. Bush and Rice pushed the summit by exploiting the need for a common front against Iran by so called moderate Moslem states (such as extremism funding Saudi Arabia) and Israel.

8. Israel was to be compelled by Bush and Rice to sit down with a number one against sixteen mainly Moslem countries, including terror sponsoring Syria and human rights violating Saudi Arabia. The very week that Bush invited the Saudi government to attend, Saudi Arabia ordered a young 19-year-old woman, who had been gang raped by twenty-one Moslems, to be flogged with 200 lashes (initially 90, but raised to 200 when the international media was alerted). The US State Department under Rice admitted the victim was going to be mercilessly whipped under the Islamic law of savage Saudi Arabian 'House of Saud' barbarianism, who are business associates with the Bush family.

None of this, of course, matters to Bush, but the political injustice was not the beginning of the Annapolis betrayal committing Israel to creating a second Palestinian state. It promises to be like the first one, Jordan, and be another non-democratic Islamic state that persecutes Christians and continues its support of terror, courtesy of the American government, oil interests, and the European Union.

As we witness in the biblical books of Daniel, Zechariah, and

Revelation – these political events are the mere result of dark spiritual forces in the heavens as Ephesians chapter 6 describes them.

Apostasy Paves the Way

In 2007 the Roman Catholic Arch Diocese of Los Angeles agreed to pay $630 million in compensation after Cardinal Mahoney protected pedophile clergy at the expense of the children whose lives these sex criminals destroy. A similar huge settlement was made a week later by the Arch Diocese of San Diego (indeed, nearly every Roman Catholic diocese in the USA, with their bishops have been similarly found liable in court; a saga repeated globally).

In spite of this, Pope Benedict XV, who as Cardinal Joseph Radzinger issued the 'Criminale Solicitacciones' directive from the Vatican instructing bishops to protect these criminals, made a recent declaration that only Roman Catholicism was valid and other churches were not. Not a word was spoken in reaction by Chuck Colson, James Dobson and other supposedly Evangelical henchmen of ecumenical union with Roman Catholicism and its widespread sex pervert violation of children and conspiracy to cover it up and protect its pedophile priests and nuns.

Yet, this same pope, who received a letter from thirty-eight Moslem leaders, including leaders of the Moslem Brotherhood on public record for supporting terror and hatred of Jews and Christians, responded with a good neighbor letter. Yet these Moslem leaders never retracted any of their previous statements placing religious benedictions on terror, hatred of America, Britain & the West, intolerance of Christians, and murder of Jews. This is the Islamic practice of 'taq'yya': permissible lying in the struggle for Islam, disseminating misleading information to the infidel in preparation for Jihad.

At the same time, President Bush announced his departure from biblical Evangelical Christianity (which he does not appear to have ever embraced in any scriptural sense) and decreed all faiths have the same god. "I Am The Lord Your God, You Shall Have No Other gods Before Me" is erased from the Bush bible in the name of oil money and political correctness.

The prelude to the Annapolis summit however was indeed religious and spiritual. A host of apostate clergy responded to the letter by the Islamic clerics, including annihilationist John Stott, Robert Schuller (with the Moslem Grand Mofti of Damascus in his pulpit), Bill Hybels (with a Moslem imam in his), Rick Warren (after paying tribute to terrorist Syria and telling Christians to avoid end times prophecy), Emergent Church guru Brian McLaren (who mixes New Age and post modernism with mystical Christianity, and argues for a 5-year moratorium on homosexuality), and David (Paul)Yongee Cho (who combines Oriental shamanism with Christianity in his book 'The Fourth Dimension').

The letter was also signed by a leader representing the National Association of Evangelicals, an organization previously led by Ted Haggard until he was caught in a web of lies, deception, and scandal regarding his involvement with homosexual prostitutes and dangerous illegal drugs. This sad collection of theocrats issued a letter of reply to the Moslem letter that had been addressed to the pope as if he were the visible representative of Christianity. They did so even after the pope, a protector of child-molesting priests, had denounced the very existence of their churches as invalid and the Roman Catholic Church as the only true church founded by the Lord Jesus.

These so-called Christian signers were pleased to ignore the pro-terrorist history of many of the Moslem signatories and the Wahhabists signatories who impose the sentence of death becoming a Christian. They apologized to the Moslems for the

Crusades (a Roman Catholic adventure, not a Protestant one) and for the way in which 'the war on terror' has in part been pursued.

This same crowd, eager to placate Islam, stands prepared to shun Israel and support Bush and whoever succeeds him on the same course. This is not new. Disclosure of released Nixon tapes in 2006 revealed that Richard Nixon and Billy Graham were both secretly malicious anti-Semites and discussed their vehemence against Jews in the White House at some length. In his retirement, former president Jimmy Carter has become a spokesman for fundamentalist Islamic interests and a virtual defender of ant- Israel, Islamic terror paid for by Moslem oil money donated to his ' Peace Center.' Like Bush and Graham, Carter also proclaimed himself to be a 'born-again' Christian.

It is righteousness that exalts nations. How could treason in the pulpit yield anything but such de facto treason in the corridors of political power?

A day of judgment is indeed coming for corrupt governments and godless nations. A day of judgment is coming on those who curse Israel and betray the persecuted church. A day of judgment is indeed coming on Israel for her rejection of her Messiah and persecution of Jewish believers. A terrible day of judgment is coming with Gog and Magog, Armageddon, and Isaiah 17 on the Arab/Moslem world. But judgment begins in the House of God!

Chapter 3

Jewish Arab Reconciliation
in Christ

> *"Go forth from your country from your relatives, from your father's house to the land which I will show you and I will make you a great nation. I will bless you and make your name great and so you shall be a blessing, and I will bless those who bless you and the one who curses you I will curse, and in you all the families of the earth shall be blessed."*
>
> -Genesis 12:1-3

In the Bible, God gave five promises to Abraham. The Lord appeared to him at various times, but the initial calling to Abraham is what is recorded in Genesis 12. This is when the Lord spoke to Abram (before his name was changed):

- ✧ God promised him a land. This promise was reiterated to his descendants Isaac and Jacob. (Avraham, Yitzak and Ya'akov in Hebrew.)
- ✧ God promised to make him a great nation and God would bless him.
- ✧ He promised him a great name.
- ✧ God also said "the one who will bless you, I will bless and I will curse the one who curses you".
- ✧ And lastly God said, "Through you all the families of the earth will be blessed."

At one time Spain was the number one world power. Spain was the super power of its era. She dominated what was then the New World at the close of the fifteenth century after Christopher Columbus planted the Spanish flag on the island of San Salvador. Spain retained that high position until Ferdinand and Isabella gave in to the Dominicans and permitted them to carry on the Inquisition. The Jews were targeted, although they were not the only victims, they were certainly the focus of much of the treachery. And, all of a sudden Francis Drake sinks the Armada and 'Britannia rules the waves', and were then the number one power.

Great Britain had a Jewish Prime Minister who was a Christian, Benjamin Disraeli. This was not an anomaly and there were other Jews who believed in Jesus. As well as Prime Minister Benjamin Disraeli, there is Felix Mendelssohn the composer and the historian Alfred Edersheim to name but a few.

Britain was a great power and God blessed Britain. Britain issued the Balfour Declaration promising Jews the right to return to the Holy Land but later reneged on it and allowed Jews to go to the ovens. Jews burned. So did Liverpool, Coventry and London.

Jews came out of concentration camps run by the Nazis and were then put into concentration camps run by the British even after the holocaust was known. There were some British generals like General Dobbie and General Wingate who supported Israel. Moshe Dayan was trained by Lord Wingate but Glover and the others supported the Islamic Arab world against the Jews, revoking the Balfour Declaration. Britannia no longer ruled the waves. It is interesting that after the blitz, after the war, nobody could believe that Sir Winston Churchill was anything less than invincible. Seven days before the election in 1945 he said, "I want nothing more to do with the subject of Zionism." Seven days later the world was amazed he lost the election.

"I will bless them that bless thee and curse them that curse thee." Not for their sake but for the sake of God's promise to their fathers. But then, "through him all the families of the earth will be blessed." Of course, this is because of the seed of Abraham, the Messiah. Remember too that the biological seed of Abraham and the anthropological seed of Abraham became two nations, the Jewish nation and the Arab nation. God would bless all peoples through Abraham's descendants because of the Messiah.

It would be reasonable to think that the two nations and the two peoples who would be the first to accept Jesus and believe the Gospel would be Abraham's anthropological descendants: the Jewish nation and the Arab nations. However, that is not the case. According to foreign missionaries, the two kinds of people most difficult to convert to Christianity are Abraham's literal anthropological descendants: the Jews and the Arabs. The reasons for this are neither sociological nor historical. It goes well beyond that. Even though there are intellectually explicable reasons, the reasons go well beyond that. The reasons are spiritual and theological. Through Abraham, salvation would come to all nations because the Messiah, the Seed of Abraham, would be the fulfillment of that prophecy. Yet Abraham's kinsmen after the flesh, the Jews and the Arabs, are the ones who resist the Seed of Abraham the most.

The prophet Jeremiah gave a prophecy, "For My people have committed two evils against Me. They have forsaken Me the fountain of living water." The Messiah would give them the *maim chaim*, the fountain of living water as spoken by the prophet Isaiah in chapter 44 and in what Yeshua, in John chapters 4 and 7 says, *Ruach HaKodesh*, the Holy Spirit. They would reject the Messiah who would give the Holy Spirit. And they would "hew for themselves cisterns, broken cisterns that hold no water."(Jeremiah 2:13) They would invent another religion that would be spiritually bankrupt.

Two Rabbis

The Book of Acts introduces us to a rabbi named Gamaliel. Gamaliel was the Apostle Paul's tutor. He taught Paul how to be a rabbi. Gamaliel was the grandson of a very famous rabbi called Rabbi Hillel. There were two kinds of Pharisees, the school of Shammi and the school of Hillel. Paul was from the school of Hillel, was tutored by Hillel's grandson Gamaliel of whom Judaism, the Mishna, and Judaic history records his death. It was said of him that he was such a *Tzadok*, (such a righteous man), that righteousness perished from the earth when Rabbi Gamaliel died. That is how the rabbis viewed him; that is how they saw Paul's tutor. The literary and hermeneutic devices that Paul used in his epistles come from Rabbi Hillel. Paul utilized the principles of Jewish midrash in his handling of the Scriptures. Rabbi Gamaliel, this great Tzadok according to the rabbis to this day, said, "If Jesus is not the Messiah, Christianity would disappear." Well, it hasn't disappeared; He must be the Messiah!

Rabbi Gamaliel had other very famous students. One was Onkleos, a descendant of *Garim* Gentiles who converted to Judaism. Onkleos is famous because of a targum, a translation of the Hebrew Canon into Aramaic called the Targum Onkleos. There are two main Targamin: Targum Yonatan and Targum Onkleos. He was a contemporary of two other famous rabbis: Rabbi Sha'ul of Tarsus, better known as Paul the Apostle and Rabbi Yochanan Ben Zakai called the Mighty Hammer. They were classmates essentially.

Rabbi Yochanan Ben Zakai was smuggled out of Jerusalem in 70 AD during the Roman siege prophesied by Daniel and Jesus in the Olivet discourse and recorded by Josephus and Eusebius. The destruction of the temple presented a big problem to the Jewish leaders at that time. Daniel had prophesied that the Messiah would have to come and die before the second temple would be destroyed. Now they had no high priest and no temple. So Rabbi Yochanan Ben Zakai convened a conference at a place called Yavne, not far from the modern city of

Tel Aviv, to redefine Judaism and give a new interpretation to the canon of the Hebrew Scriptures. They rationalized, "But we have synagogues, we will replace the temple with the synagogue and we'll replace the Levitical priesthood with the rabbis and instead of the Korbanim, (instead of the sacrifices), we'll replace those with good works." A form of Judaism developed from that point, which later came to be known as Talmudic Judaism, or sometimes, Rabbinic. It was quite different from the Judaism of Moses and the Torah, which required the temple sacrifices, for without the shedding of blood there is no forgiveness of sins.

So Yochanan Ben Zakai thereby initiated Talmudic Judaism. The new Jewish religion was based on the old one.

A similar metamorphosis occurred in Christianity. Any newly born-again believer reading the Bible would realize that Roman Catholicism is not Biblical Christianity - neither is Liberal Protestantism or the Greek Orthodox Church. And any Jewish person who is being honest with himself recognizes the fact that Talmudic Judaism is not the Judaism of Moses and the prophets. Jewish rejection of Yeshua, of Jesus, is not the problem; it is the result of the problem. Yeshua said "if you believed Moshe, if you believed Moses, believe Me also." The problem of the Jews is not that they reject Jesus it is that they reject Moses and the Torah. If they really believed Moses and the Torah they would know He is the Messiah. The rejection of the Messiah is only the tragic consequence of the rejection of Torah.

Rabbinic literature tells us that on his death bed, Yochanan Ben Zakai, the man who began this other religion, began weeping and his disciples came to him and said, "Oh Mighty Hammer why is it that you weep?" And he responded:

"I'm about to meet God, blessed be His name,
and before me there are two roads, one to Paradise and

one to Gehenna (that is hell). I know not to which He
will sentence me."

On his deathbed, the Mighty Hammer, the founder of Talmudic
Judaism, as it became known, died terrified and in tears, not knowing
if he did the right thing or the wrong thing. Not knowing if God was
going to send him to heaven or to hell.

In contrast, his classmate Rabbi Sha'ul of Tarsus on his deathbed said
something else:

> *"I've run the good race. I've fought the good
> fight. Henceforth I know there is stored up for me a
> crown of righteousness."*
>
> -2 Timothy 4:7-8

Every Jew will follow one of these two classmates. Every Jew will
follow one of these two rabbis.

Now we come to Abraham's other children, the Arabs:

Mohamed grew up next to the well of Zumzum. The Hajj already
existed. The worship of Allah the Arabian moon god was already in
the Kabah. The Hajj was there, Allah was there, the well of Zumzum
was there! How did Mohamed begin anything? His father's name
was Abdullah the servant of Allah. What he did was go into the
Kabah and removed one stone for each day of the Lunar year and left
the Kabah one black stone. All Mohamed did was under the
influences of Judaism, Christianity and Zoroastrianism, attempt to
monotheize the pagan religions of ancient Arabia. He saw that, at
that time, Christians did not fight with each other and Jews did not
fight with each other. He thought that he could stop the Arabian
tribes from slaughtering each other by having one monotheistic
religion. As has been pointed out - Mohamed (a fact recognized by
Islam) was a pedophile. He married, at the age of fifty four, a six-

year-old girl and took her virginity at the age of nine. They call him a prophet but common sense calls him a sex criminal.

Several years ago there was a TV news documentary that featured wealthy Saudi Arabians with private jets going to India buying impoverished girls for a few hundred dollars, some of them as young as nine, taking them back to harems in Saudi Arabia. "How can you do this?" They were asked. "What's wrong with it, our prophet did it," was the reply. Now, to them, this is a prophet. I don't think God sees pedophilia as holy. He deflowered a little girl?

The guy could have been ordained as a Catholic priest these days. Why have these Catholic priests done such a thing? In Timothy, Paul says forbidding marriage is a doctrine of demons. You outlaw what's natural, people will do something unnatural. In the United States archbishops, bishops and cardinals were caught, not only covering it up, but protecting these sex criminals at the expense of not protecting the children whose lives they were destroying. And when they were caught they didn't resign; the pope didn't defrock them. This is Holy Mother the Church? Not my mother. That is not biblical Christianity. Islam is not the worship of the God of Christians and Jews and Rabbinic Judaism is not the Judaism of the Torah.

> *Then Abraham said to Lot, "let there be no strife between you and me, your herdsmen and my herdsmen for we are brothers."*
> -Genesis 13:8

Schism continually plagued Abraham's family and his people and his tribe, with Lot, then between Ishmael and Isaac and ultimately his grandchildren Esau and Ya'akov (Jacob).

There is a theological term some of you may have heard called the corporate solidarity. That's the theological expression for when one person represents a larger group of people. The name of the patriarch becomes a metaphor for the nation that comes from the patriarch. That is why, for instance, the great tribulation is called the time of Jacob's Trouble. Jacob wrestled with the Metatron, the Angel of the Lord, Yeshua, an Old Testament manifestation of Christ, and his name was changed from Jacob to Israel.

You and I have two names. The name we were born with before we met the Lord and the name we were given when we met Him, the name in the Book of Life, according to Revelation. When we behave like new creations, God calls us by our new name. When we revert to the flesh, He calls us by our old name. And so it is in Genesis when Jacob behaves like a spiritual man, God calls him Israel. When he is back to his old carnal ways he is called Jacob.

When Jacob wrestled with the Angel of the Lord, it was the dark night of his soul, when he split his family into two tribes, *mahaneim* meaning two camps in Hebrew. Jacob wrestled to the end of the night. In biblical typology the night is the most common metaphor for the great tribulation. "Watchman, watchman how far is the night?" "The sun and moon did not give their light." "Work while you have the light, for the night will come no man can work." "He is coming like a thief in the night." The wise virgins needed oil in their lamps to see in the night. In the Song of Solomon, the bridegroom comes for the bride in the night. Jacob wrestles to the end of the night. Unbelieving Israel goes through the whole tribulation. The Church is rescued out.

> *The Angel of the Lord said to her further, behold you are with child and you shall bear a son and call his name Ishmael (God has heard – Ish-ma-el) because the Lord has given heed to your affliction. The lad will be a wild donkey of a man, his hand will*

be against everyone and everyone's hand will be against him. He will live to the east of his brothers. (Notice the east)

-Genesis 16:11-12

His seed will be divided - that's Ishmael! God would later tell Abraham, "Take your son, your only son." God recognizes nothing that is done in the flesh. He only recognizes what is done in the Lord. He does not recognize Ishmael. Yet, because he is Abraham's descendant, God gives him a promise of the land to the east, but there is more to that than this.

> *"But an uncircumcised male, who is not circumcised in his flesh of his foreskin, that person shall be cut off from the covenant he has broken."*

-Gen. 17:14

> *Then Abraham took Ishmael, his son and all his servants who were born in the house and all who were bought with money, every male among them in Abraham's household and circumcised the flesh of their foreskin, that very same day, as God had said to him.*

-Genesis 17:23

Notice Ishmael was included in the covenant at that point.

God's Covenant

Then God told Abraham:

> *"Know your wife, Sarah shall bear you a son, you shall call his name Yitzak (Isaac) and I will establish My covenant with him, for an everlasting covenant for his descendants after him."*

-Genesis 17:19-20

Islam, of course, substitutes Isaac with Ishmael and it substitutes Christ with Mohamed. It actually says the Messianic prophecies about the Messiah in the Old Testament are about Mohamed not Jesus. However, verse 20 gives God's promise to Ishmael:

> *"And as for Ishmael, I have heard you, behold I will bless him and make him fruitful and will multiply him exceedingly. He will become the father of twelve princes and I will make him a great nation."*

The Jews began with twelve princes, the descendants of Isaac through Jacob and so do the descendants of Ishmael. Ishmael is incorporated into the covenant by *brit milah*, by circumcision. There is a promise to both.

> *"The son of the maid, I will make into a nation also because he is your descendant. I will make him a nation."*
>
> -Genesis 21:13-18

> And God heard the lad crying and the Angel of God, *(the definite article) called to her. "What's the matter with you Hagar? Do not fear for God has heard the voice of the lad where he is. Arise, lift up the lad and behold, hold him by his hand for I will make him a great nation."*
>
> -Genesis 21:17

So, you've got the first split between the sons, Isaac and Ishmael with promises to both for the sake of Abraham. By continuing the line through Abraham and Isaac something else happens:

> *The Lord said to her "two nations are in your womb. Two peoples shall be separated from your body, and one people shall be stronger than the other.*

*The older shall serve the younger." And when her
days to be delivered were fulfilled, behold there were
twins in her womb. Now the first came forth red, all
over like a hairy garment; and they named him Esau.
And afterward, his brother came forth with his hand
holding on to Esau's heel, so his name was called
Jacob;* (from the Hebrew word a'kov. Ya'kov
meaning heel) *and Isaac was sixty years old when she
gave birth to them.*

-Genesis 25:23

Now look at verse 12 of that chapter. "These are the records of the
generations of Ishmael." Notice that Genesis, by divine inspiration,
is keen to track the genealogy of both Ishmael and Isaac, with
promises to both and nations from both beginning with twelve
princes. But in verse 23 - "Two nations are in your womb." These
twins are struggling in their mother's womb.

This harkens back to the fall of man in Genesis 3. The husband is the
head of the wife (as Christ is the head of the Church). Because of the
fall of man, something has happened to us. Many things have
happened. One of them is that because of the fall, men have become
insensitive and women have become hyper-sensitive. When a
husband and wife get saved, most of the time it's the wife who gets
saved first. There are exceptions to this however. If a husband gets
saved first, water normally takes the shape of its container; the wife
will usually, eventually get saved. However, if the wife gets saved
first, it's very often much harder to see the husband get saved. Why
are women more likely to get saved? If a husband and wife pray
together for direction, it will usually be the wife who hears the voice
of the Lord first and clearest. Why? Men are insensitive. Men are
reliant on female sensitivity.

However, anything God intends for good, the world, the flesh and the
devil will always use for evil. Because it is easier for women to hear

the voice of the Holy Spirit, because they are more sensitive, it is also easier for women to be seduced by a counterfeit spirit. Leadership is male because men are less vulnerable to spiritual seduction. Remember, the serpent beguiled the woman. Any time a man did not take responsibility spiritually for his marriage and family, there was a disaster. Not just for him, but something that was perpetuated; Adam and Eve, and Abraham and Sarah. She puts him up to it and after he gives in to her nagging - "Get that woman out of my house." That principle will be true for us if the husband and father do not take responsibility for the spiritual leadership of the family. You are going to hurt not only yourself but you will perpetuate that into your own offspring, until it's dealt with biblically.

That is partly what happened with Abraham, going back to the fall Satan uses the same tricks over and over but the ramifications of what you see in the middle east now date back to this conflict in a women's womb all these centuries ago? Yes! Two nations, twins, they look so much alike. We can still see that today. Sephardic Jews and Arabs look so much alike. There are Jews in Israel who speak Arabic as their mother tongue. Sephardic music, Yemenite music, the cuisine, it's almost the same as Arab culture.

> *Then Isaac, his father, answered and said to him, "behold away from the fertility of the earth shall be your dwelling and away from the dew of heaven from above. By your sword you shall live and your brother you shall serve but it shall come about when you become restless that you shall break his yoke from your neck."*
>
> -Genesis 27:39-41

So Esau bore a grudge.

We are told about the sin of Esau in the New Testament. It is reiterated. He despised his birthright. Now Jacob was a conniver who was always trying to appropriate the blessing and promise of God by his own scheming. But, every time he did, he wound up the man on the back of the proverbial eight-ball. He was slick! He was clever! When Laban tried to con him, he conned Laban. He was slick, but he kept ending up in muck up to his neck.

The Birthright

Look at the history of the Jews. Why the holocaust? Why the inquisition? Why the pogroms? Why in their own land do they have no peace? The curse of the law! You either keep the Torah, which you can't since 70 AD or you accept the Messiah who fulfilled it, otherwise you are under the curse. Every Jew is under one covenant or another - no exceptions. If they say they don't believe, it doesn't matter. They are under the curse of the law. Mankind is accursed but Israel becomes God's teaching tool. They couldn't keep the Law of God. The purpose of the Torah was to point them toward the Messiah who would save them from the inability to keep God's law. The law teaches us through the example of the Jews about our fallen nature, our need for salvation, and our incapacity to get redemption for ourselves. They're under the curse of the law. I've read Hasidic rabbis who admit that. "These things happen to us because we haven't kept the Torah." What they don't tell you is that they **can't** keep the Torah. They have gone the way of Rabbi Yochanan Ben Zakai. That was Jacob. But his brother despises his birthright.

God gave the Arabs a lot more land than He gave the Jews. There are no more than fourteen million Jews in the world. And there are well over one hundred and forty million Arabs just in the nations that surround Israel. So, counting land and demographics, He blessed the Arabs a lot more than He blessed the Jews. But then there is wealth. The Kuwaiti government alone recycles fifty-five billion per annum alone in petro-dollars through the city of London. In terms of wealth He has blessed the Arabs more than He has blessed the Jews. All that land, all those people, all that wealth and they despise their birthright. They covet a little strip of land.

How does God see this? Now notice what it says about Esau, "By your sword you shall live." Mohamed's goal was to see the Arabian tribes stop fighting each other. The only way for the Arabian tribes to stop fighting each other is to reverse the curse put on Ishmael and Esau. But that curse can only be broken in the same way the curse of the law can be broken for their Jewish brothers: the cross of the Messiah - the one Jews call Yeshua HaMashiach. The one Arabs call Yesua. Mohamed however, tried to break that curse by putting a Surah in the Koran called Umma, saying "we are one nation and one people."

I used to live among the Arabs in London and I used to preach among them every Sunday and when I was in seminary I'd go down there with my stepladder. I was down there during the war in the Gulf and when the Muslims began to gather I would say, "If you are one nation and one people like the Koran says, why did King Hussein of Jordan exterminate 18 thousand Palestinians in twelve days? I'll tell you why. Because the 'Ketab' (Judeo Christian bible) is right and the Koran is wrong.

"Tell me, how come one and a half million Muslims died in the jihad, as they called it, between Iran and Iraq? You say, 'it's not jihad.' Go to Iran and say it wasn't a jihad. They will kill you. Let me tell you why one and a half million died, because the Bible is true and the Koran is false. You are not one nation and one people like the Koran says. You are a divided nation and a divided people like the Bible says and you will be until you accept the Seed of Abraham."

"How come Kuwait has just been invaded by Iraq?" I asked them. "I'll tell you why, because the Bible is true and the Koran is wrong." By that time, I was surrounded by dozens and dozens of increasingly incensed Arabs and they began to scream louder. So, I began to praise the Lord, in Arabic, which only made them angrier. They were going nuts, vehement! One guy was spitting and saying they were going to kill me. And I said , "You're not one nation and one people. I saw the king of Saudi Arabia on TV – 'Help England! Help America! Help Christian nations! Save me from the jihad! Save me from my Muslim brothers! Protect the tomb of the prophet! Save the Kabah!' From whom? Your Islamic brothers! 'His sword will be against everyone, his seed will be divided.' There is no Umma. You want to break that curse? The only one who can break it is the Seed of Abraham."

And likewise, I say to my Jewish friends and family, "Zionism is not the way of salvation. You lived in terror in Europe, now you live in terror in you own land. You want to break that curse? - the Seed of Abraham!" and believe me, they can get almost as angry.

In Genesis 28 verse 9, Esau went to Ishmael and married. Anthropologically you have intermarriage between the descendants of Ishmael who are already cousins, and the descendants of Esau, and we know the nations which they settled, the lands to the east. So, how does God see this? One of the longest chapters in the Bible is Genesis 36. It is the lineage and pedigree of the Arab nations. Why does God give so much space in His Word to the Arabs? Only the Jews get more mention. Why - because they are Abraham's descendants and He has a prophetic destiny for them but, there are terrible things prophesied to happen in the Middle East, to the Jew and the Arab. There are unfulfilled prophecies of devastation that are coming to both the Jewish and the Arab nations.

God sees the dispute over land and has determined whose land is whose. God told Moses:

> "Command the people saying you will pass
> through the territory of your brothers, the sons of
> Esau, and live in Seir and they will be afraid of you so

*be very careful. Do not provoke them for I will not
give you any of their land even as little as a footstep,
because I've given Mt Seir to Esau as a possession.
You shall buy food from them, with money, so that you
may eat and you shall also purchase water from them,
with money, so that you may drink. For the Lord your
God has blessed you in all that you have done. He has
known your wanderings through this great wilderness.
These forty years the Lord your God has been with you
and you have not lacked a thing." So we passed
beyond our brothers the sons of Esau...* (In the eyes of
God, Jews and Arabs are brothers) *and we turned
through and passed through by the way of the
wilderness of Moab. And the Lord said to me, "Do not
harass Moab or provoke them for I will not give you
any of their land as a possession because I've given Ar
to the sons of Lot."*

-Deuteronomy 2:4-9

"These are your kinsmen! Don't take your brother's land! I've given
you this land, that land to the east belongs to your Arab brothers!
They are your brothers, that's theirs, don't you touch what belongs to
them!" God told the Jews. All that land, all that wealth, all those
people - Moab, Edom and Amman are modern Jordan. "Don't touch
it! Don't take it! I gave it to them." God promised them land. He
promised them a birthright. But like Esau they despise it. Instead of
cultivating it they intentionally turned it into desert. But what comes
next? Then they want to usurp what God gave to their brothers, the
Jews.

This is also recorded in the Book of Numbers:

> *From Kadesh, Moses then sent messengers to
> the king of Edom. "Thus your brother Israel...."* (your
> brother)   -Numbers 20:14

"Treat me like a brother and I'll treat you like a brother. We'll have trade, we'll be good neighbors, we'll be friends and we'll be brothers!" That's what God wanted. But Jacob connives and Esau despises.

> "*Thus your brother Israel has said, 'You know all the hardship that has befallen us, that our fathers went down to Egypt and we stayed in Egypt a long time and the Egyptians treated us badly and our fathers badly, but when we cried out to the Lord He heard our voice and He sent an Angel and brought us out of Egypt. Now behold, we are at Kadesh* (it's a word for holy in Hebrew) *a town on the edge of your territory. Please let us pass through your land. We will not pass through your field or your vineyard. We will not even drink water from a well. We will go along the king's highway (which is still there in Jordan to this day) not turning to the right or to the left until we pass through your territory.' Edom however said to him, 'You shall not pass through us lest I come out against you with the sword.' And again, the sons of Israel said to him, 'We shall go up by the highway and if I and my livestock do drink any of your water then I shall pay its price. Let us only pass through on our way, nothing else.' But he said, 'You shall not pass through.' And Edom came out against him with a heavy force, with a strong hand. Thus Edom refused to allow Israel to pass through his territory. So Israel turned away from him.*
>
> *Now when they set out from Kadesh, the sons of Israel, the whole congregation, came to Moses, and the Lord spoke to Moses and Aaron at Mount Horeb, by the border of the land of Edom saying, 'Aaron shall be gathered to his people and Aaron would die.'"*

Numbers 20:14-24

This was a bad time for Israel. Aaron was about to die. They were just trying to get by and their own brothers said "you can't come here!" "But we want good relations. You are our kin. We are descended from Abraham. If you don't want to sell us water, fine. We just want to go by." "No!"

Look what God said to the Hebrews concerning the Canaanites. "Wipe them out!" The Amalekites: "Wipe them out!" The Philistines: "Wipe them out!" The Arab, "Don't touch him, he is your brother, I gave that to him. That's his. He is not being too kind to you, but I'll deal with him. Don't you touch him." Yet he despised his birthright and he despises it to this day. In the character of Jacob, in the character of Moses, Israel had tried and tried and tried to get along peaceably.

How does this end?

But, we know how it ends in Zechariah 12. However, it's not the end of the story - Zechariah 14 is. That speaks of the millennial reign of Jesus, when the nations will come to Jerusalem and celebrate Sukkoth, the Feast of Booths. The Feast of Booths is a picture of the millennial reign, according to Zechariah. That is why at the transfiguration, Peter wanted to build three booths. He thought it was the beginning of the millennium, the Messianic Kingdom. Here is Moses, here is Elijah and here is the Messiah. You've got a man who is raptured, a man who is resurrected and Jesus. This is the Millennium. "Let me build three booths." He thought that this was the Messianic fulfillment of Tabernacles.

During this period, the nations will come and worship the Messiah in Jerusalem. Jerusalem is not even mentioned in the Koran. It is mentioned dozens and dozens of times in both Testaments. There is a place called *Al Quds* in Arabic but there is no proof that it is

Jerusalem. No, it does not end with the return of Christ. Something else happens. This is what the Middle East will come to. The United Nations won't bring this about. The United States won't bring this about. The Arab League won't bring this about. The European Union won't bring this about. No man will bring this about. No man can bring this about. This will be brought about by one thing and one thing only, the return of Jesus to reign from the throne of David.

The 19th chapter of the book of Isaiah tells us what will happen during the millennial reign of Christ:

> *In that day there will be a highway from Egypt to Assyria. The Assyrians will come into Egypt and the Egyptians into Assyria, and the Egyptians will worship with the Assyrians. In that day Israel will be a third party with Egypt and Assyria, a blessing in the midst of the earth whom the Lord of Hosts has blessed saying "Blessed is Egypt My people, and in Assyria the work of My hands and Israel My inheritance."*
>
> -Isaiah 19:23

"Egypt, My people? Assyria the work of My hands? Israel My inheritance?" That's how it will end! There will be peace when the Prince of Peace reigns on the throne of David. Before that there will be a false peace, but this will be a real peace.

The Book of Genesis gives us a glimpse of what happens when Jacob is reconciled to Esau. Jacob is indeed reconciled to Esau, when he wrestles with the Angel of the Lord at Peniel. Something happens. Jacob is left alone at the darkest and most terrible hour of his history. He sees Esau coming, so he divides his children into two camps in case some get wiped out, others will survive. He thinks Esau is going to wipe him out. But instead, something happens:

> *Esau runs to meet him, grabs his neck, and kisses him, embraces his neck and they wept and he lifts his eyes and sees the women and children. "Who are these with you?" "The children God has graciously given your servant!"* (Your servant?) *And the maids came near with their children and they bowed down. And Leah likewise came with her children and they bowed down. And Joseph came near with Rachel and they bowed down. And He said, "What do you mean with all this company?" And he said, "To find favor in the sight of my lord." But Esau said, "I found plenty, my brother. Let what you have be your own." And Jacob said, "No! Please, if I have found favor take my present for I see your face as one sees the face of God and you have received me in favor."*

-Genesis 33:4-10

For centuries, the rabbis have said correctly, that as Jacob and Esau were reconciled, in the days of Messiah the Jewish and Arab nations will be reconciled. Can you imagine the Jew and the Arab calling each other brother, trying to outdo each other in grace, in righteousness and brotherly love? Can you imagine the Jews saying "you take this" and the Arab saying "no, you take this?" Can you imagine a Jew saying to an Arab "when I look at you, I see the face of our Maker?" That will come about one day.

God cannot lie, but you know, I don't have to wait for that to happen. I see that happen every time a Jew puts his faith in Yeshua the Messiah, the Seed of Abraham. Every time an Arab puts his faith in Yeshua, the Seed of Abraham, that happens. I've seen Jews and I've seen Arabs walk in fellowship as brothers. Oh! It will happen some day, but it is also happening this day. Our ministry in Israel supports evangelism. The evangelists that we help sponsor witness to both Jews and Arabs. I don't have to wait for it to happen. The Seed of Abraham is already making it happen. I don't care what the Israeli government says. I don't care what the Arab governments say. I don't care what the UN says. I don't care what the White House or Number 10 says. I care what the Bible says. I know what's going to happen!

Governments will not have their way in the Middle East. International bodies will not have their way in the Middle East. And above all Satan will not have his way in the Middle East. God is going to have His way in the Middle East!

Chapter 4

The Curse of Obadiah

And The Islamic Terrorist Bombings in London

"For the Day of The Lord draws near on all the nations. As you have done, it will be done to you. Your dealings will return on your own head."
                                                                -Obadiah 1:15

In the book of Obadiah a prophetic curse is placed on the Arab nations descended from Esau and on their dwelling in southern Jordan, Edom, (so named not only for the redness of Esau's hair or complexion but for the red color of the mountains of Seir surrounding Petra where he and his descendants dwelt). The inhabitants had always taken a rather nasty disposition towards their Israelite brethren, who only wanted to befriend them and have peaceful trade relations and the right to transit to their own promised land, but the Israelites were not to respond with hostility or touch the land God promised to their brothers/cousins who were also descended from Abraham. (Deuteronomy 2:2-5)

Obadiah's curse had specific meaning to the land of Edom when Edom gloated over and effectively supported the Babylonian captivity of the Jews circa 585 BC. The pattern was typical. God would use a heathen nation with a heathen religion to judge His own people for their sin, but then He would judge and even destroy those heathen nations.

It is the same pattern we witness today. As a lover of America, of Britain, and of Israel – it is personally difficult for me to face up to the fact that Islam and its barbaric cruelty is a judgment on the Judeo-Christian world for their rejection of the God of the Judeo-Christian Scriptures. Also as one who had a family member murdered by the radical Islamists in the Twin Towers in New York on September 11th, it is not without a deep sense of compassion for those who also lost family and friends in the July 2005 Islamic terror attacks in London, that I ponder this Scripture. It is not a judgment against individuals, but against nations and godless societies that God allows these murdering savages to infiltrate and rise up against, using senseless violence in the name of their religion.

I cannot as a believer in Jesus incite hatred against Muslims. But it is no less a fact that their religion (Islam) has perpetrated open genocide against Christians in East Timor, the Molukan Islands, the Southern Philippines, Eritrea, Northern Nigeria, Saudi Arabia (which hangs, flogs and beheads Christians), Iran (which is racing to build a nuclear bomb) and Egypt which is supposedly moderate, but arrests and persecutes people for becoming Christian, and cannot reasonably be described as anything short of satanic, by Christian standards. May more Muslims come to know Christ and may the Western world wake up to the reality of Islam (based on the writings of the Koran) and its destructive goals for the west and the world.

Eschatologically however, in verse 15 of its solitary chapter, the book of Obadiah expands the prophecy to all nations, predicting that as we approach The Last Days, Divine retribution will fall upon other nations in accordance with their maltreatment of Israel. This directly relates to God's promise to Abraham in Genesis 12:1-3 and reiterated to Jacob to "curse those cursing and bless those blessing Abraham's descendants" via the lineage of Isaac and Jacob. It also points ahead to Jesus coming to save the surviving Jews of "the time of Jacob's Trouble," which occurs during the Great Tribulation in the Book of Zechariah chapters 10-12.

The tragic events that transpired in London when British born Muslims became suicide bombers because of their Islamic beliefs must be viewed in this light. There is a Divine retribution and God is trying to wake up the Western World not only to the reality of Islam's global persecution of Christians, but to its own sin and indeed blasphemy. It is for sure that the BBC would not have dared to broadcast a Jerry Springer Opera at Ramadan with Mohammed saying that he was a "little bit gay" as they ascribed to Jesus at Christmas. Such dual standards at the BBC accurately portray not only its cowardice but also hypocrisy: BBC = Bias Blasphemy Cowardice. It is not only the British media, campuses, and church that continually denounces Israel in its struggle to live in a land that archaeological records prove is historically theirs. It is the government too! No one would dare say Apaches occupy Arizona or Maoris occupy New Zealand or that the Irish occupy Ulster. The rights of others to live in New Zealand, Arizona, or Ulster is not in dispute, but only in regards to Israel do academics, theocrats, politicians, and distorting propagandists, who masquerade as journalists, call the indigenous an occupation.

What drives the political left? Whether it be it the Galloways or Sizers, or Goerings, or Fisks (or even a now failed Islamic aligned Tory politician like David Mellor) it certainly cannot be left wing ideology or a genuine concern for human rights. If that were the case they would be focused not against Israel, a state safeguarding not only the human rights of homosexuals and religious minorities, and of Muslims living in Israel, but against the Islamic nations who do no protect such human rights.

Galloway once made a statement supportive of Saddam Hussein who, like Hitler, used chemical agents against women and children (Kurdish Muslims). Galloway was later forced to withdraw in the face of Hussein's slaughter of hundreds of thousands of Muslims. The Fisks and Goerings seem to expect the world to ignore that the only orchestrated campaigns of genocide against the Palestinian

Arabs were carried out, not by Israel, but rather by Jordan in Black September of 1970 (after Arafat tried on King Hussein what he would later try on Israel), by Kuwait after the Palestinian Arabs supported the Iraqi invasion and rape of Kuwait, and by other Palestinian Arabs in their own civil war in Lebanon. They also expect us to ignore the fact that prior to the intifadas, the World Health Organization determined that in terms of everything from life expectancy to infant mortality and employment, the standard of living of West Bank Arabs improved by 320% under the Israelis and by 370% among Gaza Arabs above what it had been under Islamic rule. Left leaning politicians expect the world to pretend that there were Palestinian Arabs in the West Bank before 1967, when in fact they were called Jordanians and 70% of the population in Jordan today is "Palestinian Arab." They expect the world to forget that from 1948 until 1967, the West Bank, Gaza, and East Jerusalem were all in the hands of Arab Muslims.

If the Muslim world really wanted a second Palestinian Arab Muslim state in addition to Jordan, why did the Arab Muslim world not simply establish one when they had the opportunity of nearly 20 years to do so? Instead of asking the obvious however, we are called to subscribe to the rewriting of history by revisionist liars and unprincipled journalists. Stephen Sizer and his Sabeel movement and the Presbyterian Church of America say little or nothing about the horrific persecution of Arab Christians in Muslim countries. Instead they gang up on little Israel, a country which protects the rights of Arab Christians, and has the courage to stand up to this same radical Islamic oppression that kills Christians. It is difficult to account for such a conspicuous and willful blindness to fact. But combine this with an irrational response to the issues of human rights in the Middle East and this is simply a case of historical European anti-Semitism and Jew hatred operating under a guise of concern for the downtrodden. The reality is that it is the Christian communities of the Islamic world who are the downtrodden, persecuted, and repressed.

Recently Britain has had a glimpse of what the Christian communities of the Islamic world constantly experience. They have seen terror promoter Abu Hamza preaching hatred, and what makes it even worse is that he has been doing this at the expense of the British tax payer courtesy of the British government. The refusal of the British government, in the opinion of many, to link asylum policy with the terror threat, and to link the high rate of Muslims on the dole with the dhimmi (an Islamic tax penalty tax on non-Muslims), is not the only reason for the rise of Islamic terror in the UK.

Indeed, the London suicide terrorists were British born Muslims, like John Walker Lindh in the USA, dispelling the silly myth that Western Muslims do not share the same intolerance as those in Muslim nations but are more civilized; which is plainly not the case. Such attacks also dispel the myth that suicide bombing is the action of uneducated Muslims, when in fact; some of these bombers were university graduates.

These attacks drive the suspicion into people's minds that every Muslim, western born or not, educated or not, is a potential terrorist and may be a fanatical religious killer. This indeed may often be the case, although not necessarily always the case. While I can only consider fundamentalist Islam to be a terrorist religion, as a Christian must love my enemies and do not condone the hatred of Muslims. However, It also needs to be understood that literally thousand of sections of the Koran and Hadith condone murder, killing and hatred of Christians and Jews. Because of this I hate the (false) religion of Islam.

Neither is the problem only the result of the failure to crack down on radical Islam after thousands of barbarians took to the streets of London demanding the murder of a British citizen for writing a book they did not like.

The real trigger for the Islamic attacks on London is the 'seed faith' principle of reaping as one sows; what happened in London on July 7th, 2005 was Obadiah 1:15 in action as were the attempted attacks two weeks later, in Sham el Shak, Egypt, killing British tourists. This is what can be expected. Cheri Blair, wife of the Prime Minster made a statement sympathetic of Islamic suicide bombers in Israel. As a barrister she defended the demands of a fundamentalist Muslim to wear a veil over her face in defiance of a school's dress code. London's mayor Ken Livingstone invited Sheikh Yusuf Al Qaradawi, often called "the Islamic theologian of terror" who supported suicide bombers in Israel, to London telling him "he was most welcome." Well Mr. Livingstone, you welcomed a supporter of terror to London, so terror itself came to London under your leadership!

With a woman like Cherie Blair in Number 10, and with a Livingston in the seat of London's mayor, combined with a David Galloway in Parliament representing a London constituency, how could such attacks not come to London?

God says: "As you have done it will be done to you, your dealings will return to your head." Churchill was dramatically removed from office a week after turning his back on the Zionist cause of Jews who survived the concentration camps and needed a homeland. When Britain revoked the Balfour declaration and broke its promise to Jewry, allowing Jews to burn in ovens instead of returning to the home the British crown and God had promised them, London, Liverpool, and Coventry also burned. When Britain took the Jews who survived the Nazi concentration camps and placed them in British internment camps on Cyprus, the Empire began to crumble quickly.

When the Mayor of London Ken Livingston made statements akin to those of Omar Bakri Mohammed and Arjem Choudary, blaming British foreign policy for the suicide attacks, he came close to justifying suicide bombing. Livingston also took the occasion to point the finger at Israel falsely accusing them of the indiscriminate slaughter of Muslim women and children, which is of course a lie. To find the indiscriminate slaughter of Muslim women and children one would rather need to look to Islam and the terrorism in Iraq perpetrated by Muslims against Muslim women and children. Livingston also referred to the Israeli soldiers protecting their nation and their families from the same Islamic terror that murdered 57 in London as "Jewish Boys', potentially inciting further anti-Semitic attacks in London by Muslims. Livingston went on to say that Palestinian Muslim youth become suicide bombers because they don't have a vote, implying that this is Israel's fault. In fact, Livingston did not speak the truth. Israeli Arabs do have a vote and Gaza Muslims voted for Mahmoud Abbas and Ismail Haniyeh. It is unlikely such persons will abandon their wickedness and hypocrisy, hence, lest they do, we pray the swift judgment of God on Livingston, Galloway, and Blair and their ilk as well as upon the biased elements of the media. We pray for a Divine judgment. The Divine judgment we yearn for is not for their death (that is the prerogative of God) or physical harm but removal from the corridors of power, least these wicked people bring further retribution on all of us.

The July 2005 attacks took place during the G 8 summit and eclipsed both the summit and the Live 8 concerts. Yet the very day after the attacks, Tony Blair reacted in precisely the same way that George Bush and his oil interest owned administration reacted to September 11th. These politicians did what politicians seem to do best – lie!

Both immediately praised Islam as a religion of peace and tolerance knowing that not a single Islamic country will give Christians and Jews the freedom they receive in Britain, America, Israel, Australia or any other western country. The Saudis fund the radicalism that breeds terror and finance the construction of mosques all over America and Britain with the de facto blessings of men like Bush and Blair, (while Bush and Blair remain silent when the same Saudis arrest, beat or execute people for becoming Christians as recent headlines have shown). Yet these demonic radical savages will not allow one church to be built in Saudi Arabia. Blair and Bush know these facts. They also know that we are in a conflict of cultures and there are three times as many conflicts involving Islam as all of the other people groups put together. In Islam it is simple – Muslims have rights, others do not. Left wing politicians seem to now agree this should also be the case in the UK. Radical Islam sees Western principles of democracy and tolerance as weaknesses in our culture to be exploited.

Blair's second reaction was to use the event to revoke a law 'inciting to religious hatred' (That is designed in the admission of his former home secretary for use against evangelical Christians) making it illegal to speak against Islam making religious vilification a hate crime.

Blair's solution is simple - since Muslims do not allow freedom of religious expression in Islamic countries, in order to placate the Islamic community we should also not allow it here! Using the Blair government, Islam seeks to deprive British citizens of the freedoms denied in Islamic countries. This can affect evangelism to Muslims, and campaigning for the human rights of persecuted Christians in Islamic countries. A case can emerge, where instead of protecting Salman Rushdie; the British police will now be obligated to arrest him if a complaint is made against him.

It is also interesting to note that the Muslim Council of Great Britain sent a delegation to Mr. Blair demanding that in exchange for their condemnation of the London attacks, public reading and preaching from passages of the Koran and Hadith calling for the murder of Christians and Jews be excluded from the incitement law. The situation is clear! If Christians cite passages calling for Muslims to murder Christians and Jews, it is incitement to religious hatred, yet when Muslims read those same passages it somehow becomes religious freedom. This type of action has already been effectively decreed by Judge Michael Higgins in Melbourne, Australia where a similar anti-vilification law already exists and is being used to persecute Christians.

We sympathize with those in Australia believing that Higgins should be sent to Saudi Arabia. Those who legislate and adjudicate against democracy, do not deserve to live in a democracy. Higgins issued opinions that were not purely legal, but theological and out of his scope of expertise, and he did so even though 88 Australians came home from vacation in Bali in coffins courtesy of a 'religion of peace and tolerance.' It should also be noted that the militant leader of the Jemaah Islamiyah branch of Al Qaeda responsible for the bombing got two years in prison in the Islamic nation of Indonesia, and the leader of the fundamentalist group who bombed the Australian embassy got three years, and a young Australian woman, (whose guilt is questionable) got 20 years for transporting cannabis.

Higgins handed down convictions of two Christian pastors for vilifying Islam while across town an Islamic bookshop was selling Islamic literature calling for "Christians to be trampled under foot". Indeed, it is reasonable for Higgins to be 'transported' to Saudi Arabia. Since he doesn't believe in the free expression of religious opinion as a matter of democratic values, he should do the honorable thing and live in an Islamic country like Saudi Arabia where he won't have any religious freedom.

Mr. Blair's third reaction was the most ludicrous of all. The day after the London bombings, the Palestinian Authority TV (of which Mahmoud Abbas had authority over) broadcast a sermon by an Islamic cleric calling for terror attacks on Britain. Blair's response was to join with Bush in giving another $3 billion to Abbas and his Palestinian Authority (PA), whose Al Aqsa Brigade faction was continuing its terror war against Israel in violation of a supposed cease fire that the British media blamed Israel for ending when it returned fire in self-defense. The billions already stupidly given to the PA by the USA and Europe were stolen, squandered, or used to finance terror and violence. So, Blair decided the day after the London bombings at the G8 summit to give them more money at the same time their TV station broadcast calls for more terror attacks on Britain.

Although Britain and the USA (as well as Germany, Japan France, Russia, and Canada) are facing major budget deficit problems, Saudi oil revenues have doubled. Yet Bush and Blair think it should be the West (throwing good money after bad) helping an Islamic cause that hates America and Britain. This same scenario was seen during the tsunami that hit the Indian Ocean. It was to be the West, not the Saudis or oil rich Gulf States, who flooded Asia with Tsunami aid, despite most of the victims being Muslims. Somehow, it is the West, instead of the oil rich Islamic countries who are expected to absorb and support Islamic asylum seekers from Somalia and elsewhere.

Such a response was rivaled only when Bush continued to import Saudis under the easy access express visa program for a full year after September 11th, and when his father's Secretary of State, James Baker (who left Saddam Hussein in power in 1991 to placate the Saudis, leaving Iraq in its present debacle) became defense attorney for the Saudi Arabians against the families of the September 11th victims in a class action litigation.

As Mr. Bush continues to respond to Islamic terror by bullying Israel to bow the knee to Islamic terror and forfeit it's God given right, and what the archaeological record proves is its historical homeland to Islam, God's judgment falls on America in Iraq because of Bush and his oil crony administration. While the Judeo-Christian Scriptures establish that the land (less than 1% of the land the Arab Muslim nations have) belongs to the Jews, Israel can also make a legal and historical claim to the land as the archaeologically supported indigenous people. Islam's claim can not be based on any archaeological evidence, but is based only the terrorist doctrine of jihad, demanding others acquiesce and submit to the dominion of their religion with its culture of human rights violation. It is a demand which the oil controlled American government and Bush family seem to be supporting by their actions and political decisions.

Adding insult to injury, the Australian education minister now wants to force Australian taxpayers to fund the education of Islamic clergy in Australia in order to help prevent radical jihadist preaching in mosques. Australia does not publicly fund the training of Christian or Jewish clergy, but Australian politicians in Canberra want Australian Christians and Jews to pick up the bill for educating Muslim clergy in Australia, supposedly to control terrorist theology. But thinking people can only ask "what kind of barbaric religion has a terrorist theology to begin with?" Australia's highly taxed citizens are already forced to fund the imprisonment of many Muslims in jail and the disproportionately high Muslim population on the dole and on public benefit. Now, the Australian taxpayers are to be handed the bill for training their clergy, when a growing number of Australians would prefer to pay for the deportation of radical Muslims. Such madness and injustice continues to be fueled by the lunacy of politicians and biases of the left wing media.

The fear of an increasing number of people in Britain, Europe, Australia, and America is that the refusal of elected governments to carry out deportations, stop Islamic immigration and asylum seeking, and close radical mosques and institutions that have had terrorist links such as the Council for American Islamic Relations, only alienate working class taxpayers and engender support for racist neo Nazi and national front type extremist political parties in elections. The Bush administration gave over $50,000 in US tax payer money to Islamic organizations in order to train them how to apply for more federal grants. Like their predecessor Bill Clinton (whose library was funded in large measure by Saudi interests), it is not the Saudis who should fund the Palestinian Authority, whose people danced in the streets celebrating the murder of nearly 3,000 Americans on September 11th, and whose Al Aqsa Brigade continue their campaign of terror and murder.

It is the deficit strapped American working man whose country Muslims attacked on September 11th and whose sons come home in body bags from a new Vietnam in Iraq. And why? Because George Bush Sr. left Saddam Hussein in power in 1991, at the behest of his Saudi oil partners in the Carlyle enterprise who did not want regime change. It is not Republican rich kids who usually come home in body bags (neither Bush and Cheney served in Vietnam nor opposed it). It is the working man and woman getting stabbed in the back, whose kids get killed, and who are then expected to finance those wishing to kill them.

Our purposes as a ministry are theological not political, but theologically we must examine world events in light of biblical prophecy (despite the dangerous and false assertions of Rick Warren that we should not).

When Americans died in Vietnam, it was a corrupt Republican Watergate administration elected with the backing of Billy Graham and Evangelical Christians that traded with the Soviets under détente while the Soviets supplied the North Vietnamese with the hardware to kill Americans. Now, they are at it again, as another Republican administration, once more engrossed in scandal and elected with the support of Evangelical Christians is in bed with the same Saudis who fund the fundamentalism that breeds support for terror. The Republicans lost Vietnam and now they are losing the war on terror for the same reasons of corruption and betrayal. I have little doubt; this is a judgment on a backslidden America and on its backslidden church.

On top of this, America's placation of evil Islam at the expense of Israel is bringing the curse of Obadiah 1:15 upon the United States.

Just as in Billy Graham's now revealed anti-Jewish dialogue with Nixon, we have another so-called Christian Republican engaged in anti-Jewish dialogue, demanding the forfeiture of Jewish land to Islam. Despite the majority of the 9/11 suicide hijackers being Saudi, the Bush administration continued to import Saudi fundamentalists into the USA as the easy entry express visa program for Saudis was continued for over one year. Such a policy of madness in itself is part of God's judgment. Politicians in America, Britain, and Australia open the gates to our enemies because these fundamentalists are agents of God's wrath just as Babylon was to ancient Judah, but the basis of guilt and blame is not with political parties or conniving politicians but with a church that is no longer salt and light.

We have the money grabbing tele-evangelists and the ecumenical treason of Chuck Colson. We have the market driven, psychology, and New Age drivel of Rick Warren and Purpose Driven 40 Days of Purpose, and similar escapades of Bill Hybels, Robert Schuller, and the "emergent church" of Brian MacLaren, as well as Ken Blanchard's hybrid of New Age and the Gospel. What we do not have is a church that is being salt and light that Jesus commanded, but rather darkness and vomit. With such delusion abundant in the church, what can be expected from mere politicians in the White House or at Number 10? When ancient Israel and Judah had corrupt clergy among the Levites, it had corrupt kings and God brought judgment from nations like Babylon (Iraq) and Edom (proto Arabs). Now the Christian church has a twisted clergy and hence twisted political leaders and judgment once more arises from those same nations, evil as they are, as agents of reproof against the stiff necked Judeo-Christian world.

Unless America, Britain, and Australia wake up they will not be immune and indeed the virus seems to already be at work among us. Yet we know that the Christians will not wake up unless their churches do, but their churches won't unless the church leaders do. But that just isn't happening!

We have asked for prayer that God's wrath would rather fall on the Bush administration than fall on America because of the Bush administration decisions and actions against Israel, and the Lord is moving. Along with Grover Norquist, Carl Rove is a political kingpin in the Bush administration who is often seen as an arch Saudi bootlicker and political manipulator representing oil interests inside the White House. Yet it has been Rove who has pushed Bush the most, to distance himself from the Evangelical right once the elections were over, and when they were no longer needed for electoral reasons.

Now, Rove is at the center of a scandal exposing the identity of a secret intelligence agent that would, if proven, constitute a criminal breach of federal law. Unless he turns from his sell out to Islam and his betrayal of Israel for the price of a no longer cheap barrel of Saudi oil, may the judgment of God continue to fall on the Bush administration and on Rove.

We are seeing continual betrayals and contradictions worldwide. At the time when a series of Islamic attacks took place in London, Islamic scholars in Britain debated if or not suicide bombing was permitted in the Koran. We have witnessed Islamic postgraduate students in Atlanta cheering on September 11th when the Twin Towers came down. It is also evident that there is far more sympathy for Islamic terror among British, American, and Australian Muslims than the politicians want to admit or the media wants to report. The media continually compound the situation and despite September 11th, the Bali bombings, the Lockerbie bombings etc. all taking place before the Anglo American invasion of Iraq, some in the biased media and Islamic community are proposing the illogical and ludicrous assertion that the invasion has caused the avalanche of Islamic terror that has preceded it!

What we are seeing is political hypocrisy, judicial hypocrisy, academic hypocrisy, and journalistic hypocrisy. Add to this ecclesiastical hypocrisy on a level that would have been unimaginable a generation ago. It then produces what we are see Obadiah 1:15 warning us about.

The predictive promise of God in Obadiah 1:15 is literal and will continue. In any climate of heightened anxiety induced by the climate of fear terror engenders, mistakes can happen. While the British media and politicians linked with Islamic interests blame Israel for its self defensive actions in killing terrorists before the terrorists kill them, now the British have realized that Islamic terrorists must be shot dead in the streets of London as they have had to be shot dead on the streets of Tel Aviv and Jerusalem. Only they fault Israel for shooting terrorists. On a London subway the British police accidentally shot dead a completely innocent man in a small taste of the atmosphere of continual tension Israelis have had to live with for years.

A time will come when the western media will not be denouncing Israel for sending tanks into Jenin or Gaza in response to Islamic terror because the British government will be forced to send tanks into Bradford and Birmingham for the same reasons. It is also with little doubt that Canada will reap what it has sowed in its giving abode to Islamic radicals and pandering to them in its media such as the CBC. What they have condemned Israel for doing; such nations will be forced to do themselves. They will now see just how peaceful and tolerant Islam really is; a religion they have repeatedly preached is peaceful and tolerant! Yet the proven action of Islamic nations says otherwise as Western politicians lie in support of them. They know that from September 11th to the murder of Theo Van Gough in Holland to the Islamic gangs of Sydney and Malmo, Sweden, hardly a single civilized country that has allowed Islamic immigration has not reaped violent consequences and threats to their freedom because of the sizeable radical elements.

They will now see just how peaceful and tolerant Islam is; again a religion they have preached is peaceful and tolerant. As has come upon Israel, now comes upon Israel's critics. If western societies and their churches will turn their backs on cries of the martyrs, persecuted for the name of Jesus in Islamic countries in order to befriend the faith of their persecutors, they will suffer at the hands of Islam themselves. The media and the politicians in Washington and Whitehall will tell the public everything but the truth. The Word of God however does tell us the truth, and the truth is again Obadiah 1:15. Our sincere condolences to all who lost loved ones on July 7th 2005 and we assure our Muslim friends that we do not hate them; we only despise their wicked evil terrorist religion (again we make this last statement based on the authoritative teachings of the Koran and Hadith) that is leading them to eternal hell and we pray that they will come to know the true faith of the God of Israel through Jesus. Our purpose is not to editorialize along political lines, but to examine these prophetically significant events biblically. We also urge prayers for Mr. Blair, Mr. Bush, Mr. Olmert, and Mr. Howard in accordance with the teachings of Scripture. Above all we pray that, in the mercy of God, Tony Blair's war on religious freedom and democracy in placation of Islamic pressure will again be stopped in the House of Lords and that he will not be able to misuse the Parliament Act to force his ban on free religious speech into law. May the speedy wrath of God come upon this Christian persecuting, Jew hating religious culture of Islamic fundamentalism and may God deal with its defenders in the media and in the governments of free nations.

Chapter 5

A Prophet Like Moses

> *"I will raise up a Prophet from among their countrymen like you, and I will put My words in His mouth, and he shall speak to them all that I command Him."*

-Deuteronomy 18:18

Distinguishing between real and false prophets

> *"But the prophet who shall speak a word presumptuously in my Name, which I have not commanded him to speak, or which he shall speak in the name of other gods, that prophet shall die."*

-Deuteronomy 18:20

It does not matter if people predict something in the Name of the Lord because they are inspired by a demon, or if they do it by the futility of their own mind. Either way, a false prophet is a false prophet.

> *"And you may say in your heart, 'How shall we know the word which the Lord has not spoken?' When a prophet speaks in the Name of the Lord, if the thing does not come about or come true, that is the thing, which the Lord has not spoken. The prophet has spoken it presumptuously; you shall not be afraid of him."*

-Deuteronomy 18:21-22

> *Then Jeremiah the prophet said to Hananiah the prophet, "Listen now, Hananiah, the Lord has not sent you, and you have made this people trust in a lie. Therefore thus says the Lord, 'Behold, I am about to remove you from the face of the earth ......'"*
>
> -Jeremiah 28:15-16

Hananiah predicted things that did not happen.

> *Then the Lord said to me, "The prophets are prophesying falsehood in my Name. I have neither sent them nor commanded them nor spoken to them; they are prophesying to you a false vision, divination, futility and the deception of their own minds."*
>
> -Jeremiah 14:14

These false prophets were deceived by what was in their own mind. There were a lot of false prophets during the time of Jeremiah, but even after their prophecies were proven to be false, people continued to follow them:

> *"The prophets prophesy falsely, and the priests rule on their own authority; and my people love it so! But what will you do at the end of it?"*
>
> -Jeremiah 5:31

It does not say they are not His people, nor that they are not prophets, but He does say that they prophesy falsely and the people love it so!

Now, when Jesus warned about false prophets in the Last Days, many people think He was talking about the Jehovah Witnesses, the Mormons, the Hare Krishnas, etc. There is no doubt that the proliferation of these cults is of some prophetic significance, and they are certainly false prophets, but those are not the false prophets Jesus was warning about. He said:

For false christs and false prophets will be raised, and they will give signs and wonders in order to lead astray, if possible even the elect.

-Mark 13:22

Jesus - A Prophet like Moses

The Talmud, Midrash Tanhuma, Targum Yonatan and Ralbag (14th century) all say that Deuteronomy 18:18 is about the Messiah:

"I will raise up a Prophet from among their countrymen like you, and I will put My words in His mouth, and he shall speak to them all that I command Him."

We know that it is about Jesus - Yeshua!

Let us compare Moses and Jesus, a prophet like Moses:

Born under oppressive foreign rule

Now a new king arose over Egypt, who did not know Joseph. And he said to his people, "Behold, the people of the sons of Israel are more and mightier than we. Come let us deal wisely with them, lest they multiply and in the event of war, they also join themselves to those who hate us, and fight against us, and depart from the land." So they appointed taskmasters over them to afflict them with hard labor. And they built for Pharaoh, storage cities, Pithom and Raamses.

-Exodus 1:8-11

Moses was born under an oppressive, foreign rule.

> *Now it came about in those days that a decree went out from Caesar Augustus, that a census be taken of all the inhabited earth. This was the first census taken while Quirinius was governor of Syria.*
>
> -Luke 2:1-2

Jesus was also born under an oppressive, foreign rule.

Threatened by a wicked king

> *Then the king of Egypt spoke to the Hebrew midwives, one of whom was named Shiphrah and the other was named Puah; and he said, "When you are helping the Hebrew women to give birth and see them upon the birthstool, if it is a son, then you shall put him to death; but if it is a daughter, then she shall live."*
>
> -Exodus 1:15-16

A wicked king decreed that Moses and other male Jewish children be killed.

> *Then when Herod saw that he had been tricked by the magi, he became very enraged, and sent and slew all the male children who were in Bethlehem and all its environs, from two years old and under.*
>
> -Matthew 2:16

A wicked king decreed that Jesus and other male Jewish children be killed.

The faith of the parents

And the woman conceived and bore a son; and when she saw that he was beautiful, she hid him for three months.

-Exodus 2:2

By faith Moses, when he was born, was hidden for three months by his parents, because they saw he was a beautiful child; and they were not afraid of the king's edict.

-Hebrews 11:23

Moses' life was saved and preserved through the faith of his parents.

Now when they had departed, behold, an angel of the Lord appeared to Joseph in a dream, saying, "Arise and take the Child and His mother, and flee to Egypt, and remain there until I tell you; for Herod is going to search for the Child to destroy Him." So he got up, took the Child and His mother during the night and left for Egypt.

-Matthew 2:13-14

Jesus' life was saved and preserved through the faith of His parents.

Protected in Egypt

And the child grew, and she brought him to Pharaoh's daughter, and he became her son. And she named him Moses, and said, "Because I drew him out of the water."

-Exodus 2:10

Moses received protection in Egypt for a time.

> *And he arose and took the Child and His*
> *mother by night, and departed for Egypt; and was*
> *there until the death of Herod, that what was spoken by*
> *the Lord through the prophet might be fulfilled, saying*
> *"Out of Egypt did I call My Son."*
>
> -Matthew 2:14-15

Jesus received protection in Egypt for a time.

His wisdom not surpassed

> *Then Miriam and Aaron spoke against Moses...*
> *"Has the Lord indeed spoken only through Moses?*
> *Has he not spoken through us as well?" Now the man*
> *Moses was very humble, more than any man that was*
> *on the face of the earth.*
>
> -Numbers 12:1-3

There were people trying to compete with Moses because of his wisdom.

> *And it came about that after three days they*
> *found him in the temple, sitting in the midst of the*
> *teachers, both listening to them, and asking them*
> *questions. And all who heard Him were amazed at His*
> *understanding and answers.*
>
> -Luke 2:46-47

From His youth, Jesus demonstrated tremendous wisdom and understanding, and others wanted to compete with Him, but they could not do it.

Rejected by the Jews

> *Now when the people saw that Moses delayed to come down from the mountain, the people assembled about Aaron, and said to him, "Come, make us a god who will go before us; as for this Moses, the man who brought us up from the land of Egypt, we do not know what has become of him."*
>
> -Exodus 32:1

Moses was rejected for a time by the people of Israel.

> *But the governor answered and said to them, "Which of the two do you want me to release for you?" And they said, "Barabbas." And Pilate said to them, "Then what shall I do with Jesus who is called the Messiah?" They all said, "Let Him be crucified!"*
>
> -Matthew 27:21-22

Toward the end of His life, Jesus told the Jews:

> *"You shall not see Me until you say, 'Blessed is he who comes in the name of the Lord.'"*
>
> -Matthew 23:39

> *"For I do not want you, brethren, to be uninformed of this mystery, lest you be wise in your own estimation, that a partial hardening has happened to Israel until the fullness of the Gentiles has come in."*
>
> -Romans 11:25

Jesus was rejected for a time by the people of Israel.

Accepted by the Gentiles

> *And he (Moses) went out the next day, and behold, two Hebrews were fighting with each other; and he said to the offender, "Why are you striking your companion?" But he said, "Who made you a prince or judge over us?"...... When Pharoah heard of this matter, he tried to kill Moses. But Moses fled from the presence of Pharoah and settled in the land of Midian ...... And Moses was willing to dwell with the man, and he gave his daughter Zipporah to Moses.*
>
> -Exodus 2:13,14,15,21

Moses was rejected by the Jews, but accepted by the Gentiles.

> *Quite right, they were broken off for their unbelief, but you stand by your faith. Do not be conceited, but fear.*
>
> -Romans 11:20

> *"I permitted myself to be sought by those who did not ask for Me; I permitted Myself to be found by those who did not seek me." Therefore, thus says the Lord God, "Behold, My servants shall eat, but you shall be hungry. Behold, My servants shall drink, but you shall be thirsty. Behold, My servants shall rejoice, but you shall be put to shame. Behold, My servants shall shout joyfully with a glad heart, but you shall cry out with a heavy heart, and you shall wail with a broken spirit. And you will leave your name for a curse to My chosen ones, and the Lord God will slay you. But My servants will be called by another name."*
>
> -Isaiah 65:1,13-15

Jesus was rejected by the Jews, but accepted by the Gentiles.

Criticized by his family

> Then Miriam and Aaron spoke against Moses because of the Cushite woman whom he had married, for he had married a Cushite woman.
>
> -Numbers 12:1

Moses married a Cushite - a black African woman.

> Then Jesus entered a house, and again a crowd gathered, so that he and his disciples were not even able to eat. When his family heard about this, they went to take charge of him, for they said, "He is out of his mind."
>
> -Mark 3:20-21

Moses was criticized by his family because he took a Gentile wife. Jewish people criticize Jesus because, in figure or in type, He took a mainly Gentile wife, the church. The book of Ruth is read in the synagogues on the day of Pentecost - the story of a Jewish man taking a Gentile wife and a baby born in Bethlehem, who was called 'the redeemer.'

Willing to bear their sin

> Then Moses returned to the Lord, and said, "Alas, this people has committed a great sin, and they have made a god of gold for themselves. But now, if Thou wilt, forgive their sin and if not, please blot me out from Thy book which Thou hast written!"
>
> -Exodus 32:31-32

Moses prayed to God to forgive the sins of his people and Moses was willing to bear the consequences of their sin and their guilt.

But Jesus was saying, *"Father, forgive them; for they do not know what they are doing."*

-Luke 23:34

For you have been called to this purpose, since Christ also suffered for you, leaving an example for you to follow in His steps, who committed no sin, nor was any deceit found in His mouth; and while being reviled, He did not revile in return; while suffering, He uttered no threats, but kept entrusting Himself to Him who judges righteously; and He Himself bore our sins in His body on the cross, that we might die to sin and live to righteousness; for by His wounds you were healed.

-1 Peter 2:21-24

Jesus prayed to God to forgive the sins of His people and He was willing to receive the consequences of their sin and their guilt.

Fasted forty days and nights

So he was there with the Lord forty days and forty nights; he did not eat bread or drink water. And he wrote on the tablets the words of the covenant, the Ten Commandments.

-Exodus 34:28

Moses fasted for forty days and forty nights to bring a covenant to God's people.

And after he had fasted forty days and forty nights, He then became hungry.

-Matthew 4:2

Jesus fasted for forty days and forty nights to bring a covenant to God's people.

Face to face with God

> *Since then no prophet has risen in Israel like Moses, whom the Lord knew face to face.*
>
> -Deuteronomy 34:10

Moses had a face to face relationship with God.

> *No man has seen God at any time; the only begotten God, who is in the bosom of the Father, He has explained Him.*
>
> -John 1:18

Jesus had a face to face relationship with God.

His face shone

> *Whenever Moses came out and spoke the sons of Israel would see the face of Moses, that the skin of Moses' face shone. So Moses would replace the veil over his face until he went in to speak with Him.*
>
> -Exodus 34:34-35

When Moses met God face to face, he glowed supernaturally.

> *And He was transfigured before them; and His face shone like the sun, and His garments became as white as light.*
>
> -Matthew 17:2

Jesus glowed supernaturally like Moses.

A voice was heard

In Exodus we read that God spoke to Moses directly from heaven and a voice was heard.

> *And Jesus answered them, saying, "The hour has come for the Son of Man to be glorified ...... Father, glorify Thy name." There came therefore a voice out of heaven: "I have both glorified it, and will glorify it again."*
>
> -John 12:23,28

God spoke to Jesus directly from heaven.

Tomb guarded by an angel

In the epistle of Jude, verse 9, we read that an angel guarded the tomb of Moses.

> *And behold, a severe earthquake had occurred, for an angel of the Lord descended from heaven and came and rolled away the stone and sat upon it. And his appearance was like lightning, and his garment as white as snow; and the guards shook for fear of him, and became like dead men. The angel answered and said to the women, "Do not be afraid; for I know that you are looking for Jesus who has been crucified. He is not here, for He has risen."*
>
> -Matthew 28:2-6

An angel also guarded Jesus' tomb.

Revealed God's name

> *Then Moses said to God, "Behold, I am going to the sons of Israel, and I shall say to them, 'The God of your fathers has sent me to you.' Now they may say to me, 'What is His name?' What shall I say to them?" And God said to Moses, "I AM WHO I AM"; And He said, "Thus you shall say to the sons of Israel, 'I AM has sent me to you.'"*
>
> -Exodus 3:13-14

Moses revealed God's name to God's people.

> "I manifested Thy name to the men whom Thou gavest Me out of the world ...... And I am no more in the world; and yet they themselves are in the world, and I come to Thee. *Holy Father, keep them in Thy name, the name which Thou hast given Me, that they may be one even as we are. While I was with them, I was keeping them in Thy name which Thou hast given Me......"*
>
> -John 17:6,11,12

Jesus revealed God's name to God's people.

Fed the people

> *When the layer of dew evaporated, behold, on the surface of the wilderness there was a fine flake-like thing, as frost on the ground. When the sons of Israel saw it, they said to one another, "What is it?" for they did not know what it was. And Moses said to them, "It is the bread which the Lord has given you to eat."*
>
> -Exodus 16:14-15

Moses fed God's people in large numbers, supernaturally.

> *And ordering the multitudes to recline on the grass, He took the five loaves and the two fish, and looking up towards heaven, He blessed the food, and breaking the loaves He gave them to the disciples, and the disciples gave to the multitude, and they all ate and were satisfied.*
>
> -Matthew 14:19-20

Jesus fed God's people in large numbers, supernaturally.

Showed signs and wonders

> *Since then no prophet has risen in Israel like Moses, whom the Lord knew face to face, for all the signs and wonders which the Lord sent him to perform in the land of Egypt against Pharaoh, all his servants, and all his land, and for all the mighty power and for all the great terror which Moses performed in the sight of all Israel.*
>
> -Deuteronomy 34:10-12

Moses did miracles, signs and wonders as no other man before him had ever done.

> *"But the witness which I have is greater than that of John; for the works which the Father has given Me to accomplish, the very works that I do, bear witness of Me, that the Father has sent Me."*
>
> -John 5:36

The Lord Jesus did works, signs, wonders and miracles, as no one else has ever done.

Made a covenant with blood

> *Then he took the book of the covenant and he read it in the hearing of the people; and they said, "All that the Lord has spoken we will do, and we will be obedient!" So Moses took the blood and sprinkled it on the people, and said, "Behold the blood of the covenant, which the Lord has made with you in accordance with all these words."*
>
> -Exodus 24:7-8

Moses went to a mountain, made a covenant with blood and covered God's people with that blood.

> *And while they were eating Jesus took some bread, and after a blessing, He broke it and gave it to the disciples and said, "Take, eat; this is My body." And, when He had taken a cup and given thanks, He gave it to them, saying, "Drink from it, all of you; for this is My blood of the covenant, which is poured out for many for forgiveness of sins."*
>
> -Matt. 26:26-28

> *But when Christ appeared as a high priest of the good things to come, He entered through the greater and more perfect tabernacle, not made with hands, that is to say, not of this creation; and not through the blood of goats and calves, but through His own blood, He entered the holy place, once for all, having obtained eternal redemption.*
>
> -Hebrews 9:11-12

The Lord Jesus went to a mountain, made a covenant with blood and covered His people with that blood.

Jesus - A Prophet like Moses

There were many great men of God in the Old Testament - Elijah, Isaiah, Jeremiah, Samuel, David - just to name a few.

But there was only one prophet like Moses, the Lord Jesus Christ - the true Messiah of Israel.

Chapter 6

One Messiah: Two Comings

Why Jews reject Jesus

There are two main reasons why the Jewish people will reject Jesus as the Messiah. One is the unfortunate history of "Christian" anti-Semitism, usually carried out by the Roman Catholic Church and the Eastern Orthodox Church, but with the unfortunate exception of Protestant Martin Luther, whose works inspired Adolf Hitler in writing *Mein Kampf*.

Luther in one of his final sermons taught that every Jew should be herded into a corral and forced to confess Christ at the point of knife. He said; "we, the German people, are to blame if we do not murder the Jews to prove we are Christians."

The second reason most Jews will reject Jesus as the Messiah is because Jesus did not bring in worldwide peace. He did not subdue the enemies of Israel, or establish the Messianic kingdom in Jerusalem, or bring justice to the nations, or prosperity and tranquility to the world.

If He is the Messiah, where is the Messianic reign in the character of David?

To the end there will be war

The answer is found in Daniel 9. The Messiah would have to come and die before the Second Temple would be destroyed.

It was not the purpose of the Messiah to bring worldwide peace at His first coming. It was His purpose to deal with the source problem - sin. It will be at His second coming that He will bring in worldwide peace.

> *And its end will come with flood and even to the*
> *end there will be war and desolation's are determined.*
> -Daniel 9:26

According to Judaism (the Midrash Bereshith on page 243 of the Warsaw edition), the Messiah was to exit in 33AD. We read confirmation in the Talmudic literature also, confirming that the Messiah should have come and died before the Second Temple was destroyed. We read that the Sanhedrin wept and said:

> "Woe to us! Where is the Messiah? He had to
> have come by now."

Rabbi Leopold Cohen

Rabbi Leopold Cohen, a very senior, ultra-orthodox rabbi, sought to understand the meaning of Daniel chapter 9.

He found two things in the Rabbinic literature of the ancient sages. One is that the Messiah was supposed to have come already. The other is that there is a curse on anybody who reads Daniel chapter 9. So Rabbi Leopold Cohen did the only honorable thing he could. He became a Baptist minister.

Christian anti-Semitism

"How can you expect me to believe that Jesus is the Messiah when Christians murdered my grandparents?"

The way you deal with the issue of "Christian" anti-Semitism is to know and show the real Jesus - Jesus the Jew, Rabbi Yeshua Ben Yosef of Nazareth, and be reminded that Jewish people murdered their own prophets in the name of Moses.

It was in the name of Moses that they put Jeremiah in prison, sawed Isaiah in half and killed Zechariah.

Should you reject Moses because of what Jews did in his name?

Should anyone reject Moses because of the orthodox Jew who in 1994 went into a mosque in Hebron with an automatic weapon and murdered thirty Muslims? Do I blame Moses for that and for other times when people murdered in his name?

Well, then we cannot blame Jesus for what people have done over the centuries in His name.

I have to accept Moses and the Torah on the basis of what Moses said. I also have to accept or reject Jesus and the New Testament on the basis of what He said and did.

Fulfilling all the prophecies

The other subject though - Why the Messiah did not bring in worldwide peace - is another issue. For Jesus to be the Messiah, He has to fulfill all the Messianic prophecies of the Old Testament.

There are two kinds of Messianic prophecies in the Old Testament - the "Suffering Servant" prophecies (seen in the Servant Songs of

Isaiah and elsewhere, and in some of the psalms of David), and also the "Davidic Messiah" of the conquering triumphal King who will subdue the enemies of God, establish the Kingdom and bring in worldwide peace, reigning from Jerusalem.

If Jesus is not the Messiah of the Jews, neither is He the Christ of the church. They mean the same thing: "Christ" and "Messiah," - the "Anointed One."

Jesus has not fulfilled all of the Old Testament prophecies as yet. He has only fulfilled the "Son of David" prophecies in a spiritual sense, not yet in an historical sense. For Jesus to be the Messiah, He must fulfill all the prophecies.

The "Suffering Servant" Messiah is called HaMashiach Ben Yosef, the Messiah, the Son of Joseph. The "Conquering King" Messiah is HaMashiach Ben David, the Messiah, the Son of David.

Palm Sunday

We see this in the Jewish background of Palm Sunday. Passover was one of three pilgrim feasts where the Jews sing something called the *Hallel Rabah* (from Psalms 113 to 118).
The highlight of the *Hallel Rabah* is:

> *Hosanna, hosanna, blessed is He who comes in the name of the Lord. We bless you from the house of the Lord. Give thanks to the Lord, for He is good, for His loving kindness endures forever. Hosanna, hosanna.*

The Jews were meant to sing that on Passover, with their hands waving. They were also meant to sing it at the Feast of Tabernacles, while waving palm branches in their hands.

On Palm Sunday, the Jews began to celebrate Passover (which teaches about the Messiah who was the Lamb who would be slain), as if it were the Feast of Tabernacles, which corresponds, in the typology of the Jewish calendar, to the Millennium.

The Feast of Tabernacles (seen in John 7:2), drawing on the background of Ezekiel 47, is associated in Jewish thought with the Davidic Kingdom.

That is why, when Jesus was transfigured with Moses and Elijah, Peter wanted to build three booths, three tabernacles. Peter was saying, "Here is the Messiah. Now let's set up the Kingdom!"

When Jesus came on Palm Sunday, they wanted somebody who was going to get rid of the Romans, in the same way as the way the Maccabees had gotten rid of the Greeks, and set up the Messianic Kingdom. So they began to celebrate Passover, as if it were the feast of Tabernacles.

In His first coming, Jesus fulfilled the first three (Spring) holidays in the Jewish calendar: Passover, First Fruits (which was the Resurrection), and the Feast of Weeks (which was Pentecost).

In His Second Coming, Jesus will fulfill the last three (Autumn) holidays: the Feast of Trumpets, the Day of Atonement, and finally and ultimately, the Feast of Tabernacles.

One Messiah, Two Comings

The Jews of His day did not want to know about a Suffering Servant Messiah, who was going to come as the Passover Lamb to be slain. They wanted a conquering King, who was going to set up the Millennium.

The suffering servant Messiah is called "the Son of Joseph," *HaMashiach Ben Yosef*. The conquering king Messiah is called "the Son of David," *HaMashiach Ben David*.

In other words, it is one Messiah, two comings. In His first coming Jesus came as the Son of Joseph, the suffering servant. In His Second Coming He will return as the Son of David, the conquering King who will set up His Kingdom.

False doctrine: Amillennialism and Postmillennialism

The doctrines of Amillennialism and Postmillennialism were the invention of the Roman Catholic Church, following the errors of Constantine and Augustine, at the time when Christendom was made the religion of the state. Amillennialism and Post Millennialism are totally unbiblical.

From the original Jewish perspective of the New Testament, only a Premillennial position is tenable.

If there is no Millennium, Jesus is not the Messiah. And, if He is not the Messiah for the Jews, neither is He the Christ for the church. He must fulfill all the Old Testament prophecies and, so far, He has only fulfilled the Son of Joseph prophecies.

Restoring the kingdom

What the apostles were really asking with the question, "Lord, is it at this time you are restoring the Kingdom?" was: "We know that you are the son of Joseph, but when are you going to be the son of David? When are you going to restore the kingdom the way David did?" Even John the Baptist could not understand this:

> *And summoning two of his disciples, John sent*
> *them to the Lord, saying, "Are You the Expected One,*

or do we look for someone else?"

Even the apostles, after the resurrection, on the Mount of Olives at the Ascension, were unable to understand that it is one Messiah, but two comings.

In His first coming, the Lord Jesus was the Messiah, the Son of Joseph. In His second coming, He will be the Messiah, the Son of David, the conquering king who will fully establish the kingdom.

Let us look at Jesus, the son of Joseph:

Beloved of his father

> *Now Israel loved Joseph more than all of his sons.*
>
> -Genesis 37:3

Joseph was the beloved son of his father.

> *And behold, a voice out of the heavens, saying, "This is My beloved Son, in whom I am well pleased."*
>
> -Matthew 3:17

The Messiah, the son of Joseph, was the beloved son of His Father.

Fellowship and service

> *Then he [Jacob] said to him [Joseph], "Go now and see about the welfare of your brothers and the welfare of the flock; and bring word back to me." So he sent him from the valley of Hebron, and he came to Shechem.*
>
> -Genesis 37:14

Joseph lived in *Hebron* which, in Hebrew, means "the place of fellowship." Joseph dwelt with His father at the place of fellowship and was sent by his father to seek the welfare of his brothers.

> *Have this attitude in yourselves which was also in Christ Jesus, who, although He existed in the form of God, did not regard equality with God a thing to be grasped, but emptied Himself, taking the form of a bondservant, and being made in the likeness of men.*
> -Philippians 2:5-7

> *For God so loved the world that He gave His only begotten Son, that whoever believes in Him should not perish but have eternal life.*
> -John 3:16

Jesus dwelt with His Father in the place of fellowship and was sent by His Father to seek the welfare of His brothers.

His brothers' sin

> *And Joseph brought back a bad report about them to his father.*
> -Genesis 37:2

Joseph testified to his father about the sins of his brothers, and his brothers hated him.

> *"If the world hates you, you know that it has hated Me before it hated you. If you were of the world, the world would love its own; but because you are not of the world, but I chose you out of the world, therefore the world hates you."*
> -John 15:18-19

Jesus testified about the sins of His brothers and so they hated Him.

They hated him still more

>*Then Joseph had a dream, and when he told it to his brothers, they hated him even more.*
>
> -Genesis 37:5

Joseph revealed to his brothers the exalted position he was to receive. They already hated him for testifying against their sins, but now they absolutely despised him.

>*And then the sign of the Son of Man will appear in the sky, and then all the tribes of the earth will mourn, and they will see the Son of Man coming on the clouds in the sky with power and great glory.*
>
> -Matthew 24:30

>*And the scribes and chief priests tried to lay hands on him that very hour, and they feared the people; for they understood that he spoke this parable against them.*
>
> -Luke 20:19

Jesus revealed to His brothers the position of glory that He would receive and so His brothers hated Him.

Foretold that he would rule

Joseph told his brothers:

>*"We were binding sheaves in the field, and lo, my sheaf rose up and also stood erect; and behold, your sheaves gathered around and bowed down to my sheaf."*
>
> -Genesis 37:7

Joseph foretold that one day he would rule.

>*"You shall see the Son of Man sitting at the right hand of Power."*
>
> -Matthew 26:64

Jesus foretold that one day He would rule.

Rejected and condemned
> *When they saw him from a distance and before he came close to them, they plotted against him to put him to death.*
>> -Genesis 37:18

Joseph was rejected and condemned to die.
> *"We do not want this man to reign over us!"*
>> -Luke 19:14

> *But they kept on crying out, saying, "Crucify, crucify Him!"*
>> -Luke 23:21

Jesus was rejected and condemned to die.

Out of His mind
> *And they said to one another, "Here comes this dreamer!"*
>> -Genesis 37:19

Joseph was accused by his brothers of being a dreamer.
> *And when His own people heard of this, they went to take custody of Him; for they were saying, "He has lost His senses!"*
>> -Mark 3:21

They said of Jesus, the Messiah, the son of Joseph, that He had lost His senses.

Sold for silver

> *And Judah said to his brothers, "What profit is it for us to kill our brother and cover up his blood? Come and let us sell him to the Ishmaelites and not lay our hands on him; for he is our brother, our own flesh."*
>
> *And his brothers listened to him. Then some Midianite traders passed by, so they pulled him up and lifted Joseph out of the pit, and sold him to the Ishmaelites for twenty shekels of silver.*
>
> -Genesis 37:26-28

Judah betrayed Joseph and sold him for twenty pieces of silver.

> *Then one of the twelve, named Judas Iscariot, went to the chief priests, and said, "What are you willing to give me to deliver Him to you?" And they weighed out for him thirty pieces of silver.*
>
> -Matthew 26:14-15

Judah betrayed Joseph for twenty pieces of silver. Judas (same name as "Judah" in Hebrew) betrayed Jesus, for thirty pieces of silver.

Servant's heart

> *So Joseph found favor in his sight, and he became his personal servant; and he made him overseer over his house, and all that he owned he put in his charge.*
>
> -Genesis 39:4

Everything Joseph did, he did as a servant. Luke 22:25-27 and Philippians 2:7 tell us that everything Jesus did, He did as a servant.

Everything to prosper

> *And it came about that from the time he made him overseer in his house, and over all that he owned, the Lord blessed the Egyptian's house on account of Joseph.*
>
> *-Genesis 39:5*

The Lord caused all that Joseph did to prosper.

And the good pleasure of the Lord will prosper in his hand.
-Isaiah 53:10

God shall cause all that Jesus, the son of Joseph does to prosper.

Tempted

> *And it came about after these events that his master's wife looked with desire at Joseph, and she said, "Lie with me." But he refused and said to his master's wife, "Behold, with me here, my master does not concern himself with anything in the house, and he has put all that he owns in my charge. There is no one greater in this house than I, and he has withheld nothing from me except you, because you are his wife. How then could I do this great evil, and sin against God?"*
>
> *-Genesis 39:7-9*

Joseph was tempted to the utmost, but he endured and would not sin.

> *Then Jesus was led by the Spirit into the wilderness to be tempted by the devil   Then Jesus said to him, "Be gone, Satan! For it is written, 'You shall worship the Lord your God, and serve Him only.'" Then the devil left Him...*
>
> *-Matthew 4:1-11*

The Messiah, the son of Joseph, was tempted to the utmost, but He endured and did not sin.

Falsely accused

> When she saw that he had left his garment in her hand, and had fled outside, she called to the men of her household, and said to them, "See, he has brought in a Hebrew to make sport of us; he came in to me to lie with me, and I screamed. And it came about when he heard that I raised my voice and screamed, that he left his garment beside me and fled, and went outside."
>
> -Genesis 39:13-15

Joseph was falsely accused and lied about.

> Now the chief priests and the whole Council kept trying to obtain false testimony against Jesus, in order that they might put Him to death; and they did not find any, even though many false witnesses came forward.
>
> But later on two came forward and said, "This man stated, 'I am able to destroy the temple of God and rebuild it in three days.'"
>
> And the high priest stood up and said to Him, "Do You make no answer? What is this that these men are testifying against You?"
>
> But Jesus kept silent. And the high priest said to Him, "I adjure you by the living God, that You tell us whether You are the Messiah, the Son of God." Jesus said, "You have said it yourself; nevertheless I tell you, hereafter you shall see the Son of Man sitting at the right hand of Power, and coming on the clouds of heaven."
>
> Then the high priest tore his robes, saying, "He has blasphemed! What further need do we have of

witnesses? Behold, you have now heard the
blasphemy ..."

-Matthew 26:59-65

Yeshua, the Messiah, the son of Joseph, was also accused falsely and
lied about.

Predicted life and death

> Then the cupbearer and the baker for the king of
> Egypt, who were confined in jail, both had a dream the
> same night, each man with his own dream and each
> dream with its own interpretation. Then Joseph said [to
> the cupbearer], "This is the interpretation of it: the three
> branches are three days; within three more days
> Pharaoh will lift up your head and restore you to your
> office; and you will put Pharaoh's cup into his hand
> according to your former custom when you were his
> cupbearer . ."
>
> Then Joseph answered and said [to the baker],
> "This is its interpretation: the three baskets are three
> days; within three more days Pharaoh will lift up your
> head from you and hang you on a tree; and the birds will
> eat your flesh off you."

-Genesis 40:5-19

Joseph predicted that one of these criminals would live and that the
other one would die.

> And one of the criminals who were hanging
> there was hurling abuse at Him, saying, "Are You not
> the Christ? Save Yourself and us!" But the other
> answered, and rebuking him said, "Do you not even
> fear God, since you are under the same sentence of
> condemnation? And we indeed are suffering justly, for
> we are receiving what we deserve for our deeds; but

this man has done nothing wrong."

> *And he was saying, "Jesus, remember me when You come in your kingdom!" And He said to him, "Truly I say to you, today you shall be with Me in Paradise!"*

-Luke 23:39-43

Jesus was condemned with two criminals and, as He predicted, one lived and one died.

Promised deliverance

> *Then Joseph said to him, "This is the interpretation of it: the three branches are three days; within three more days Pharaoh will lift up your head and restore you to your office; and you will put Pharaoh's cup into his hand according to your former custom when you were his cupbearer."*

-Genesis 40:12-13

Joseph promised deliverance to a condemned man.

> *And he was saying, "Jesus, remember me when You come in Your kingdom!" And Jesus said to him, "Truly I say to you, today you shall be with Me in Paradise!"*

-Luke 23:42-43

Yeshua, the son of Joseph promised deliverance to a condemned man. And that same son of Joseph is promising deliverance to condemned men today if they will repent and ask Him to forgive them, and follow Him.

Joseph was betrayed by his Jewish brothers into the hands of Gentiles, but God took this betrayal and turned it around and made it a way for all of Israel, and the entire world, to be saved.

So too, the Messiah, the son of Joseph, was betrayed by His Jewish brothers into the hands of Gentiles. God took this betrayal and turned it around, making it a way for all Israel, and the entire world, to be saved.

Forgotten by those he helped

> *Yet the chief cupbearer did not remember Joseph, but forgot him.*
>
> -Genesis 40:23

Joseph was forgotten by those he helped

> *And Jesus answered and said, "Were there not ten cleansed? But the nine - where are they? Was no one found who turned back to give glory to God, except this foreigner?"*
>
> -Luke 17:17-18

Yeshua, the son of Joseph was forgotten by those He helped.

Raised to glory

> *Then Pharaoh sent and called for Joseph, and they hurriedly brought him out of the dungeon; and when he had shaved himself and changed his clothes, he came to Pharaoh.*
>
> *So Pharaoh said to Joseph, "Since God has informed you of all this, there is no one so discerning and wise as you are. You shall be over my house, and according to your command all my people shall do homage; only in the throne I will be greater than you."*
>
> -Genesis 41:14,39-40

Joseph was taken from a dungeon, a place of death, and he was raised by the king to the place of glory in one day.

> *I pray that the eyes of your heart may be enlightened, so that you may know what is the hope of*

His calling, what are the riches of the glory of His inheritance in the saints, and what is the surpassing greatness of His power towards us who believe.

These are in accordance with the working of the strength of His might which He brought about in Christ, when He raised Him from the dead, and seated Him at His right hand in the heavenly places, far above all rule and authority and power and dominion, and every name that is named, not only in this age, but also in the one to come.

-Ephesians 1:18-21

Joseph was raised from a place of condemnation to a place of glory in one day, and the son of Joseph, the Messiah, the Lord Jesus, was raised from a place of condemnation to a place of glory in a single day.

Wonderful counselor

So Pharaoh said to Joseph, "Since God has informed you of all this, there is no one so discerning and wise as you are!"

-Genesis 41:39

Joseph proved to be a great counselor. In Isaiah 9:6 we read about Jesus that: *"His name will be called Wonderful Counselor."*

Highly exalted

And Pharaoh said to Joseph, "See I have set you over all the land of Egypt!"

-Genesis 41:41

Joseph was promoted to glory and honor and given a new name.

> *Therefore also God highly exalted Him, and*
> *bestowed on Him the name which is above every name.*
>
> -Philippians 2:9

Jesus was promoted to glory and honor and given a new name.

Took a Gentile bride

> *Then Pharaoh named Joseph Zaphenath-*
> *Paneah; and he gave him Asenath, the daughter of*
> *Potiphera priest of On, as his wife. And Joseph went*
> *forth over the land of Egypt.*
>
> -Genesis 41:45

After being exalted, Joseph took a Gentile bride.

> *For the husband is the head of the wife, as*
> *Christ also is the head of the church, He Himself being*
> *the Savior of the Body.*
>
> -Ephesians 5:23

Jesus, after exaltation, took a Gentile bride - in figure, the Gentile church.

That is why the book of Ruth - the story of a Jewish man taking a Gentile bride - is read in the synagogues at Pentecost, which we call "the birthday of the church."

And, in both cases, the brides were given to share the glory.

About thirty years of age

> *Now Joseph was thirty years old when he stood*
> *before Pharoah, king of Egypt.*
>
> -Genesis 41:46

Joseph was 30 years old when he began his work.

> *And when He began His ministry, Jesus Himself was about thirty years of age...*
>
> -Luke 3:23

Jesus, the Messiah, the son of Joseph was 30 years old when He began His work.

"Do whatever He says"

> *So when all the land of Egypt was famished, the people cried out to Pharoah for bread; and Pharoah said to all the Egyptians, "Go to Joseph; whatever he says to you, you shall do!"*
>
> -Genesis 41:55

> *His (Jesus') mother said to the servants, "Whatever He says to you, do it!"*
>
> -John 2:5

Of Joseph it was said "Do whatever he tells you." Of the son of Joseph it was said, "Do whatever He tells you."

Every knee shall bow

> *Then Pharaoh took off his signet ring from his hand, and put it on Joseph's hand, and clothed him in garments of fine linen, and put the gold necklace around his neck. And he had him ride in his second chariot; and they proclaimed before him, "Bow the knee!" And he set him over all the land of Egypt.*
>
> *Moreover, Pharoah said to Joseph, "Though I am Pharoah, yet without your permission no one shall raise his hand or foot in all the land of Egypt."*
>
> -Genesis 41:42-44

When he was exalted, every knee bowed to Joseph and he was given all power and glory.

> *Therefore also God highly exalted Him, and bestowed on Him the name which is above every name, that at the name of Jesus every knee should bow, of those who are in heaven, and on earth, and under the earth, and that every tongue should confess that Jesus Christ is Lord, to the glory of God the Father.*
> -Philippians 2:9-11

> *And Jesus came up and spoke to them, saying, "All authority has been given to Me in heaven and on earth!"*
> -Matthew 28:18

Every knee shall bow to Yeshua, the Son of Joseph, and He has been given all power and glory.

The Bread of Life

> *So when all the land of Egypt was famished, the people cried out to Pharoah for bread; and Pharoah said to all the Egyptians, "Go to Joseph; whatever he says to you, you shall do."*
> *When the famine was spread over all the face of the earth, then Joseph opened all the storehouses, and sold to the Egyptians; and the famine was severe in the land of Egypt, And the people of all the earth came to Egypt to buy grain from Joseph, because the famine was severe in all the earth.*
> -Genesis 41:55-57

> *Jesus said to them, "I am the bread of life; he who comes to Me shall not hunger, and he who believes in Me shall never thirst!"* -John 6:35

> *And there is salvation in no one else; for there
> is no other name under heaven that has been given
> among men, by which we must be saved.*
>
> -Acts 4:12

The whole world had to get their bread from Joseph - there was no other way the people could be saved. And there is no way for us to be saved except through the son of Joseph.

Knows his brothers sinful history

> *Now they were seated before him, the firstborn
> according to his birthright and the youngest according
> to his youth, and the men looked at one another in
> astonishment.*
>
> -Genesis 43:33

Why? Because Joseph knew the past sinful history of his brothers.

> *But Jesus, on His part, was not entrusting
> Himself to them, for He knew all men, and because He
> did not need anyone to bear witness concerning man
> for He Himself knew what was in man.*
>
> -John 2:24-25

Jesus the Messiah is like Joseph, knowing the past history and sins of his brothers.

Not recognized first time

However, as we read in Genesis, Joseph's brothers do not recognize him at the first coming. They recognized him at the second.

> *Then Joseph could not control himself before
> all those who stood by him, and he cried, "Have*

everyone go out from me." So there was no man with him when Joseph made himself known to his brothers. And he wept so loudly that the Egyptians heard it, and the household of Pharoah heard of it.

Then Joseph said to his brothers, "I am Joseph! Is my father still alive?" But his brothers could not answer him, for they were dismayed at his presence.

Then Joseph said to his brothers, "Please come closer to me." So they came closer. And he said, "I am your brother Joseph, whom you sold into Egypt!"

-Genesis 45:1-4

Joseph's brothers did not recognize him at the first coming, but at the second.

"And I will pour out on the house of David and on the inhabitants of Jerusalem, the Spirit of grace and of supplication, so they will look upon Me who they have pierced; and they will mourn for Him, as one mourns for an only son, and they will weep bitterly over Him, like the bitter weeping over a first born."

-Zechariah 12:10

The Jewish people, the brothers of Jesus the Messiah, the son of Joseph, on the most part did not recognize Him at His first coming, but they will at the second, realizing the one they betrayed is now the exalted one who will save them.

The one who was crucified is the one who is the Redeemer, the King. The son of Joseph is also the son of David.

The Suffering Servant is also the Conquering King

When his brothers repented, he forgave them. And when Jesus' brothers, the Jewish people repent, He forgives them.

In the beginning Joseph used the Egyptian people, the Gentiles, to give bread to his brothers, but a time came when the Gentiles were sent away and he revealed himself to his brothers.

Right now the son of Joseph is using Gentiles, Christians, to send the food, the Bread of Life, to His brothers, but a time will come in the Great Tribulation when the son of Joseph will personally reveal Himself to His brothers.

All power to the King

> *Joseph, after his exaltation, turned around and delivered all into the hands of Pharaoh.*
>
> -Genesis 47:20

> *Then comes the end, when He delivers up the kingdom to the God and Father, when He has abolished all rule and authority and power.*
>
> -1 Corinthians 15:24

Joseph gave all rule and authority and power into the hands of the king. The Messiah, the son of Joseph, will give all power and rule into the hands of the King.

Savior

> *So they said, "You have saved our lives! Let us find favor in the sight of my lord, and we will be Pharoah's slaves!"*
>
> -Genesis 47:25

Joseph was acknowledged to be the people's savior.

> *For the grace of God has appeared, bringing salvation to all men, instructing us to deny ungodliness and worldly desires and to live sensibly, righteously*

and godly in the present age, looking for the blessed hope and the appearing of the glory of our great God and Savior, Christ Jesus; who gave Himself for us, that He might redeem us from every lawless deed and purify for Himself a people for His own possession, zealous for good deeds.

-Titus 2:11-14

The Messiah, the son of Joseph, the Lord Jesus Christ, is acknowledged to be the Savior of all mankind.

Not recognized
When Joseph was adorned (Genesis 41:42) with the garments of Egyptian royalty, he became totally unrecognizable to his Hebrew brothers. (Genesis 42:8).

After the first century, Jesus was taken and made king of the Gentiles. It was forgotten that He came as King of the Jews and He became totally unrecognizable to His Hebrew brothers.

One Messiah : Two Comings

Joseph was given a new name upon his exaltation (Genesis 41:45). The Gentiles call *Rabbi Yeshua Ben Yosef* by a new name - Jesus - a Greek name, not His original one.

One Messiah : Two Comings

The Jews did not recognize Joseph at the first coming but at the second. And they will recognize Jesus, the son of Joseph at the second coming, seeing the one who was betrayed and crucified as the one who has indeed come to bring salvation.

One Messiah : Two Comings

Jesus is coming back as the son of David. Every eye will see Him. The Jews will look upon Him whom they have pierced and mourn as one mourns for an only son.

Those who look upon Jesus, whom we have all pierced, and mourn now as one mourns for an only son, will have the same blessing and promise that He gives to His own people.

The Messiah, the son of Joseph, will return as the Messiah, the son of David and He will restore the kingdom to Israel.

Chapter 7

Metatron: The Angel of the Lord

Then Jacob was left alone, and a man wrestled with him until daybreak. When he saw that he had not prevailed against him, he touched the socket of his thigh; so the socket of Jacob's thigh was dislocated while he wrestled with him. Then he said, "Let me go, for the dawn is breaking." But he said, "I will not let you go unless you bless me." So he said to him, "What is your name?" And he said, "Jacob." He said, "Your name shall no longer be Jacob, but Israel; for you have striven with God and with men and have prevailed." Then Jacob asked him and said, "Please tell me your name." But he said, "Why is it that you ask my name?" And he blessed him there. So Jacob named the place Peniel, for he said, "I have seen God face to face, yet my life has been preserved." Now the sun rose upon him just as he crossed over Peniel, and he was limping on his thigh.

-Genesis 32:24-31

The femur is the strongest bone in the human body and in a healthy adult male, it will not break under the weight of a Volkswagen. God dealt with Jacob's human strength by dislocating his femur. This has a double meaning - it illustrates the "Dark night of the soul" experience, which happened to Jacob and to every believer at some point in their life, but it also foreshadows the Great Tribulation, the Time of Jacob's Trouble. The church will be taken out of the Tribulation; while the unsaved Jews go through it. This was Jacob's trouble, when he went through this dark period to the end of the night. He sees God face to face at *Peniel*, which means "come out" in Hebrew. On our Holy Land tours we take people to this particular brook where this occurred - the brook of *Jabbok, Peniel*, where Jacob wrestled with the Angel of the Lord.

There are many angels of the Lord, but there is only one called "the Angel of the Lord," *HaMelech Adonai*, with a definite article. The Rabbis identify this man as the Angel although he appears as a man. Repeatedly, angels have been known to take human form, such as at the tomb of Jesus where angels appeared as men. And in fact, fallen angels known as the *Nephilim* actually procreated with human beings as is recorded at the beginning of the book of Genesis and also sited in Jude, as well as in the Apocryphal book of Enoch.

The Angel of the Lord is an enfleshment of someone whom Jacob says has the face of God. In no way does that diminish the uniqueness of the Incarnation of Jesus in the womb of the virgin handmaiden that fulfilled the prophecies of Isaiah 7:14. God took on humanity and became a man such as we are. Though He was without sin, He was in the likeness of sinful flesh. There was something very special and unique about the Incarnation of the subsequent nativity of Jesus. However, the Incarnation was not the first time God became a man, even though it was the first time He came via an embryonic conception. There have been other enfleshments of God in the Old Testament.

When Adam and Eve heard God walking in the garden, I am convinced from Proverbs 8 and John 1 that it was Jesus. And when Abraham saw three men, he was not looking at the Trinity, it was more likely Jesus and the two angels that accompany Him, like at the garden tomb. Again, that does not diminish the significance of the Incarnation inside Mary's womb, when God became a man, as we are, but it is not when God first became a man.

In witnessing to Jews or Arabs, there are two problems: tri-unity and incarnation; one God in three, three in one and the idea of God becoming man. When witnessing to Muslims, it is never a good idea to start by telling them that Jesus is the Son of God. To them that means that God had relations with an evil woman and it is blasphemous to them. It is seen as a pagan concept, like Hercules being the offspring of a relationship between Zeus and a human female. Sonship has to be explained in other terms when witnessing to a Muslim. When talking to Jews, successfully defending the Trinity and the deity of Jesus is a bit different, sometimes the Rabbis do our work for us, and they can be quoted.

When Rabbi Menachem Schneerson was alive, the rabbis used to say of Jesus, "What, he rose from the dead - what are you crazy?" Rabbi Menachem Schneerson was the rabbi of the Lubavitch branch of the main Hasidic movement. One day I spoke to the Hasidim at their display cabinet at the Ben Gurion airport in Tel Aviv. They were handing out information and forms to fill out if you wanted to become a Hasid. All over Israel there are portraits of the now deceased Jewish Rabbi Menachem Schneerson, also known as *Melech Meshiach* - King Messiah they call him.

The Hasidim believe their rabbi, called the *Tsadek* or the *Rebbe*, has the reincarnated spirit of the founder of the Hasidic movement, Rabbi Bal Shem Tov (also known as the Besht, an acronym from letters of his name bet ayin shin tet). This spirit they believe passes from father to son. Menachem Schneerson was said to have the spirit of *"The Besht"* by his followers. This is all Gnosticism and reincarnation. Hasidic Jews are very occultic. He was not a direct descendant of *The Besht* himself, but was someone married to a descendant of *The Besht* and he had no son or daughter and therefore no heir.

So I told them at the airport in Hebrew, "you have a problem - no one can be the rabbi instead of him." And they replied, *"hu Yakum M'hametim"* - meaning "he's going to rise from the dead." To that I said, "You mean you are telling me that you believe a Jewish Messiah will raise from the dead? That's all I wanted to know!"

The founding Rebbe of the Chabad branch of the Hasidic movement is considered to be Shneur Zalman of Liadi, and Menachem Schneerson who is referred to above was the seventh Lubavich or Chabad Rebbe.

This idea of God coming in human form is also seen regarding Melchizedek who received a tithe and had neither father nor mother. This is certainly a type of Jesus, more like a *Christophany*, the Old Testament manifestation of God in some human form. In mystical Judaism's Cabalah, its primary work is known as the *Zohar* and it can be quoted to demonstrate the belief that God can take on human form.

So what do you do with Orthodox Jews? How do you convince them that the idea of God becoming a man is not just a Christian concept but a Jewish one? You can say that the resurrection of the Messiah who has to die and come to life is not just a Christian invention, because they believe it themselves.

The place to start is in the book of Malachi, whose name can be co-equally translated "my messenger" or "my angel." The Greek word *angelos* simply comes from the Hebrew idea of angel. All angel means in Hebrew is messenger. But the Messiah would be a unique messenger. Malachi says:

> *Behold I will send My messenger,* (my Malachi) *and he shall prepare the way before Me and the Lord, whom you seek, shall suddenly come to His temple, even the angel of the covenant whom you delight in. He shall come sayeth the Lord of Hosts.*
>
> -Malachi 3:1

This "angel of the covenant" is the Lord, who is at the temple and being worshipped therein. In Judaism there is a concept called *dvar*. Its Aramaic equivalent was *mamre* and its Greek equivalent was *logos*. In John's gospel in Greek it is *en archae*: in the beginning, *kai ho logos*: was the Word. The beginning was the Word, the Word was *Theon*; it was God. That is *mamre, dvar* - both the Greeks and the Jews understood this idea of God's Word and God's incarnation being identical. The Hebrews understood the *dvar* or the *mamre* - the incarnate Word as being God's agent of Creation and God's agent of Salvation. The Greeks might have gone along with that as well, but in verse 14 of John, "and the Word became flesh" (*sarx* in Greek, *besor* in Hebrew), they would have had a problem because they thought God was impassible.

Middle of the throne

The Word of the Lord is not only called *melech habrit*, (the Angel of the covenant), but also the **Metatron**, from Greek *meta* - middle of the throne.

There are two Greek concepts for the throne: the throne of judgment and the throne of reward. Unsaved people appear before the throne or the seat of judgment. God's people appear before the *bema*, which is the same word used for the judges of the Greeks when they were enthroned to give out the rewards for those who successfully competed in the Olympics.

Rabbi Simeon Ben Yochai taught that according to the Zohar, volume 3, page 227 of the Amsterdam edition, the middle pillar in the Godhead is the **Metatron**, who has accomplished peace above, according to the glorious state there. They identify this Angel, with whom Jacob wrestled and who appears in Malachi, as God Himself. They say it is through Him that God shall bring peace on earth as He has brought it in heaven and it further says that God would answer prayers offered in the name of the **Metatron**.

Cabalah teaches that God is plural, one God in three persons, or as we say in Hebrew *"shma Israel Adonai Elohenu Adonai eched, baruch haShem kvodo u malchuto la'olam v'ed amen."* When the Jews asked Yeshua what was the greatest command, He said "Hear O Israel, The Lord our God is One; ye shall love the Lord your God with all your heart, all your soul and all your strength." - *"Shema Israel Adonai Elohenu."* Now we see Adonai, the Hebrew is *Yahweh*, they consider the name of God to be ineffable. The Lord our God, not *Elohym*, there is no Hebrew word for God, only gods. There is an abbreviated form *El*, but there is no Hebrew word for God in the singular. We have *El - Eliyon* or *El-Shaddai*, but there is no Hebrew word for God; only gods.

"Shema Israel Adonai Elohenu Adonai echad." A heretical Rabbi, an Aristotelian in the Middle Ages, around the year 1100, called Rambam, Moshe ben Maimonides, changed the meaning of the Hebrew word *Echad* and *Yahid. Yahid* is the Hebrew digit numeral one in biblical Hebrew. In modern Hebrew, the number one is *echad*. Rabbi Moshe ben Maimonides the Rambam, changed it because he wanted to point away from the deity of Jesus.

If I were to transliterate the *Shema* instead of translate it, I would say "Hear O Israel, the Lord our gods is one in unity." That word *echad* is the same one used for Adam and Eve, the husband and wife shall become one flesh. „ *echad*, cling to is *devik*. It is the same word *echad*, a plural oneness. In the Psalms, "how good and how pleasant it is when brothers dwell together in unity,"- *"hine Ma Tov U'Manaim Shevet Achim Gam Yachad,"* is the same idea. It is not the number one, it is a plural oneness, like becoming one flesh, like unity; as in *"achdut."* The *Shema* not only allows for, but supports, the plurality of the Godhead and Judaism itself teaches that God is one God who is plural in nature.

So the Rabbinic arguments that Christian belief in Jesus, the Messiah, being God, is a Gentile belief of pagan origin can be refuted. It does not pervert the Jewish Scripture; nor are these ideas alien to Jewish thought, contrary to what the Rabbis want people, Jew and Gentile, to believe. They may still reject the Messiahship of Jesus, but they cannot reject His deity based upon the idea being alien to Jewish thought. To do so would be a rejection of their own Jewish sages.

Some rabbis have been influenced by writers like Rabbi Samuel Levene who wrote "You Take Jesus, I'll take God." However, scholarly rabbis and Jewish professors in universities who have investigated the New Testament from a Jewish perspective do not dismiss it as *goyisha*, a Gentile distortion of Jewish thought or Jewish Scriptures. Men such as Professor Pinkus Lepede, the late Professor David Fluesler in Israel, Jacob Neusner from the United States and Jewish scholar Gesev Remnesh from the Dead Sea Scrolls Commission at Oxford, all accept the Jewishness of it. In fact, Jacob Moisna argues that it is pivotal Jewish literature that provides the crucial link between the Intertestamental literature, like the Maccabees with the Apocrypha and the early Midrashim. Some rabbis even say it is crucial Jewish literature. They have no problem dealing with this.

Orthodox Rabbi Pinkus Lepede, professor of Hebrew at Hebrew University, admits that the resurrection of Jesus from a Jewish perspective is undeniable when speaking academically. But when it comes to personal faith, even the Jewish scholars have a problem. They get around it by saying that Jesus was the Messiah for the Gentiles, but not for the Jews. However, the reality is that if they reject Christianity as non-Jewish, then they would have to reject Judaism as non-Jewish.

God is worshipped in his plurality according to the Zohar. The Cabalah talks about the tree of life; prayers are answered in the name of the **Metatron**; and it is the **Metatron** who will bring peace. In Exodus 24:1 it says: "And he said unto Moses, Come up unto the Lord." Rabbi Bechai taught the following:

God said to Moses, come up unto the Lord. This is **Metatron**. He is called by his name **Metatron** because in this name are implied two significant things which indicates his character. He is both Lord and messenger. There is also a third idea implied in the name **Metatron**. It signifies a keeper. For in the Chaldee (which is Aramaic), a keeper or watchman is called "Matherath" and because he is the keeper or preserver of the world he is so called the keeper of Israel.

The significance of his name is shown in Psalm 121:4 where we learn that he is Lord over all the world, because all of the hosts of heaven and the things of the earth are put under his power and might. This **Metatron**, the Angel of the Lord, who becomes human according to Judaism, who brings peace on earth as he does in heaven, in whose name we pray, will have all power and authority on heaven and earth. He who keeps Israel neither slumbers nor sleeps. That's the **Metatron**, say the Rabbis; "Hine Lo Yanum Veh Lo Yshon Shomer Israel" - "He who keeps Israel neither slumbers nor sleeps." Who keeps Israel? The **Metatron**!

So we see that in Exodus 24:1, the God who is exalted is the God who is speaking to Moses, "sayeth unto him that he should come up to Jehovah, Adonai, Yahweh," which is **Metatron**. So the **Metatron**, the Messenger of Yahweh, the Angel of the Lord, is Yahweh who is oftentimes connected to the name of God, alluding to the Shekinah, the glory of the Lord. Hence God is in the Shekinah, the Holy Spirit, Ruach HaKodesh. Somehow the **Metatron** God and Shekinah are the same. They are all Jehovah, but they are nonetheless separate persons. The Shekinah, the **Metatron** and God are all Yahweh. They are all one, echad; not yachid,

-column 1 of the Amsterdam edition (pg 114)

Is that Christianity? That is Judaism!

The Redeemer

When He said "come up," it is as if He said "ascend to the place of glory" where there is the Angel, the Redeemer. Remember, no one can come to the great God, for it is written in Exodus 33:20: "there shall no man see me, and live." We Jews believe Moses was instructed in all divine knowledge by none other than the **Metatron** (Haraba Dalet from the Mentuah edition). And the **Metatron** is not only God, but the Redeemer, and Jacob sees this **Metatron** and lives because the **Metatron** comes in a human form, the only way you can see God and live to tell about it.

-Haraba Dalet from the Mentuah edition

Think of the New Testament. John the Apostle was a physical relative of Jesus. He knew Jesus, followed Jesus, walked with Jesus. He was discipled by Jesus and knew him personally; but when he saw Jesus in his manifest glory on Patmos he was terrified. You can't look upon that. Then God says "come up here" and I'll show you the place. He had to be translated; he had to be raptured, taken up and shown. He couldn't see it in his human form and live. He could see Jesus, God who became a man, but he couldn't see Jesus as God without undergoing some supernatural transformation to make it possible.

In the **Metatron** is the *goyel*, the Redeemer. A *goyel* in Hebrew means literally one who "buys back." Reading from the Zohar:

Rabbi Simeon Ben Jochai took me into the inner chambers of mystery, mystical Judaism. This is of the saving marriage of God, and instructed me that **Metatron** existed from eternity. He took me to the chamber of mystery. Not just ordinary mystery, but mystery of the saving knowledge of God, God's salvation, the mystery of salvation and he showed me that the **Metatron** is the Redeemer but more than that, he pre-existed.

So according to the Zohar, Breshiet (page 126) Midrash K'olam, the **Metatron** existed from eternity.

In Micah 5:2 we read: "but as for you Bethlehem, house of bread, Ephratah, though little among the clans of Judah, you will go forth from me to be ruler of Israel. His goings forth are from long ago, from the days of eternity." Notice that his goings forth are from long ago, from the days of eternity. The Messiah would be born in Bethlehem and he would be a pre-existent being.

-Rabbi David Kimche - (*this is Messiah*; Targum Palestine)

"out of these Messiah shall go forth."

"Well that's just the Christian interpretation, or a Christian distortion of our Hebrew Scriptures" some may argue. No, that is Rabbi Simeon Ben Zoccai who wrote the Zohar. Christians did not write the Zohar!

Informed Jews must reject Judaism in order to reject Christianity. To reject Jesus is to reject Torah. The problem for unsaved Jews is not that they reject Jesus; the rejection of Jesus is a consequence of their problem. The problem is that they reject Moses and the Torah. Jesus said, "If you believe Moses, you would believe me also." Their problem is a rejection of Judaism, real Judaism, and Torah. They believe another Judaism, invented by the Rabbis after the destruction of the second temple, beginning at the Council of Yavne, by Rabbi Yochanan Ben Zakai. That is what they believe; they do not believe the Torah.

In Genesis 24:2, we read: "And Abram said unto the oldest servant of his house..." Who is the servant referred to in this verse? Rabbi Nehori said that it is in no other sense to be understood than expressed by the word *avdo* from Hebrew, meaning "servant." His servant, the servant of God, the nearest to his service - **Metatron**. He is appointed to glorify the bodies which are in the graves. This is the meaning of the words, Abraham said to his servant, to the servant of God. This servant is **Metatron**, the eldest of God's house. He was the first begotten of the creatures of God, who is the ruler of all. The ruler of all that God has because God has committed to him the government over all of his *savaot* that is, over his hosts. This is what Judaism teaches about this **Metatron**.

-Rabbi Simeon Ben Yochai - Zohar,
Genesis (pg 126) (midrash b'olam)

He is appointed to glorify the bodies which are in the graves. What does Job say?:

> *"Though my flesh decay, even with my own eyes shall I see God."*
>
> -Job 19:25-27

Judaism teaches that the only way that Job could see God with his own eyes and not another after his flesh decays in the grave was that he shall see the **Metatron**.

So, we have this unique messenger of God, who was the middle pillar of the Godhead, who pre-existed from eternity, prayer is answered in this name, and he will bring peace to earth as he has in heaven. He is the Redeemer. He is in the *Shekinah* and the *Shekinah* is in him. He is

God's agent of salvation. He is identified with the *Dvar* (also known as *Mamre*). And, now he will somehow glorify the bodies which were dead in the grave.

Judaism teaches that after the time of the Maccabees during the second temple period, a deeper knowledge of the Word of God came to be understood by the ancient sages. With this the New Testament agrees. There was a growing awareness of things already in Scripture such as the resurrection, eternal judgment and salvation of the Gentiles. Jesus came along and developed these concepts even further. In other words, the discovery of these deeper things in Scripture paved the way for the Messiah to come. Hence, ideas that all nations shall believe in the Jewish God became popular and widely known. Also the concept of the coming of a Messiah is seen in the Old Testament but never in the way that the New Testament speaks of the Christ. It is something that is there, but not fully understood at the time of Jesus.

Christianity teaches that this awareness was passed onto the Apostles. Jesus said that the keys would be taken from the Jewish leaders, and given to another - the apostles - *Ha Schlechim*.

What Zohar does, Cabalah does, mystical Judaism does: they try to take the lost knowledge of the ancient rabbis and give it back through mysticism and the occult. So the rabbis admit they lost their keys. Remember Jesus told them the keys would be taken "from you and given to another." In Judaism, the rabbis admit they lost a deep understanding of the Bible and the way to interpret it. In spite of the midrashim, they admit they lost it. We know that Jesus gave it to his apostles, who were also Jews. What Cabalah seeks to do is to restore those lost mysteries. Cabalah has lots of occult and lots of crazy stuff - astrology, numerology. It is more Hellenistic than Hebraic.

But to the extent that the rabbis have tried to rediscover the lost knowledge that disappeared when the temple was destroyed, they arrive at the conclusion that everything depends on the **Metatron**. The pre-existence of God, who is the redeemer, who brings peace, the government will be on his shoulders, and God will answer prayers in his name. *"Always learning, but never coming to a knowledge of the truth."* (2 Timothy 3:7)

King of Kings

Rabbi Akiva, a very early and a very important rabbi, after Rambam the most important Rabbi in the history of Judaism, tells us about the **Metatron's** title, which reveals his nature in Mennachi, page 37, column 2. He says the **Metatron** is the Angel of the Prince of God's countenance; The Angel, the Prince of the Law, the Angel of the Prince of Life, the Angel of the Prince of Glory, the Angel of the Prince of the Temple, the Angel of the Prince of Kings, the Angel of the Prince of Lords, the Angel of the Prince of the high exalted mighty princes in the heavens and the earth.

It goes on to say that **Metatron** is a ruler over all rulers, over all kings ruling with power, therefore the Cabalah, the hasidic Cabalah, and Zohar, call him **Metatron**, *'Merya sis."* It signifies ruling and governing with might and dominion because he is the beginning of the ways of God, citing Proverbs 8:22:

> *The Lord possessed me at the beginning of his way before the works of old. From everlasting I was established; from the beginning, from the earliest times of the earth. When there were no depths, I was brought forth, when there were no springs abounding with water, before the mountains were settled, before the hills I was brought forth. While he had not yet made the earth and the fields or the first dust of the world. When he established the heavens I was there, when he ascribed the circles on the face of the deep. When he*

made firm the skies above, when the springs of the deep became fixed. When he set to the sea its boundaries, so that the waters should not transgress his command. When he marked out the foundations of the earth. There I was next to him, a master workman and I was daily his delight, rejoicing always before him; rejoicing in the world, his earth and having my delight in the sons of men. Now therefore sons listen to me, for blessed are they who keep my ways. Heed instruction and be wise and do not neglect it. Blessed is the man that listens to me, watching daily at my gates, waiting at my doorposts. He who finds me finds life and obtains favor from the Lord. He who sins against me injures himself and all those who hate me love death.

The rabbis teach that this is the **Metatron**. What does it say? What does the New Testament say? In the beginning was the Word and the Word was God. All things were made though him, without him not anything was made. In him was life and the life was the light of men.

He who finds me, finds life, finds the **Metatron**. You have to find the **Metatron**, say the rabbis if you want to have life. And if you sin against the **Metatron** and curse the **Metatron** by calling him nasty names like Yeshu, instead of his real name Yeshua, you will find death. But then Exodus 20:19 could read: "they said to Moshe Rabbeinu speak to us yourself and we will listen, but let not God speak lest we die. Speak with us and we will hear, but not God, we will burn."

Reading this passage and knowing that my nation, the children of Israel, never approached God without the mediation of a priest or a high priest, I went to Rabbi Simeon Ben Yochai to enquire whether any mortal and sinful man dare to approach God without a mediator. I received the following instruction: This is an extract from the

Cabalah, the Zohar volume 2 on Exodus page 51 of the Amsterdam edition.

"To keep the way of the tree of life, there is but one mediator between God and man and that is **Metatron**." Yet the high priest is a mediator, but somehow he is not a good enough mediator. What does it say in the book of Hebrews? We have a more perfect high priest from a different order. It was Melchizedek, i.e., the **Metatron** - the only mediator between God and man; the middle pillar of the Godhead; that pre-existed, through whom God made the world and sustained it; that God would only answer prayers made in his name, that the government would be on his shoulders, that the mystery of salvation is in him. He is the Redeemer, and the only mediator between God and man. And Jews ask where do we Christians get this? The Zohar!

Tree of Life

Central to Cabalah is the tree of life. A Messianic Jew, or a Jewish believer in Jesus, reading the gospel of John at the end of the first century would have recognized it as a Midrash on the creation in Genesis or *Berashith* - John 1, 2 and 3 is the Midrash on Genesis 1, 2 and 3.

He would have said God walked the earth in the creation in Genesis, now God walks the earth in the new creation in John. The Spirit moves on the water and brings forth the creation in Genesis; the Spirit moves on the water and brings forth the new creation in John - one of water and Spirit. There is the small light and the great light in the creation in Genesis. And in the Gospel John the Baptist is the little light and Jesus the Messiah is the great light in the new creation. He would say God separated the light from dark in the creation, and He separated the light from dark in the new creation. Born of water and of spirit, God became a man. Then he would have seen the same

Midrash in the wedding at Cana. Jesus spoke the miracle with the water at the wedding supper in Cana on the third day and on the third day of creation God did the miracle with the water.

In the 47th chapter of the book of Ezekiel, the tree of life is mentioned in a millennial context, as it is in the book of Revelation. It is in the Garden of Eden to begin with in Genesis. The rabbis tell us that the tree of life is represented by a fig tree. So when Jesus tells Nathaniel that "I saw you under the fig tree," He was referring to a lot more than a literal fig tree. Midrashically, in Jewish metaphor, Jesus was telling him "I saw you from the garden, from the creation, from the foundation of the world."

Midrash only brings out what is in the text that wouldn't be seen without an understanding of a Hebraic perspective. The Bible clearly teaches that those who are predestined are born anew before the foundation of the world. The Midrash illustrates that doctrine that is already taught directly in Scripture.

The tree of life is also spoken of by the rabbis of the Cabalah. It tells us the following: "Who is the way to the tree of life? It is the great **Metatron**. He is the way to the great tree of life." It also is written in Exodus chapter 14:19: "The Angel of God which went before the camp of Israel removed and went after them." The **Metatron** is another name for the Angel of God.

So Jewish Cabalists are saying in order to eat of the tree of life you have to go by way of the **Metatron**? The same revelation was spoken by Jesus who said, "he who comes to me, I will give him to the right to eat of the tree of life."

"Come and see" said Rabbi Simeon:

> "the holy one, blessed be he who hath prepared
> for himself a holy temple, above in the heavens, a holy

155

city, a city in the heavens, a heavenly Jerusalem, the holy city where every petition to the king must be sent through the **Metatron**. You can't go to that holy city, that heavenly Jerusalem unless the **Metatron** brings you there. Every message of petition must first go the **Metatron** and from thence to the king. **Metatron** is the mediator of all that cometh from heaven down to the earth or from the earth up to heaven."

If it doesn't go through the **Metatron**, say the rabbis, you're wasting your breath; it doesn't go.

> And because he's the mediator of all, it is written in Exodus 14:19, "And the Angel of God which went before the camp removed that is before Israel which is above." This Angel of God is the same of whom it is written in Exodus 13:21, "Jehovah went before them to go before them, to go by day and night as the ancients have expounded."
> -Rabbi Menachem of Recanati (pg 123 section dshla)

What does it say? In the *Shekinah*, God himself is in the *Shekinah*, going before them. But how was God in the *Shekinah*? The **Metatron**! God, **Metatron**, *Shekinah* - Is there one God or three? The idea of the Trinity is not just a Christian concept exclusive to New Testament Christianity. It is seen in the Old Testament and elaborated upon in the mystical Jewish writings in the Cabalah; a fact rabbis today would rather not have to reckon with.

It is written in Psalm 121:4. The Almighty has revealed himself in none other than the **Metatron**. God is going to reveal himself to Israel and mankind, from only one, the **Metatron**. However, The **Metatron** is also the uncreated self-existing *memre* in Aramaic, which is also called the *Melech Habrit*, who is the **Metatron**. That is

Almighty, *El Shaddai* who has revealed himself in **Metatron**, not two **Metatrons**, but God *El Shaddai* has revealed himself in the **Metatron**, who is uncreated and self-existing Word, who was there from the beginning. In the beginning was the Word, the Word was with God and the Word was God. The garment of the Almighty is the **Metatron**. That is seen in 2 Corinthians and also in 1 Timothy 3:16. I guess the Cabalah must have read the New Testament, since the New Testament is older than Cabalah, at least in its written form.

Secret Society

The Cabalah teaches that the **Metatron** is the Son of God. "I could not mention many secrets respecting **Metatron** into which my teachers have led me." You see, Cabalah is based on secrecy, somewhat like its "Christian" counterpart: Freemasonry. There are secret initiation rites to understand this stuff and it takes years before Yeshiva boys are taught these secrets. Probably just about a week before they die in some cases because they don't want to tell anybody else that the Almighty has revealed Himself in the **Metatron**.

In the commentary of the Rabbi Moses Moishe Butalari on the book of (Sefra Yitzirah) are these words:

> The Cabalists call the second Sephira **Metatron**, the keeper, which is the inferior name of his name, the Son of God. When Joshua said "art thou for us or for our adversaries" he said "nay as a prince of the Host of the Lord, I am come."

The **Metatron** appeared to Joshua:

> *Now it came about when Joshua was by*
> *Jericho, he lifted up his eyes and looked and he saw a*
> *man, and behold the man was standing opposite him*

with his sword drawn in his hand and Joshua went up
to him said "are you for us or for our adversaries?"
And he said "No, rather I indeed come now as captain
of the Hosts of the Lord." (shevaot) And Joshua fell on
his face to the earth and bowed down......

-Joshua 5:13-14

Now when the Hebrews would worship *histachavot* they would bow down in an act of worship. (The Roman Catholic practice of bowing down before statues is idolatrous, it is exactly what we were told not to do.) *"What has my lord to say to his servant?"* And the captain of the Lord of Host said *"remove your sandals from your feet for the place you are standing is holy. And Joshua did so."*

This was the **Metatron** that Joshua bowed down before. "The middle pillar in the Godhead has revealed himself as the Son of God, having penetrated thus far the mystery of the nature of God and seeing what the faith of my fathers had been at the time when the candlestick was burning, in all of its essence and glory in the sanctuary, I look to the second psalm which speaks of no other than the **Metatron**, the Son of God." Consider the 7th and 12th verses of Psalm 2:7 - "I will surely tell of the decree of Lord. He said to me, Thou art my Son, today I have begotten thee... Do homage to the Son, lest he become angry and you perish in the way. For his wrath may soon be kindled but blessed are they who take refuge in the Son."

-Commentary of the Rabbi Moses Moishe
Butalari on the book of Sefra Yitzirah

Yet Jews say today that God has no son? Yet the Psalms say he does and the rabbis tell us that the Psalms tell us he does. More than that, the rabbis tell us that God's son is also the **Metatron**. We read in the book of Proverbs:

> *"Who has ascended into heaven and descended, who has gathered the wind in his fist?* (Ruach in Hebrew, Spirit). *Who has wrapped the waters in his garment, who has established all the ends of the earth? What is his name and what is his son's name?"*
>
> -Proverbs 30:4

The Son of God is the **Metatron**!

> *I will declare the decree, the Lord has said unto me, Thou art my Son; this day have I begotten thee..... Kiss the Son, lest he be angry and ye perish from the way, when his wrath is kindled but a little. Blessed are all they that put their truth in him.*
>
> -Psalm 2:7,12
> Midrash Tehilim (Rabbi Udan; Talmud: Sukka 52a)

In whom? In the **Metatron**.

I search the matter in which the word *hayom*, this day, is used by the sacred writers and found that sometimes it expresses eternity as in Isaiah 43:11 "Yea, before the day was, I am He." That is from eternity as Yonatan Ben Uziel translates. "I am also from eternity." thus *hayom* used from the second psalm in the sense of day of eternity. The Greek word here is *hemera aniones* - day of eternity so that he who is here called by God my Son must be from eternity. That is **Metatron**.

- Jacob wrestled with the **Metatron**, God in a human form.
- Joshua fell down before Him upon entering the Promised Land - the **Metatron**.
- The **Metatron** is the middle pillar of the Godhead.
- The **Metatron** is Jehovah.
- The **Metatron** is in the Shekinah; the Shekinah is in the **Metatron**. Jehovah God, **Metatron**, Shekinah, three in one, one in three.
- The **Metatron** is the Redeemer;
- The **Metatron** is the only way to God.
- The **Metatron** is the only one in whose name He will answer our prayers.
- The **Metatron** is the only one to whom God has committed the future of Israel into his hands.
- The **Metatron** is the only agent of God's salvation.
- The **Metatron** is the only one who has the right to give the way to the tree of life.
- The **Metatron** is the only one in whom if you take refuge you will be saved.

Who is the **Metatron**? Yeshua HaMashiach, Jesus the Messiah. The New Testament? Yes! Is that what I think? It is what I know. If you don't want to believe me, believe your own rabbis.

My dear Jewish friends, if you are reading this, the **Metatron** is the Messiah; the **Metatron** is God who became a man. The **Metatron** is the only one who can give you salvation. The **Metatron** is the only one who can bring you to the Jerusalem above that your rabbis teach you about. The **Metatron** is the only one, the only way, the only future you have. Embrace the Son, blessed are all those who take refuge in the **Metatron**. Yeshua HaMashiach, Jesus, the Jewish Messiah.

Chapter 8

Jesus in the Talmud

A distressing phenomenon is occurring in modern day Christendom: many Christians who love Israel and who have a heart for the Jewish people often confuse love for the people of Israel with love for the government of Israel. More seriously, many confuse loving the Jews with loving the religion of the Rabbis, Talmudic Judaism, and don't see that the modern-day Judaism of the synagogues is not in any sense the Jewish religion of Moses and the Torah.

One way to understand modern Judaism is to compare it to Roman Catholicism or Eastern Orthodoxy. Those churches claim to be Christian, but if one reads the New Testament it is quickly obvious that they are not at all Christian; rather they are built from largely pagan traditions which have little or nothing to do with the original teachings of Jesus and the Apostles. These are religions that come in the guise of Christianity, bearing the title "Christian Church," but are in no way true to what Jesus taught. Similarly, in no sense is the Judaism of today the same religion that was taught by Moses.

The Spirit of Antichrist

> *I know your tribulation and your poverty, but you are rich; and the blasphemy of those who say they are Jews and are not, but are a synagogue of Satan.*
>
> -Revelation 2:9

The same message can be found in the second chapter of Romans and in the book of Jeremiah: "He is not a Jew who is one outwardly …… but he is a Jew who is circumcised of heart." (Romans 2:28-29) Even the Talmud admits that people who are anthropologically or genetically Jews would know their Messiah if they were true Jews, or Jews in heart. Jesus called the Judaism that rejects its own Messiah a "synagogue of Satan." When you pass a Jehovah's Witness Kingdom Hall, it is a place of Satan. When you pass a mosque; that too is a place of Satan. When you go by a Roman Catholic Church, it is a place of Satan. When you pass a Hindu Temple; that is a place of Satan. A synagogue is also no less a place of Satan.

There is something in Orthodox synagogues called *ha bierkat ha minim*; they call it a blessing, but in reality it is a curse. There is also something known in the synagogue liturgy called the *shmona asrey*: Jesus is called Yeshu instead of Yeshua; they shorten His name to an acronym to mean "May His name be blotted out." They pray that the *minim*, a collective term for theological dissidents within the Jewish community that includes Messianic Jews, will be blotted out of the Book of Life. To Jewish believers in Jesus therefore, it is very confusing to see fellow believers who are in philo-Semitic organizations, lifting up Judaism and shaking hands with Rabbis. They watch other Christians stand on platforms and give speeches that make it seem as if Judaism is good and Islam is bad. How would you feel if your brethren in Christ stood up on platforms at the Feast of Tabernacles or some such thing, shaking hands with and making speeches on behalf of people who pray that your name and the names of your children would be blotted out of the Book of Life?

> *Who is the liar but the one who denies that Jesus is the Christ? This is the Antichrist, the one who denies the Father and the Son. Whoever denies the Son does not have the Father; the one who confesses the Son has the Father also.* -1 John 2:22-23

162

In Scripture there are prophecies of the rise of a man known as the Antichrist who will show up at the time of the end. The Apostle John also says that there are already many antichrists – those who have "the spirit of antichrist" – in the world at any given time. He identifies them as any who deny that Jesus is the Messiah. The Judaism of the Rabbis is a false Judaism that denies Jesus as the Messiah. In addition, John says that whatever denies the Father-Son relationship is also antichrist. On the Dome of the Rock on the Temple Mount there is a quote from a Surah in the Quran which declares, "God has no son." Islam denies the Father-Son relationship; it is an antichrist religion. The Judaism of the Rabbis today – not to be confused with the Judaism of Moses and the prophets – is also an antichrist religion.

There is a terrible history of "Christian" anti-Semitism. This is sadly true; nonetheless, man is fallen. In Israel today Orthodox Jews are perfectly capable of doing to non-Jews what anti-Semites did and still do today. They do even worse to Jewish believers in Jesus, whom they are trying to deport back to Russia. It is true that terrible crimes were perpetrated against the Jews in the name of Christ, but false religion is false religion no matter what guise it comes in: Islam, Roman Catholicism, Hinduism, Rabbinic Judaism – they are all antichrist.

Maimonides, the Rambam (1135-1204), known as the "greatest Rabbi" taught:

> Gentiles with whom we are not at war: One must not directly cause their death, but it is forbidden to save them if they are about to die. For example, if one sees a Gentile falling into the sea, it is forbidden to pull him out, for in Leviticus 19:16 it says, "You shall not stand by the blood of your neighbor," and that Gentile is not considered your neighbor.
> - *Yad ha-chazaka*, the Laws of Murder and Protection of Life

The same word for "neighbor" is used in Leviticus 19:18 in the famous phrase, "Love your neighbor as yourself," but Maimonides, a medical doctor, was telling Jews that Gentiles are not really your neighbors.

Maimonides also said:

> One is not permitted to heal Gentiles, even for payment. But if the Jewish doctor is afraid of them, or if there is concern about arousing hostility, then he may heal for payment, but not free of charge.
> -*Yad ha-chazaka*, Laws of Idolatry, chapter 10 verse 2

Joseph Caro, who compiled the *Shulchan Aruch*, which is the basic "set table" or codification of *chalachic* Jewish law, said this:

> A woman in birth is considered like a sick person whose life is in danger, for whom the Sabbath may be violated for any of her needs in giving birth to her child, such as lighting a candle; but one must not assist a non-Jewish woman in giving birth on the Sabbath.
> -*Shulchan Aruch, Or Hayim*, Law of the Sabbath 330:1, 2

Hafetz Hayim, (also known as Israel Meir Ha Cohen) 1838-1933, founder of Avodat Israel, and a 20th century *chalachic* authority on *chalacha* (Jewish law), elaborated on the preceding item in his commentary *Mishnah Berurah*, which means "the clarification of the Mishnah." He wrote:

> One must not assist a Gentile woman in birth, not even for payment; for in the weekdays one assists them in birth only to avoid hostility, and the Magen

Abraham (the Shield of Abraham, which is a commentary on the *Shulchan Aruch*) has written that even where there is concern for hostility, one is only permitted to do activities that do not entail a violation of the Sabbath; and I want you to know that the more acceptable (literally, more kosher) Jewish doctors do not observe this at all, for every Sabbath they travel many miles to heal Gentiles and they write a prescription personally or prepare medication; but they have no *chalachic* Jewish law, upon which to base such actions as treating or writing a prescription for a sick Gentile. For even if one is permitted to violate a Rabbinic prohibition in order to prevent Gentile hostility, one is certainly not permitted to violate a Rabbinic prohibition, and they are considered intentional violators of the Sabbath – God spare them.

In a parallel column entitled *ha* or *chalacha*, the author of the *Mishnah Berurah* adds:

The same law also applies to Muslims (literally Ishmaelites) and even to Karites (Jews who do not accept *torah b'al pei* - the oral law.) Everyone agrees that one may not violate a Rabbinic prohibition of the Sabbath in order to save their life.

Fortunately today most Jews and even many moderate Orthodox Jews do not actually believe such hate-mongering dogma. But in its ultra-orthodox form, this is a bigoted, racist religion from the pit of hell. It not only denies the Messiah, it even curses Him. It prays that those faithful Jews who do accept Him as Messiah, and are the true faithful remnant of Israel, would be blotted out of the Book of Life. God called Rabbinic Judaism an antichrist religion, and Jesus called it a "synagogue of Satan." Their own literature shows that it is as equally bigoted, racist, and vile as Luther, the Roman Catholic Church, or anyone else who has claimed to be Christian and committed crimes against the Jews. They are no better and no different than the apostate forms of Christianity whose anti-Semitic adherents for centuries persecuted and killed countless innocent Jews. Even in its more moderate expressions, rabbinic Judaism points God's covenant people away from their Messianic redeemer whose Messiahship is the reason for the covenant.

The people who publish literature in favor of modern Judaism do not know what they are talking about; they have no idea what Talmudic Judaism really is. The only valid Judaism today is the Messianic Judaism which fulfills the Torah, and its Jewish believers in Yeshua who are the righteous Jews because they have the imputed righteousness of Messiah. Once again, Yeshua told us exactly what this counterfeit Talmudic Judaism of the rabbis is: it is a "Synagogue of Satan," misleading precious Jewish souls away from the true salvation of their Messiah and into the eternal damnation of Satan.

We must make a distinction between the religion and the people who are trapped in it. I love Roman Catholics, and because I love them, I hate Roman Catholicism. I love Muslims, and because I love them, I hate Islam. I love Jews, and because I love Jews I hate Rabbinic Judaism, which is not the Judaism of Moses; and as we shall see, they know it is not the Judaism of Moses.

Two Schools of Thought

The Rabbis also teach hostility against Jesus in their rhetoric against Christianity.

They say things like: "The Gentiles have taken our Scriptures and twisted them to make it seem like they are speaking of Jesus" and "If you read the original context of the Jewish Scriptures you see that it is not talking about Jesus, and they have gotten it all wrong." They can make some pretty convincing arguments in that regard, but the truth is that real Christianity does not distort the Scriptures and the teachings of Jesus were not alien ideas from Jewish thought, that no Rabbi would believe. In fact, the Rabbis confirm the Christian interpretation of these Scriptures. In defense of their positions, the Rabbis try to show some *chalacha* or some other Midrash, or some other Talmud, or some other Rabbinic commentary to refute Christian interpretation of Scripture. This is known as *pilpul*, which is the way that the Rabbis devised to argue the *chalacha*, which comes from the Hebrew word *la lechet* meaning "to walk," or the way you live your life.

The Gospels report that at the end of the Sermon on the Mount the people were astounded because Jesus taught "as one with authority, and not as the scribes and Pharisees." What that meant was that Jesus would not engage in *"pilpul."* He simply said, "This is what God says," and would not engage in legalistic nit-picking and searching for loopholes, because it was an endless road to nowhere. He referred to this style of teaching as "leaven" and warned people to "beware of the leaven of the Pharisees."

Jesus did use Midrash, the Jewish way of interpreting the Scriptures, but in moral legislation. He would not engage in *pilpul* – with one exception. The Apostle Paul also refused to engage in *pilpul*, with the same exception: they used it to provoke the Pharisees and Sadducees into fighting with one another. Jesus knew, for example, that the Pharisees believed in the Resurrection while the Sadducees did not; therefore He would quote, "I am the God of Abraham, Isaac, and Jacob" and ask "is He the God of the living or of the dead?" knowing that this would start them arguing. It is almost as if He was poking fun at them, to show them how ridiculous it all was.

Again, those who will argue with you, will always find a rabbinic commentary that's says a text does not "necessarily have to mean what you say it does" and the discussion can go around and around. The main thing is to show that they cannot sweep your view out the window and that the facts speak for themselves: the New Testament was written by Jews; Jesus was a Jew; the apostles were Jews; the first Christians were Jews; and the last Christians will be Jews. The only reason that non-Jews believe in Jesus, in His Gospel, and in the New Testament, is that Jews wrote the New Testament and taught them that Jesus is the Messiah. No one can deny this historical fact, although some Jews will try to claim that Christianity is a Gentile fabrication (but they have no facts to go on).

The Rabbinic Literature Regarding Yeshua

There is a place in the Rabbinic writings called Yoma 39 b, where the rabbis taught that in the forty years prior to the destruction of the Temple, the following happened: on Yom Kippur, the Day of Atonement, they would hang a scarlet cord (probably associated in some way with Isaiah 1:18) before the Holy of Holies, when the High Priest entered to make the sacrifice. They believed that this scarlet cord would turn white if the sin of the people was forgiven; if they were not forgiven, the cord would remain red. The ninth chapter of Daniel says that the Messiah had to come and die before the second Temple was destroyed; Jesus echoed this in the Olivet Discourse (Matt. 24, Luke 21). The Rabbis taught:

> During the last forty years before the destruction of the Temple – (which happened circa 70 A.D.) - the scarlet thread did not become white, nor did the Western lamp in the Temple shine; and the doors of the Holy of Holies would fling themselves open of their own accord. For the forty years before the destruction of the Temple, the scarlet thread never turned white, but remained red.
> -Yoma 39b

The second Temple was destroyed in 70 A.D. Forty years previous would have been circa 30 A.D./C.E. In other words, from the time of Jesus until the destruction of the Temple, according to Judaism, the people's sin was never forgiven. Since then they try to justify themselves by works, but Isaiah 64:6 tells us that "our righteous deeds are as filthy rags." The literal Hebrew term for "filthy rags" in this passage is actually a comparison to a blood-soiled menstrual cloth. Scripture uses very coarse language to describe human righteousness and religion. On the other hand, Messiah's righteousness is not human; it is a divine righteousness imputed through faith in the Jewish Messiah Yeshua.

> During the last forty years before the destruction of the Temple, the lot for the Lord did not come up in the right hand, nor did the crimson-colored strap become white; nor did the Western-most light shine, and the doors to the Hekal, the Temple, would open by themselves, until Rabbi Yochanan ben Zakai rebuked them, saying, "Hekal, Hekal, why wilt thou be the alarmer thyself? I know about thee, that thou wilt be destroyed, for Zachariah Ben Ido has already prophesied concerning thee. Open thy doors, O Lebanon, that the fire may devour the cedars."

What this is saying is that Rabbi Yochanan ben Zakai is said to have asked the doors why they were predicting their own destruction.

In the Menahot it says:

> By the morning, the oil in the lamps had burnt out. The priests came in and cleaned out the lamps, removing the old wicks and putting in new wicks, and pouring oil into them, ready for the kindling in the evening. The Western lamp, however, although it had no more oil than the other lamps, miraculously continued to burn the entire day long, so that when the lamps were to be kindled in the evening, they were kindled from this one. The western lamp itself was

then extinguished, cleaned out, a fresh wick put in, oil poured in, and then relit. Thus the lamp provided the fire for lighting the other lamps, and yet was the last to be cleaned out. This miracle has testified to the Divine Presence in Israel.

According to these entries, during the forty years prior to the destruction of the second Temple in 70 A.D., the Western lamp which was the lamp that lit the other lamps – in other words, Jesus, the true Light of the world – went out, which is an indication that the Shekinah cloud had left as well. Also, the doors to the Holy of Holies would fling themselves open. Furthermore, the scarlet thread that was tied to the door of the Temple never became white, indicating that the sins of Israel were not forgiven. This took place from the time of the crucifixion of Jesus to the time of the destruction of the Temple; Yoma 39b.

A Tale of Two Rabbis

"A Tale of Two Rabbis" gives us an understanding of what happened in the Jewish religion. Once upon a time, there was a very famous rabbi whose name was Rabbi Hillel. There were two main kinds of Pharisees from two academies where Rabbis were educated: one was the School of Hillel and the other was the School of Shammai. They had certain differences in their emphasis, but they were the two main schools of Pharisaic thought. The School of Hillel had a number of very famous graduates. Hillel was the grandfather of another very famous rabbi who was his successor, Rabbi Gamaliel. Rabbi Gamaliel is mentioned in the Talmud, which says of him that when he died righteousness perished from the earth.

The New Testament quotes Gamaliel in Acts 5 saying that if Jesus was not the Messiah, Christianity would disappear; and if it did not disappear, the Jews who opposed it would be working against God. Rabbi Gamaliel from the School of Hillel was associated with something called the "Midot of Hillel," which St. Paul used in his teaching methods. Gamaliel had a number of famous students, one of whom was Onkleos, who did a famous translation of the Targum into Aramaic. He also had two other very famous students, one or the other of whom every Jew who came after them would follow, causing the Jewish religion to have a schism. The first of these students was Rabbi Yochanan ben Zakai, who said after the destruction of the Temple (in paraphrase), "We have a big problem: we cannot practice the Jewish faith that Moses gave any more." To this day, on every Orthodox Jewish synagogue you will find the term Ichabod - "the glory has departed, the Shekinah has gone." They know very well that without a Temple they cannot practice the faith of their fathers. On the Passover, the Pesach, instead of taking the Passover seder with lamb, they take it with chicken because they have no priesthood and no Temple.

Rabbi Yochanan ben Zakai had a council at Yavne, near modern Tel Aviv, at which the rabbis decided the following: instead of the Levites and priests, the rabbis would be the new spiritual authorities, ergo the new leaders of Israel. Also, instead of the Temple being central, the synagogues would become central (synagogues having begun developing after the Babylonian Captivity). Thus another religion began to evolve from that point, based in tradition.

There was a classmate of Rabbi Yochanan ben Zakai whose name was Rabbi Shaul of Tarsus, better known to some as St. Paul the Apostle. He was likewise a disciple of Gamaliel, but he said that the Law was fulfilled by the Messiah. Jesus paid the price for our sins, and thus the curse of the Law and the consequences for breaking it were laid on Him. Every Jew is under one law or another. Think of an unsaved Jewish person as a kind of backslider. Although he is in a covenant relationship with God, he is not keeping that covenant. He may be an atheist, but he is still under the curse of the Law. If you want to know what happened to the Jews, read Leviticus 26 and Deuteronomy 28 – their entire history is therein foretold. The Jews are under a national curse because they reject Jesus; they are under the curse of the Law.

By the time the Temple was destroyed, Daniel's prediction that the Messiah would come and die beforehand was fulfilled. Every Jew then had one of two choices: he either accepted Jesus as Messiah, or he began to practice a Judaism that was not Scriptural. The entire future of the Jewish faith to this day is based on these two classmates: Rabbi Yochanan ben Zakai and Rabbi Shaul of Tarsus.

At the end of his life, the Talmud tells us, Rabbi Yochanan ben Zakai was weeping. His disciples came to him and said, "O Mighty Hammer, why are you weeping? Why is your soul in distress?" And Rabbi Yochanan ben Zakai said:

> "I am about to meet Ha Shem – God – blessed be His name, and before me are two roads: one leading to Paradise (Heaven) and the other leading to Gehenna (Hell); and I do not know to which road He will sentence me."

The founder of Rabbinic Judaism admitted that he had absolutely no assurance of salvation. He said that he did not know if God would sentence him to Hell for what he did, so at the end of his life he was terrified to die. It is the same for all the Jews who follow in his footsteps.

Then there is Rabbi Shaul of Tarsus, who said at the end of his life:

> *"I've run the good race. I've fought the good fight. Henceforth I know there is stored up for me a crown of righteousness."*
>
> -2 Timothy 4:7-8

He had the assurance of his salvation, and so does every Jew who follows in his footsteps.

Your King Comes to You, Righteous and Having Salvation

That is what happened in the Jewish faith, and what is going on to this very day.

As early as the Talmudic era, the sages knew that the Messiah should have already come. They cried, "All the predestined dates for the Redemption have passed, and the matter now depends only on repentance and good deeds." – Sanhedrin 97 beht. They were faced with major prophecies that were well past their dates for fulfillment. Jesus was the only person who claimed to be the Messiah who could actually in His time prove Davidic descent. This is not only recorded in the New Testament, but also referred to in Sanhedrin 43 aleph: "With Yeshu (Jesus), it was different: He was connected with the government. This is an ambiguous phrase, which has actually misled some people to believe that it actually refers to royal lineage." God spent 1000 years promising Abraham and David that the Messiah would descend from them; therefore, when He allowed all of the genealogies to be destroyed with the second Temple, it was obvious that the Messiah had to have come.

So we read, "And the Sanhedrin wept: '*Oy vevoy*, woe to us! For the Temple is destroyed, and the Messiah has not come.'"

-The Midrash Bereshith on page 243 of the Warsaw edition

> "*The scepter shall not depart from Judah, nor the ruler's staff from between his feet until Shiloh comes; and to Him shall be the obedience of the people.*"
>
> -Genesis 49:10

Shiloh is one of the places in which the Ark of the Covenant dwelt, but it became an appellative for the Messiah in Judaism. Every tribe of Israel had its own tribal staff, a scepter, with the tribe's name inscribed upon it. This represented judicial power. The removal of the scepter therefore occurred when Herod the Great – a non-Jew – became king, and the Sanhedrin had its power limited. These things both happened during Jesus' lifetime. The name Shiloh is the name of the Messiah, according to the Talmud, Sanhedrin 98 b.

The prophecy of Genesis 49:10 declares that the Messiah had to have come prior to the removal of the scepter from Judah. Therefore, either the Messiah has already come and gone or God lied. God cannot lie; so whoever the Messiah is, according to the Talmud, He had to have already come by that point. Again, the Talmud mentions how 40 years before the destruction of the Temple the Sanhedrin was moved from the Hall of the hewn stones to a place outside; you may read this in 41a and in the Avodat Zerah 8b. Whoever the Messiah is, He had to come and die prior to 70AD/CE.

After five centuries of accumulated oral teaching was passed down, Rabbi Yehudah ha Nassi (meaning "Judah the President") and his disciples wrote down selected material from the oral law, calling it "Mishnah." This was not done until 230 A.D. The Talmud, in other words, was not even written down at all until 230 A.D. What the rabbis teach is this: the Talmud – what they call the *Torah b'pei* - was given to Moses on Mount Sinai, although he did not write it down. However, in Joshua 8:35, among other places, we read this:

> *There was not a word of all that the Lord had commanded Moses which Joshua did not read before the people of Israel.*

So the Torah says that Moses wrote it all down, but the rabbis deny this and claim that the oral law was given without being written down until a later date. They go so far as to say that the opinion of one rabbi is more important than the opinions of a thousand prophets, because the prophets were only messengers and secretaries, while the rabbis had to interpret the messages and divulge their meaning.

Each generation continued to raise new questions, so there were experts, one of whom was Rabbi Yohochanan, of the same college as Tiberias. He compiled these new rabbinic decisions in about 330 A.D. When this was done, he called it the *Gimmorah*, taken from the Hebrew word that means "to finish," or "completion."

The Mishnah and the Gimmorah were put together and named the "Jerusalem Talmud" - this was the first Talmud. Through the centuries, however, there has been much tampering with the Talmud, and there are all kinds of critical arguments as to what the original actually said in some cases.

Teaching as Doctrines the Precepts of Men

During the Dark Ages – from about 900 to 1500 A.D. – other things began to develop. Few Jews could understand the Hebrew or Aramaic text, so commentaries and codifications were written on the Talmud. These codifications were condensed into systematic codes of law, and from here we have things called the *Torim*, the *Riff* , the *Schulhan Aruch, Ha kitzor Ha Schulhan Aruch*, the *Mishnah Torah*, etc. Rambam was the main rabbi at this time; preceding him was Rashi in France. They got continually further away from the Word of God, and began developing along the same lines as Roman Catholicism.

Around 1000 A.D. there was also a rebirth of Aristotelianism in the Muslim world. Thomas Aquinas totally redefined Roman Catholicism in Aristotelian terms when he wrote *Summa Theologia*, in which he said that the opinion of the "church" was more important than the opinion of the Bible, just as the Rabbis declared the opinion of a rabbi more important than that of all the prophets. Reacting against Aquinas, who was a terrible heretic, were people like the Reformers who came from the Humanists.

What Aquinas did for Roman Catholicism, Rambam did for Judaism. He wrote a book called *A Guide for the Perplexed,* followed by something called *Mishnah Torah*, in which he Aristotelianized Judaism with totally Hellenistic ideas that were alien to anything originally believed by Jews.

Some other Talmudic writers were the following: Rabbi Shlomo Itzachi, Rabbi Saida Gaon ("the Genius"), Rabbi Moshe de Nachman – (also known as Nachmanides), Rabbi David Kimchi, Ibn Ezra, Rabbi Levi Ben Gershom, etc. At this point, the Cabalah began to come on the scene. Cabalah is mystical Judaism, the chief work of Zohar. It began in Poland.

To these they added other sacred books: such as the *Pirque Rabbati*, and the *Yalkuth*, and various haggadic 13th century writings. There is also the Zohar on Moses which is held by Hasidic Jews today because it uses Gnosticism and spiritualization, which is their approach to Judaism.

"All things which are written about Me in the Law of Moses and the Prophets and the Psalms must be fulfilled"

What does God say about all this?

> *"Because this people draws near to Me with their words and honors Me with lip service, but they remove their hearts far from Me, and their reverence for Me consists of tradition learned by rote..."*
> – Isaiah 29:13

"All of the prophets prophesied only about the Messiah; the entire Old Testament is about the Messiah," according to the Talmud in Sanhedrin 99a,d. "The world was not created but only for the Messiah" – Sanhedrin 98b. In John chapter one, it says that the world was created through Jesus and by Him. Rabbi Yosef said that the Messiah would come when this gate (Rome) shall fall and be built again, and the land Israel would be overrun by enemies, in Sanhedrin 96-99. The stone cut without hands in Daniel 2:44-45 is the Messiah, according to the *Pirque Eliezar* chapter 11.

As mentioned in chapter two of this book, there was a famous rabbi named Rabbi Leopold Cohen, who was greatly troubled by Daniel 9, which said that the Messiah had to come and die before the destruction of the second Temple. He wanted to find out what this meant; so he read in the Talmud that the world would last for 6,000 years, "for a thousand years is like yesterday in Your sight when it passes by." According to Rabbi Katina, they link this with Psalm 90:4. From this they derive that the world would be 2000 years in a state of chaos, 2,000 years under the Law of Moses, and 2,000 years under the Messiah, when the Shabbat – the Millennium – will be 1,000 years of peace. Then will come the war of Gog and Magog, and the Messiah will renew the world after 7,000 years, according to Sanhedrin 96b and 99a, and Yalkut volume II p. 129d.

This is exactly what the book of Revelation teaches. The Messiah will arrive to destroy the nations and to rule the earth for a thousand years of peace when people are conducting themselves in the following manner: Those who fear sin will be abhorred; truth shall fail; children will rebel against their parents; general lawlessness will abound; Sadducaism would universally prevail. (The Sadducees denied the Resurrection, like the Bishop of Durham.) In other words, people who claim to be believers in God would deny the Resurrection on a popular level.

When David Jenkins, Anglican Arch Bishop of York, denied the Resurrection of Jesus, two thirds of the Anglican bishops defended him. Long before David Jenkins, the ancient Rabbis said that Sadducaism would prevail universally – the study of God's Law would decrease, there would be a general increase in universal poverty and despair, apostasy would increase, and there would be a growing disregard for Scripture. This comes from Sanhedrin 96b, 99a – or, if you wish, read Paul's epistle to Timothy.

Rabbi Cohen had a big problem when he went to the Talmud and read what he did. He realized that the Messiah had to have come around 32 or 33 A.D. The Talmud said two things in this regard: one was as stated above, and the other was that there is a curse on anybody who reads Daniel 9. He asked his instructors why, and looked into the Talmud, and found that it said the reason for the curse was that the time of the Messiah's coming was foretold in Daniel 9. He could not believe that God would put something in His Word and not want people to understand what it meant. Eventually Rabbi Leopold Cohen became a Baptist minister.

In the Talmud it is noted that the word *dor* in Hebrew, meaning "generations," is spelled correctly before Adam fell in Genesis 2:4, but afterward the Hebrew letter *vav* – which is also a "6," since in Hebrew the letters also stand for numbers, is missing, because Adam lost six things. The letter *vav* is then replaced in Ruth 4:18, because she was the grandmother of King David, whose son would be the Messiah. The Messiah would restore the six things lost by Adam (Bresheit Rabbah 12, p. 24b of the Warsaw Edition).

To this day, the Rabbis read the Book of Ruth at Pentecost, the birthday of the Church. Ruth is the story of a Jewish man who takes a Gentile bride and from their union the lineage of David begins – from which the Messiah would ultimately come. They knew that somehow the Messiah would, through this Gentile woman, restore what Adam had lost.

Zechariah 12:10-12 says:

> *And they will look upon Him whom they have pierced, and mourn for Him as one mourns for an only son.*

Some Jews will go to all kinds of lengths to tell you that this does not necessarily refer to the Messiah. They will try to deny that this must mean what it says, that they will look on the Messiah whom they had pierced. However, in Sukkah 52a it says directly: "They will look upon Me - the Messiah - whom they have pierced." The Talmud confirms rather than denies that this is speaking about the <u>Messiah</u> whom they had pierced.

The Messiah will arrive with the clouds of Heaven, according to Daniel 7:13, but humble and mounted on a donkey according to Zechariah 9:9. One Talmudist proposed that if Israel deserves it, the Messiah will come with the clouds of Heaven, but if Israel is not deserving, He will come poor and riding on an ass. (Sanhedrin 96b – 99a.) To this day, this is how the Rabbis get around it: they claim that the Messiah did come in the days of Jesus, but Israel was not worthy and therefore he did not reveal himself. Thus this becomes the big catch-all by which they are able to explain anything away.

"If what a prophet proclaims in the name of the LORD does not take place or come true, that is a message the LORD has not spoken"

In Deuteronomy 18, Scripture says that if you predict something that fails to happen in the name of the Lord, you are a false prophet. (I show that to the Jehovah's Witnesses right before showing them false prophecies made in their own literature.) Rabbi Menahem Schneerson , the last Lubavitch rebbe, said that Messiah was going to come at Rosh ha Shanah (September) of 1991. The day after this deadline, I called up the Chabad Center in London and asked to speak to someone who spoke Hebrew. When he came on the line, I asked in Hebrew, "Well?" – he knew what I meant. Then I went down to Stamford Hill with some of my friends from CMJ who have a Messianic testimony, bringing our tracts. We confronted the Jews there with the fact that Moshe (Moses) said that if people predict things in the name of Ha Shem that don't happen, they are false prophets who must be taken out and stoned. We then asked them if they keep the Torah. The point of this was to show them that if they remain under the Law, they must take their Rabbi Schneerson out and stone him as a false prophet; their only other choice is to accept Yeshua as their Messiah who fulfilled the Law. They didn't like that much.

I love the Talmud – it illustrates so clearly the old joke, "If you have two Jews, you have three opinions." Forget three opinions – if you have two Jews, you have thirty-three opinions! Israel would have no more Messiah because he had come in the days of King Hezekiah, according to Rabbi Hillel – not the original Hillel, but another one. (Sanhedrin 96b, 99a.) In the same passage, Sanhedrin 96b – 99a, his grandson, Rabbi Yosef, said "May God forgive my grandfather, Rabbi Hillel."

Some Talmudists, however, thought that the Messiah would come on two separate occasions, which would account for the two conflicting descriptions of his arrival – again, Moshiach ben Yosef and Moshiach ben David. It is stated that the two dates given in Daniel 12:11-12 were to date the two arrivals at 45-year intervals. (The Midrash on Ruth 2:14, p. 43b of the Warsaw Edition; also the Lost Talmud on Daniel 9, 24-27.) The ancient Talmudists knew a lot of things.

The rabbis also deny that Isaiah 52 and 53 are not about the Messiah. I showed those very passages to a Jewish girl on a kibbutz in Israel once, and she immediately said, "This is about Jesus." No one had to tell her anything or manipulate her thinking – she simply used common sense. However, the Talmudists knew that Isaiah was predicting the Messiah's appearance in Isaiah 52:14: "His – the Messiah's – appearance was marred more than that of any man, and His form more than the sons of men" Sanhedrin 97b, Yalkut volume II p. 53c and Shemoth R, 15-19. The Talmud repeatedly quotes Isaiah 53 as a prediction of the Messiah's appearance on earth.

There are two main Targums in Judaism: the Targum Onkleos and Targum Jonathan. After the Babylonian Captivity, most Jews knew Aramaic rather than Hebrew, so they translated the Scriptures into Aramaic. However, these were not simply translations, but also interpretations. It says: "Who has believed our report, and to whom has the arm of the Lord been revealed? For He grew up before Him like a tender root out of dry ground; He had no stately form or majesty that we should look on Him, nor appearance that we should be attracted to Him. The Messiah was despised and forsaken of men, a man of sorrows acquainted with grief" – it goes on and on and on, directly pointing to the Messiah in these passages. "Each of us has turned to his own way, but the Lord has caused the iniquity of us all to fall upon the Messiah." "Although He had done no violence, nor was any deceit in His mouth, the LORD was pleased to crush Him, putting Him to grief if He would render Himself as a corban – a guilt offering – He would see His offspring, He would prolong His days, and the good pleasure of the LORD will prosper in His hand, and as a result of the anguish of His soul, He will see it and be satisfied. By His knowledge the Righteous One, My Servant, will justify many and will bear their iniquities." and so on. "He Himself bore the sin of many, and interceded for the transgressors" – Sanhedrin 98b, also the Midrash on Samuel, the Lemburg Edition, p45a, and the Targum of the Kingdom of the Messiah. They knew very well that this was about the Messiah; the Targum Jonathon says so specifically.

"So I will make them jealous with those who are not a people; I will provoke them to anger with a foolish nation"

Jewish people will often accuse Christians of twisting Scriptures to make them about Jesus when they actually are not about Him. What most Rabbis will say is that these passages are about Israel and the vicarious suffering of Israel. There are a number of problems with that. One is that the same Isaiah repeatedly castigates Israel for its sin, whereas he describes this Suffering Servant as having no sin. Therefore their idea is simply incompatible with the context. There are four Servant Songs in Isaiah, and the fourth one, found in Isaiah 52-53, is different from the others. In one sense, the rabbis are right: much the same as the Church is the Body of Christ, Jesus is the embodiment of Israel. For example, when you see verses that say things like "Israel My glory, Israel My Firstborn," they are Midrashically alluding to Jesus. But only in a very abstract sense are these passages about Israel; their primary meaning, according to the Rabbinic literature, is pointing to the Messiah. When they tell you this is not about the Messiah, ask them to explain the Targum Jonathan, or the Midrash on Samuel, which say it is.

Jewish people will also accuse Christians of inventing a New Covenant that does not exist, claiming that the only covenant is the Torah. Jeremiah 31:31 says that God will make a new covenant, but when you tell them this they will try to tell you that you have misunderstood the text. At this point, you can point to the Midrash on Psalm 7, p5a of the Warsaw Edition: "God will speak through the Messiah to make a new covenant."

Psalm 2 says, "Thou art My Son; do homage to the Son, lest He become angry and you perish in the way." The Rabbis say that God has no Son; but they have to deal with Psalm 2, Psalm 110, and II Samuel 16:1, along with the Suffering Servant of Isaiah 53. These things can be read in the Midrash on II Samuel 16:1, paragraph 19 of the Lemburg Edition, p. 45; also the Midrash on Psalm 7, p. 5a of the Warsaw Edition; and Yalkut Volume II p. 90a. (These volumes can be obtained at a Yeshiva or a religious Jewish library.)

It goes on to say when it has connected Psalm 110 with II Samuel 16:1 and Isaiah 53, "Against God and His Messiah: If I find the Son of the King, I shall lay hold of Him and crucify Him with a cruel death." The Talmud actually says that the Messiah would be crucified "-*Litzlov oto*" is exactly what it says "-crucify." This is one thing they cannot answer; it shocks them.

Once again, in Genesis 49:10 Jacob predicted that the scepter would not depart from Judah nor the ruler's staff from between his feet until Shiloh comes. The Babylonian Talmud states that when this occurred, the sages said "Woe to us, for the scepter has been taken from Judah, and the Messiah has not appeared!" Rabbi Ruchman recalled that the members of the Sanhedrin covered their heads with ashes, their bodies with sackcloth, and wept when they heard these words. The Jerusalem Talmud dates this occasion at a little more than forty years before the destruction of the Temple in 70 A.D.; so they are saying that from around 30 A.D. the Messiah was pierced. – The Jerusalem Talmud, Sanhedrin Volume 24, and the Babylonian Talmud, Sanhedrin chapter 4 Volume 37.

"The sins of those who are hidden with thee will cause thee to be put under an iron yoke, and they will do with thee as with the calf. I take it upon me that no Israeli should perish; am I not flesh and blood?" – the Midrash on Jeremiah 31:8, the same as Isaiah 53. "All limits of time as regards the arrival of the Messiah are past." – Sanhedrin 96-99. The Talmud states clearly that the Messiah had to have come already.

In the Talmud it is noted that God has made various numbers significant in His plan: they noted that there were ten names for idols and prophets, ten trials of Abraham, ten generations from Adam to Noah, and ten generations from Noah to Abraham – the Avotah chapter 36. They developed from this a dating system. This Mosaic dating system of Israel is given in Leviticus 26:13-16, where a parallel to the four commandments concerning God and six concerning man are seen played out in multiples of seven (verses 18, 21, 24). The Talmudic literature examines the various historical fulfillments of this in patterns on multiples of seven times ten. For example, the Babylonian Captivity was 70 years in Daniel 9:2 when these kinds of judgments happened to Judah for these kinds of sins. Moses dated the Messiah's exit in A.D. 33 – Midrash Bresheit, Rabbah on Genesis, p. 24b of the Warsaw Edition. Their own dating system says that the Messiah had to exit in 33 A.D.

"God gave them a spirit of stupor, eyes so that they could not see and ears so that they could not hear, to this very day"

The Talmud also states that the Temple's destruction in 70 A.D. was predicted by Daniel 9:24-27. When you get into arguing with rabbis about the weeks of Daniel and what they mean – the easiest thing to say is that Daniel 9 says that the Messiah had to come and die before the second Temple was destroyed. "No, it doesn't," they will tell you, "but Yalkut Volume II p. 79d says it does, and so does Nazir 32b. The Talmud states that the destruction of the Temple in 70 A.D. was predicted by Daniel 9:24-27, when the coming of the Messiah to be cut off was predicted to precede this destruction." So the Messiah was predicted to arrive and to be killed before 70 A.D., according to the Talmud – and the Rabbis knew this.

The Talmud confirms that the stone cut without hands in Daniel 2:44, 45 is again the Messiah. "A stone to strike and a rock to stumble over, and a snare and a trap for Jerusalem." In Isaiah 8:14, God also predicted that the leaders of Israel would reject the Messiah: "Thou hast become my Yeshua; the stone which the builders rejected has become the chief cornerstone." - Psalm 118:21, 22, which is the Hillel Rabbah that they sang to Jesus on Palm Sunday.

Moses Maimonides, Rambam, considered the greatest rabbi, confirmed that Yeshua the Messiah's appearance in A.D. 30 was Israel's greatest stumbling block. In *Kings and Wars* chapter 11, the uncensored edition, (the rabbis have for obvious reasons put out a censored edition) it says:

> There has never been a greater stumbling block than this problem of Yeshua (Jesus) in 30 A.D. For three and one-half years, the Shekinah – God's dwelling, His presence – dwelt on the Mount of Olives, waiting to see whether Israel would repent, and calling on them to "Seek ye the Lord while He may be found – call on Him while He is near," but all was in vain. After three and a half years, the Shekinah returned from the Mount of Olives.
>
> – *Rabbis' Lamentation*

It is one thing when Christians say they believe that Jesus did miracles, rose from the dead, and ascended from the Mount of Olives, but what about when people who were not only non-Christians but actually anti-Christian believe all these things? You can read Roman historians such as Suetonius and Tacitus, and it is fascinating to read of how Jesus was understood by pagan Rome. Even they did not deny the things that He did. It was said to be common knowledge throughout the Roman Empire that Jesus rose from the dead. The *Avodat Zerah*, however, says that Jesus did miracles as no other rabbi, that his disciples not only healed the sick but even raised the dead in His name, that after He was crucified He rose from the dead, and that He ascended into heaven from the Mount of Olives. All of that is actually in the Talmud – even His enemies acknowledged the truth of what He did. This was written by rabbis who were trying to prevent other Jews from believing in Him; but they had to deal with the historicity of His miracles, of His disciples doing miracles, and not only of His crucifixion but also of His resurrection and ascension into heaven – the Talmud admits He did it! When an Orthodox rabbi is confronted with these things, he will not want to deal with it. However, when pressed, he will say that Jesus knew Cabalah – though this was invented centuries later, but they say it anyway – Jesus knew Cabalistic, mystical secrets and had the ineffable name of Ha Shem (the Tetragrammaton) under His tongue and under His foot and so on, and this is how He performed these miracles.

The rabbis will say that Psalm 22 does not really say "They have pierced My hands and My feet." All of Psalm 22 was fulfilled in Matthew 27, but in Hebrew there is a difference in the letter *aleph*, and they shorten a *vav* to make it a *yod*; in this way they will try to change "They have pierced My hands and My feet" into "I am like a lion's paw." This might be legitimately true, except that someone must have changed something at some point because the Talmud states the following: "At the time of the Messiah's creation, the Holy One – blessed be He – will tell him in detail what will befall him ... 'There are souls that have been put away with thee under My throne, and it is their sins which will bend thee down under a yoke of iron and make thee like a calf whose eyes grow dim with suffering.'" In other words, according to the Talmud, the Messiah would know before He was born that He was coming to die for His people. "And during the seven-year period preceding the coming of the Son of David, iron beams will be brought and loaded upon his neck until the Messiah's body is bent low. It was of the ordeal of the Son of David, who wept, saying 'My strength is dried up like a potsherd,' Ps. 22:16." In Yalkuth Shimoni, they connect "many dogs have encompassed me" (using a Midrashic principle called *"binyan ab m'shna ketubim"*) with the Book of Esther, commenting on which, Rabbi Nehemiah said "They pierced my hands and feet." Hence, the Pisgah Rabbatai 36:1,2 states directly that Psalm 22 is about the Messiah coming to die.

There are technical linguistic explanations for the translation of "like a lion" such as a textual reading adjustment called *"im crea."* In the Yalkut Shimone we find this: "Many dogs have encompassed me" – they connected this somehow with the book of Esther and the king Ahasuerus – "but the assembly of the wicked have enclosed me; *ka a'ri."* In English "they have pierced my hands and my feet." Rabbi Nehemiah quoted it this way, and the reading of "pierced" was accepted by ancient rabbis. In addition, the Peshitat Abitai says directly that Psalm 22 is talking about the Messiah suffering and dying.

Again, Isaiah 52 and 53 from the Targum Jonathon: "Behold, My servant the Messiah shall prosper; He shall be exalted, and great and very powerful." It states directly and repeatedly that this is about the Messiah.

Daniel 9, Megillah 3 aleph of the Targum of the Prophets, was composed by Jonathon ben Uzziel under the guidance of Haggai, Zechariah and Malachi, according to tradition: "And a voice from heaven came forth and said, 'Who is this who has revealed My secrets?' and he further sought to reveal by Targum the inner meaning of the Hegiographa (the portion of Scripture which includes Daniel), but a *bat kol* went forth from Heaven and said, 'Enough!' 'Why, why should we not read Daniel 9?' 'Because the date of the Messiah is foretold in it.'" And again, Sukkah 52a regarding the Messiah being pierced: "What is the cause of the mourning in Zechariah 12:12? It is well according to him who explains that the cause is the slaying of the Messiah, the Son of Joseph, since that well agrees with the Scriptures: 'And they look upon Him, because they have thrust Him through, and shall mourn for Him as one mourns for an only son.'"

There is not a single Messianic prophecy that that I could not prove, and to show that it is <u>not</u> a Christian invention in applying it to Jesus. The Talmud agrees, for instance, that Micah 5:2 is about the Messiah, who in some way had to be pre-existent:

> *O you, Bethlehem Ephrathah, are by no means least in the clans of Judah, for from you going forth from eternity will be one whose existence is from eternity.*

From the Targum of Micah 5:1 from Targum Jonathon says this:

> And you, O Bethlehem Ephrathah, you who are too small to be numbered among the thousands of the house of Judah, from you shall come forth from Me the Messiah to exercise dominion over Israel – He whose name was mentioned from before the days of creation.

In this way when one meets with the protest that Christians have read something into Micah 5:2 that it does not really say, one may respond that Christians have not read anything into it that Jews did not read into it long before Christianity was established.

From Genesis 3:1-15: "And it shall be that when the sons of the woman study the Torah diligently and obey its injunctions, they will direct themselves to smite you on the head and slay you." – right from the beginning, they believed that the Messiah had to be slain. Comments on Genesis 23:5 from the Midrash Rabbah show that Rabbi Tanhumah said, "In the name of Rabbi Shmuel Kozit, she hinted that the seed would arise from another source – the Messiah." The Midrash deals with Eve's naming of Seth, which is connected with the idea of the Messiah being bruised upon the heel and then bruising the head of the serpent.

"No one can come to Me unless the Father who sent Me draws him; and I will raise him up on the last day"

It isn't hard to undermine arguments that these things are Gentile fabrications resulting from Gentile Christians twisting the Jewish Scriptures. One can show very clearly that these things were understood by ancient rabbis in the same way in which they are understood by Christians. But there is something called "ecclentics" or convictions. "No one comes unless the Father draws him." – if you bring a Jehovah's Witness to my door, I can win every argument, but it does not mean they will get saved. The same can be said of a Mormon or of a rabbi.

The apostle Paul said that we should be "instant in season and out of season, to refute every argument." We have a long way to go, but God is doing something. We will see God work among the Jewish people in the Last Days in the same way in which He worked in the time of the early church – with not only thousands being saved, but even tens of thousands. We will see whole synagogues split over the issue of Yeshua being the Messiah. And we will also see whole churches divide over the same kind of issue.

THE MESSIAH'S PEOPLE - THE JEWS

Chapter 9

Seventy Weeks of Daniel

If you watch the news on CNN or the BBC, you see frightening images of the war in Iraq and events happening in the Middle East. We are in the last days and prophetic events are happening so fast that it often seems confusing. How do we understand the present situation in the Middle East in the light of Daniel, in light of Biblical prophecy? When we look at these things from the Bible's perspective, we get more clarity. God put these things in His Word because He wants us to have understanding.

The ninth chapter of the book of Daniel tells us:

> *"Seventy weeks have been decreed for your people and your holy city (Jerusalem) to finish the transgression, to make an end of sin, to make atonement for iniquity, to bring in everlasting righteousness and to seal up vision and prophecy and to anoint the most holy place. So you are to know and discern that from the issuing of a decree to restore and rebuild Jerusalem until Messiah, anointed One, the Prince, there shall be seven weeks and sixty two weeks; it will be built again with plaza and moat even in times of distress. Then after the 62 weeks the Messiah will be cut off and have nothing and the people of the prince who is to come will destroy the city and the sanctuary. And its end will come like a flood, even to the end there will be war and desolations are determined. And he will make a firm covenant with the many for one week*

189

but in the middle of the week he will put a stop to sacrifice and grain offering; and on the wing of abominations will come one who makes desolate, even until a complete destruction one that is decreed, is poured out on the one who makes desolate."

-Daniel 9:24-29

There are two princes in this passage. The first one, in verse 26, is obviously the Messiah, Jesus. But there are people who teach (usually extreme Calvinists) that Jesus is also the second prince. However, the second prince is Antichrist. They are confusing Christ with the Antichrist.

There are four ways to understand eschatology, the studies of the end times in Bible prophecy: preterism, historicism, poemicism and futurism.

Preterism teaches that prophetic events in the book of Revelation already happened and have no future meaning. They supposedly were fulfilled in the early church. This is the eschatology of the kingdom-now proponents who says there will be no Antichrist, no falling away, no rapture, that the Church will go from strength to strength, and Satan is already bound. (If Satan is bound, I want to know who keeps letting him go.) The Church is going to conquer the whole world for Christ before He comes - this is preterism!

There are preterists from two Christian camps: liberals and evangelicals. The liberal higher critics declare that Isaiah could not have known that a king named Cyrus would come along two hundred years later and send the Jews back to Israel from their captivity (in Isaiah chapter 44 and chapter 45) so Isaiah could not have written the Book of Isaiah. It had to be somebody they call Deutero Isaiah. He came along after the fact and took something that already happened and made it look like a prediction of a future event. The presupposition is that we can't be sure there is a God and if there is

He doesn't know the future and even if He did He wouldn't tell Isaiah. Therefore Isaiah and Daniel could not be so accurate in what they have predicted. Somebody had to come along hundreds of years later and be a make-believe Isaiah. That is what the liberals say.

From the other side of the spectrum are those who say that they are born again, are evangelical, yet believe in a form of preterism. These are the ones who say that Matthew 24 and the Book of Revelation were fulfilled in 70 AD.

The second eschatological view is historicism, which is what some of the reformers believed. Historicism teaches that there are many antichrists, not an individual person. The papacy is an ongoing institution, an antichrist institution, they say, so every pope is the Antichrist. In Northern Ireland the Presbyterians believe this and go so far as to say that ancient pagan Rome fulfilled the prophecy of the restrainer (in 2 Thessalonians) who restrains the Antichrist from rising up. When the Visigoths conquered pagan Rome in the fifth century, the papacy came to power. That is how far they take it. Now the Restrainer is the Holy Spirit but they actually say that it was imperial, pagan Rome. This is historicism.

Then there is poemicism which says that the book of Revelation is mere poetry. It is given only to encourage the Church that Jesus will come back one day. It is given to encourage us in times of persecution. We should not take it as having any specific meaning. It is just to cheer us up when times are tough. Lutherans go along with this. Luther basically rejected the book of Revelation and so Lutherans are stuck with the fact that the founder of their church did not like it. So what are they going to do? Write if off as poetry!

Then there is futurism. People like my friend the late Barry Smith and Hal Lindsey say that there will be an Antichrist, there will be a mark of the beast, and there will be a falling away.

These are the four ways that people look at Revelation in the western world, but that is not the way Jesus and the Apostles looked at it. They said that all four were true. For instance, Jesus spoke of the abomination of desolation as a past and future event:

> *"Therefore when you see the abomination of desolation which was spoken of through Daniel the prophet, standing in the Holy Place, let the reader understand then let those who are in Judea flee to the mountains."*
>
> -Matthew 24:15

By the time this was spoken of by Jesus in the Olivet Discourse, it had happened about 160 years earlier, in the times of the Maccabees. This is the Jewish Feast of Hanukah, which Jesus himself celebrated, in the tenth chapter of John. The English Bible calls it the Feast of Dedication. So Jesus knew that it already happened, yet He used a historic event and made it a prophecy. Jesus used preterism, but unlike preterists, He said that it is going to happen again; multiple fulfillments. He also used historicism. He took something that happened and said that it's going to happen again, and it did - in 70AD.

Josephus records that when the prophecies of the destruction of the Temple made by Jesus and Daniel were fulfilled, the Romans set up pagan ensigns on the Temple Mount and began to worship them on the site where the Holy of Holies had been. That was an abomination of desolation. The Emperor Hadrian came along and built the temple to Jupiter, the Roman version of the Greek god Zeus. That was another abomination of desolation. Today on the Temple mount sits the Mosque of Omar with an inscription in Arabic from the Koran that reads, "God has no son." The Bible says in the first epistle of John, that which denies the Father-Son relationship is Antichrist. Jesus used historicism.

Then there is poemicism. Jesus appeared to John on the Isle of Patmos during the persecution of the Emperor Domitian. John was the last living apostle, the others had all been martyred, and people were wondering when Jesus was coming back. They expected Him, by and large, to come in their lifetime. The Church had to be encouraged that He was coming, that He was going to keep His Word, that He did have an eternal future. Jesus used poemicism. Yet going back to the abomination, He said that it will happen again and again and again. It happened with Julian the apostate, Constantine's nephew. There have been many abominations. Each one of them is a foreshadowing of the final one. In other words, the western Church chooses to believe you can hold to one of the four, however, Jesus and the apostles were all four.

People with a preterist view say that all was fulfilled in 70 AD. When Jesus spoke the Olivet discourse on the Mount of Olives as recorded in the gospel of Matthew, He wasn't finished at the end of chapter 24 – chapter 25 is the continuation of the same message being recorded. Yes, it had a partial fulfillment in 70 AD. The believers fled from Jerusalem under Simian. They thought that would be the rapture.

So a partial fulfillment did happen. However, did Jesus separate the sheep from the goats in 70 AD? Well, they will say yes. The Jews who believed were separated from those who didn't. But then, did He give people their eternal reward, based on what they did with their talents in 70 AD? That's Matthew 25. When did Jesus give people their eternal reward based on what they did with their gifts? It never happened in 70 AD. When did the Bridegroom come for the Bride in 70 AD; the wise and foolish virgins in Matthew 25? Did Jesus come back with His Bride in 70 AD? No He did not. They take the partial fulfillment and try to make it the total fulfillment. They take the preterist portion but they forget what it means for the future.

Now that is not how Jesus handled Daniel chapter 9. Jesus said that yes, it had already happened, but it's going to happen again. He never said it was one fulfillment. It is multiple fulfillments with one final one and complete fulfillment when He comes back for the Bride.

Let's put this in context. The first thing in this context we realize is that Daniel was told that this message applied, not primarily to the Church, but to the Jews: *"70 weeks have been decreed for your people and your holy city."* I'm not saying it does not apply to the Church, but it first of all applies to the Jews. The people who go into this other error are usually people into replacement theology. They say that the Church is Israel and that God has no future purpose for the Jews. This is absurd. If God does not have to keep His promise to the Jews then He does not have to keep His promise to the Church. The New Covenant was not made with the Church but with the Jews. Jeremiah 31:31 says: *"I will make a new covenant with the House of Israel and the House of Judah."* Jesus never made a covenant with the Church. He made it with the Jews. Non Jews who accept Jesus are grafted in. Jews who reject Him are cut off from their own olive tree. But Jesus never made a covenant with the Church.

The second thing we have to understand about this context, in addition to the fact that it is for the Jews, is that there is one Messiah but two comings. Daniel 9:26 tells us that the Messiah would come and die before the second Temple would be destroyed. The Messiah would come and be cut off. The Talmudic literature refers to this in volume 2 page 79D of the Nazir edition 32B, also the Midrash Breshith, page 243 of the Warsaw edition, and confirms the Christian interpretation.

The Messiah was to exit in 33 AD. The Sanhedrin said the same thing. The Messiah was to come and die before the second Temple would be destroyed, before 70AD. The Jews expected Him to bring in the everlasting Kingdom. That was not His purpose in His first coming. That is His purpose in His second. His first coming was to be atonement for sin. But the Jews wanted somebody to get rid of the Romans the way the Maccabees did the Greeks. That will be His purpose when He comes back to bring in political dominion. It was not His purpose the first time.

The Gospel of Luke 4:17 sheds more light on this. Jesus was in His native town of Nazareth in the synagogue and the book of the prophet Isaiah was handed to Him. He opened the book and found the place where it was written:

> *"The Spirit of the Lord is upon me because He anointed Me to preach the Gospel to the poor, He sent Me to proclaim release to the captives and recovery of sight to the blind, to set free those who are downtrodden, to proclaim the favorable year of the Lord."*
> *And He closed the book and gave it back to the attendant.*

He was reading from the synagogue liturgical lexicon from the 61st chapter of the book of Isaiah:

> *"The Spirit of the Lord God is upon Me because the Lord has anointed me to bring good news to the afflicted. He sent Me to bind up the broken hearted, to proclaim liberty to the captives, freedom to prisoners, to proclaim the favorable year of the Lord and the day of vengeance of our God. To comfort all who mourn, to grant those who mourn in Zion, to give them a garland instead of ashes, the oil of gladness instead of mourning, the mantle of praise instead of the spirit of fainting, so they will be called oaks of righteousness, the planting of the Lord that He may be glorified."*

Jesus stopped half way through verse 2. He only read the first half of verse 2 and then He closed the book.

Preterists take the 27th verse of Daniel 9 that is talking about Antichrist and say that is Jesus. He stopped in the middle of the week where, according to Daniel 9:27, he will put a stop to sacrifice. Where does the ministry of Jesus break up into two halves of a week? Where do you see seven years anywhere in the Gospels or anywhere in the Bible, of Jesus? The Bible only speaks of Jesus' time of ministry as three and a half years. There is no seven year ministry of Christ. No place is the ministry of the Messiah's seven years broken into two halves. No place!

Jesus had three and a half years of public ministry and in the book of Revelation, Satan, in the person of Antichrist, will demand equal time. When did Jesus ever break a covenant? He is God. God can't break a covenant. Paul says that if God would break a covenant He would deny Himself and He can't do that. People can break covenants. Jesus never abrogated a covenant. The Bible never breaks His ministry into two halves, the seven years into two halves. He never abrogated a covenant and He never stopped sacrifice. It continued.

Now, in order to do what they do, preterists had to do two things. They had to engage at least to a degree, in the error of replacement theology; saying that God is finished with the Jews. Some are radical replacementists, some are partial. But more seriously, what they must do is engage in the ancient heresy of Gnosticism. They spiritualize a text out of context to mean something other than what it plainly states.

The basis of their error took place in chapter 9 verse 27 where they misinterpret "putting a stop to sacrifice" having to do with Jesus as the perfect sacrifice ending all continued sacrifice. Jesus indeed was the perfect sacrifice who ended the need for ongoing temple sacrifice (Hebrews 7:27) but this cannot be the context of Daniel 7.

If it were there would, of fundamental and immediate necessity, need to be a second three and one half year period of Jesus earthly ministry at His first coming (which there most certainly wasn't) and Jesus would have additionally needed to been immediately followed during that time by an abomination of desolation in the character of Antiochus Epiphanus. Nothing even remotely resembling that happened until the Romans placed pagan ensigns where the Holy of Holies once stood (foreshadowing the anti Christ) some forty years later. Events both biblical and historical line up firmly dismissing the Preterist position as pure unmitigated folly.

Now, there is typology where one thing is a symbol of another thing. But that does not negate a literal historical meaning. There is Midrash where you have a pesher interpretation but the pesher interpretation, the deeper meaning never negates the plain meaning called the peshet. Never! When you begin spiritualizing texts that way, that's Gnosticism. Calvinistic people will claim to be grammatical, historical exegesis experts. They take the Bible literally, going back to the Reformation but they are superbly guilty of the very thing they claim to be most against. Every time they see Israel they spiritualize it; that is the church - replacement Calvinism!

Not all Calvinists are replacementists but there are ones who are. Classic Calvinism is replacementist. When they see the millennial reign of Jesus: "Oh, that's only a symbol" - they spiritualize it. That's what the Catholic Church did, that's what the Gnostics did. It can't literally be a thousand years. "Well, do you believe it is literally three and a half years?" "Yes!" "Well, how come time is literal in one place in Revelation but it is only a symbol in another place?" They pick and choose!

This is reminiscent of those old aptitude tests they had in the 1940's and 1950's before we had computer tests; logic tests where they actually tried to get the pegs and put them into the holes? Square ones, round ones and triangular ones. Put this one in and that one in and it doesn't fit. Get the pen knife out. Wait a minute, we shouldn't have cut that one, we should have left it intact. It would have fitted

197

perfectly in here. Now you are stuck with this one and it doesn't go anywhere. Get the pen knife out. That's what it amounts to. It just doesn't add up. The math does not add up, the historical record does not add up and the Biblical texts do not add up.

The same deceptions and errors that came around and plagued the early Church have made a big comeback. And, as we see prophecy fulfilled, as we draw closer to the return of Jesus, the very things for which books like Daniel were given, to prevent us from being confused, are only confusing people more.

Chapter 10

End of the Gentile Age

I say then God has not rejected His people. Has He? May it never be, for I too am an Israelite, a descendant of Abraham from the tribe of Benjamin. God has not rejected His people whom He foreknew, or do you not know what the Scripture says in the passage about Elijah how he pleads with God against Israel. "Lord, they have killed thy prophets, they have torn down thine alters and I alone am left and they are seeking my life." But what is the divine response to him. "I have kept for Myself seven thousand men who have not bowed the knee to Baal." In the same way then there has also come to be, at the present time, a remnant according to God's gracious choice. But if it is by grace then it is no longer on the basis of works otherwise grace is no longer grace. What then? That which Israel is seeking for, it has not obtained, but those who were chosen obtained it and the rest were hardened; just as it is written, "God gave them a spirit of stupor. Eyes to see not and ears to hear not down to this very day" and David says, "Let their table become a snare and a trap and a stumbling block and a retribution to them. Let their eyes be darkened to see not and bend their backs forever."

I say then they did not stumble so as to fall. Did they? May it never be, but by their transgression salvation has come to the Gentiles to make them jealous. Now, if their transgression be riches for the world and their failure are riches for the Gentiles, how much more will their fulfillment be? But I am speaking to you who are Gentiles and as much then as I am an apostle of Gentiles I magnify my ministry if somehow I may move to jealousy my fellow countrymen and save some of them.

For if their rejection be the reconciliation of the world, what will their acceptance be, but life from the dead? For if the first piece of dough be holy the lump is also and if the root be holy the branches are too. But if some of the branches were broken off, and you, being a wild olive were grafted in among them and became partaker with them of the rich root of the olive tree, do not be arrogant towards the branches; but if you are arrogant, remember that it is not you who supports the root but the root who supports you.

You will say then "Branches were broken off so that I might be grafted in." Quite right, they were broken off for their unbelief but you stand by your faith. Do not be conceited but fear; for if God did not spare the natural branches, neither will He spare you. Behold then, the kindness and the severity of God; to those who fell severity but to you God's kindness if you continue in His kindness; otherwise you also will be cut off.

And they also, if they do not continue in their unbelief will be grafted in for God is able to graft them in again. For if you were cut off from what is by nature a wild olive tree and were grafted, contrary to nature, into a cultivated olive tree, how much more shall these who are the natural branches be grafted into their own olive tree? For I do not want you, brethren, to be uninformed of this mystery, lest you be wise in your own estimation, that a partial hardening has happened to Israel until the fullness of the Gentiles comes in.

-Romans 11:1-25

Notice the hardening is partial and temporary!

> *And thus all Israel will be saved; just as it is written, "the deliverer will come from Zion. He will remove ungodliness from Jacob and this is My covenant with them when I take away their sin." From the standpoint of the Gospel they are enemies for your sake, but from the standpoint of God's choice they are beloved for the sake of their fathers.* (present, continuous, active in the Greek)
>
> -Romans 11:26-28

> *For just as you once were disobedient to God but now have been shown mercy, because of their disobedience, so these also now have been disobedient in order that, because of the mercy shown to you, they may also now be shown mercy. For God has shut up all in disobedience that He might show mercy to all; all the depth of the riches both of the wisdom and knowledge of God, how unsearchable are His judgments and unfathomable His ways! For who has known the mind of the Lord or who became His counselor? Or who has first given to Him that it might be paid back to him again? For, from Him and through Him and to Him are all things. To Him be the glory for ever and ever, Amen.*
>
> *- Romans 11:30-36*

Romans 9, 10 and 11 some people say are parenthetical. In a structural sense we can say this but it's not really parenthetical. Paul talks about how the law, the Torah, is fulfilled in the Messiah in chapters one through eight and so the natural question emerges then in the context of Romans. Well what about Israel, what about the Jews, what about the ones to whom the law was given and to whom the Gospel was given? What about the Lord's own people after the flesh? Now that more non-Jews are becoming followers of Jesus than the original followers who were Jews, what happens to them? It is natural that these questions thus emerge. Now, notice the context of Romans 9, 10 and 11 is about nations not individuals.

Our Calvinistic friends are very great at that exegesis. They would claim to be the most stoic and most skeptical of things like typology or midrash for fear of any kind of spiritualization of the text out of context. Yet they themselves are the arch offenders, spiritualizing every time it says Israel - "well, that's the church." Now, the principle may apply to the church. But why do they spiritualize the text? They spiritualize the millennium. They are great spiritualizers. They are great Gnostics. The very thing they are afraid of, they are arch practitioners of, among many other problems. But their exegesis goes further, taking passages that refer to nations and miss-applying them, out of all context, to individuals. A text out of context becomes a pretext! When you read Roman 9 to 11, it's talking about nations.

For instance, one of their favorite verses is from chapter 9 verse 18:

> *So then, He has mercy on whom He desires and hardens whom He desires. You will then say to me, "why, does He still find fault? Who can resist His will?" On the contrary, who are you O man who answers back to God? The thing molded will not say to the molder, "why did you make it like this." Will it?*

They apply that to individuals, misquoting from the book of Jeremiah Chapter 18. However, Paul is talking about nations not individuals and so too is Jeremiah:

> *"Can I not, Oh House of Israel deal, with you as this potter does?" declares the Lord. "Behold, like*

the clay in the potter's hand so are you in My hand Oh House of Israel. At one moment I speak concerning a nation or concerning a kingdom to uproot, to pull it down, and to destroy it; if that nation against which I have spoken turns from its evil I will relent concerning the calamity I planned to bring upon it. Or at another moment I might speak concerning a nation or concerning a kingdom to build up or to plant it; but if it does evil in My sight by not obeying My voice then I will think better of the good with which I had purposed."

-Jeremiah 18:6-10

Now note how they love to take that thing out; the potter, the clay. One, it's talking about nations not individuals and two, when you read the text in it's context that Paul is drawing on, God will smash it if it doesn't repent, but if it repents He'll remake it and give it another chance. This directly leads into Romans 11. If you want bad exegesis go to a Reform Theological Cemetery, (I mean Seminary!)

Now, coming from a moderately charismatic, Pentecostal background, I've seen some bad exegesis. I've seen virtual Gnosticism among hyper-Charismatics, particularly in the Vineyard movement and things like this. I've seen neo-Gnosticism in the church, but what I've seen among my fellow Charismatics and Pentecostals is no worse and often no different from what I've seen from extreme Calvinists.

The biggest insanity in the church today is dominion theology, kingdom now theology, triumphalism, the notion that we are going to conquer the entire world for Christ, before He comes and sets up His Kingdom. This is post millennial. If Satan is bound for a thousand years, I want to know who keeps letting him go. The twin pillars of this insanity are hyper-charismatic people. It's definitely the Kansas City crowd and Paul Cane, Mike Bickel, absolutely. But where do they get their theology? Where do they get their eschatology? They get it from Reconstructionist Calvinists (some dead, some living) such as Rouses Rushdooney, Gary North, David Chilton, and Greg Bahson.

You have to remember something. The Charismatic movement failed to bring revival because it had no doctrine, it had no theology. It was all experiential and mysticism and emotionalism. So, where do these kooks get their doctrine? They have no doctrine of their own, so where? They get it from another kook! Makes perfect sense. When you understand replacement theology you realize what that means. - it means tearing Romans 9,10 and 11 out of the Bible!

Now, returning to Chapter 11 in essence, what Paul is doing in highlighting an olive tree, is to show that everything below the surface is the Old Testament era; everything above the surface is the New Testament era. The word that Paul uses here for the root that supports you, in Greek is *reza*. "It is not you who supports the root, the root supports you." You don't see the root. The root is under the ground. It is not visible but you know it is there. If the root was dead, biologically if those cells were dead, the tree would be dead. Wouldn't it?

If God is finished with the Jews, He's finished with the Church! The root supports you. You don't see it but it is there. The Church is roughly two thousand years old, from the time of Jesus and Pentecost etc. That's how long God spent preparing Israel for the coming of Jesus. From the time of Abraham to the coming of Christ was as old as the age of the Church. If you plant a tree there is a long time before it actually begins to push up out of the ground and then grows up. At the same time, you also know it's growing down. The roots have to be getting deeper. You don't see the root but you know it's there and you know it's alive. If it was dead the tree would die.

Now, both the root of the tree and the trunk of the tree have branches. Under the Law most of the roots were Jews like Moses and Jacob and Isaiah, etc. But you had certain non-Jews, even in the Old Testament, who were grafted in, like Ruth or Zipporah, etc. Well, the same truth is in the New Testament. The first branches, the first Christians; Peter, Paul, John are Jews. Now, when Jews reject their Messiah, they are cut off from their own tree and Gentiles replace them. Gentiles who believe in the Jewish Messiah replace Jews who reject Him. But, in no place, is it a different tree - It's the same tree! No place is it a different tree! Believing Gentiles replace unbelieving Jews, that is true. They are grafted into the tree, but they don't become a different tree. Not only that, but he says, *"I don't want you to be unaware of this mystery, that a time is going to come when the natural branches are going to be grafted in again."* The first Christians were Jews and the last Christians are going to be Jews.

This is what Revelation 7 is all about. The time of the Gentiles comes to a close. Twice the New Testament speaks of this phenomenon, of the time of the Gentiles, or the fullness of the Gentiles coming in. In the Olivet discourse, and only in Luke's version, Jesus deals with this in terms of national prophecy concerning the nation. In Luke chapter 21 verse 24; Jesus says, *"Jerusalem will be trampled down by the feet of the Gentiles until the time of the Gentiles is completed."* The Greek uses the word *ethnon*, being translated from the Hebrew word goyim, which means nations. In the time of the Gentiles, Jesus said, Jerusalem will be trampled down. Ultimately, this is bound up with the prophecies of the prophet Daniel, and the coming of the Antichrist and the defiling of the Temple and other things that are to happen. Paul deals with it salvifically or from the point of view of soteriology, that is salvation. He talks about this partial hardening, this partial blindness on Israel, that it is temporary. It's coming to an end when Jews will believe again. Now, understand something, it was never "Monday it's the time of the Jews, Tuesday it's the time of the Gentiles!" There was a period of transition. Jews continued to accept Christ in very large numbers all way until the time of Simon Bar Kochba's second Jewish revolt circa 120-132 CE/AD. More Jews came to faith in Christ in the second century than the first. Max Dimont, the popular Jewish historian, estimates that at least twenty five percent of Jews in Jerusalem believed Jesus was the Messiah by 120 AD, the time of Bar Kochba rebellion. It was a period of transition.

It begins with Acts chapter 10. Peter does not understand God's purpose for the Gentiles. "How can these goys be saved without converting to Judaism?" Then, there is the ministry of Paul and Barnabas. Then there is the *Birkhat Ha Minim* (circa 90 CE/AD) when the Jewish believers were excommunicated from the synagogue and a curse was placed on them. In 70 AD, of course, the Temple was destroyed and Biblical Judaism or Mosaic Judaism could no longer exist. From 70 AD until now, Biblical Judaism has no longer existed.

This leads to "a tale of two Rabbis." Once upon a time there were Sadducees and Pharisees. Sadducees were like liberals. They were anti supernaturalist rationalists, but the Pharisees were more Biblical. Jesus had far more in common with the Pharisees on most issues, apart from divorce and the oral tradition. You had two kinds of rabbinic academies among the Pharisees, the School of Shammi and the School of Hillel. Paul was from the School of Hillel and Rabbi Hillel's grandson, Rabbi Gamaliel was Paul's mentor. Paul had some interesting classmates at that particular time. One was Onkelos whose parents were Gentiles who converted to Judaism. Onkelos did a famous *Targum*, a translation of the Old Testament into Aramaic. We have two major *Targums*; the *Targum Yonatan* and the *Targum Onkelos*, and Paul's classmate Onkelos translated this.

Paul's other famous classmate was Rabbi Yochanan Ben Zakai. He was called the mighty hammer and when the temple was destroyed in 70 AD, Rabbi Yochanan Ben Zakai was smuggled out of Jerusalem and he convened a council at a place called Yavne, near Jerusalem where he dealt with the great Jewish dilemma; no more high priest, no more Temple. "What are we going to do? I know. Instead of 'ha Cohen', (the priest), we'll have the rabbi and instead of the Temple we'll have the synagogue. Instead of the sacrificial system we'll have the 'mitzvot' the good works."

Then, a whole Jewish legal system develops called the 'chalacha'. It did not exist at the time of Moses as it would have had to be written down (Joshua 8:35) but there was an oral law *Torah D'al Pei* at the time of Jesus which eventually gets written down by somebody called rabbi Yehuda Ha Nassi and it becomes extremely complicated. But it really began to develop prior to the Second Jewish Revolt of Bar Kochba in the second century with Rabbi Akiva. It's formal origins however were again with by Paul's classmate Rabbi Yochanan Ben Zakai.

So, as Jesus said, "the Temple is going to be destroyed." As Daniel, the prophet said, "the Temple is going to be destroyed. The Messiah would have to come before the second Temple would be destroyed."

Then once it's destroyed, you have two rabbis now, who are going to determine the future of Israel; Rabbi Shaul of Tarsus, better known as Paul the Apostle and Rabbi Yochanan Ben Zakai his classmate. Same class, same tutor. When Rabbi Yochanan Ben Zakai died, having begun Talmudic Judaism, as we know it today, he was crying, weeping on his deathbed and his disciples came and said to him "Oh mighty hammer why do you weep?" And he said:

> "Because I'm about to meet Ha-Shem, (God) blessed be His name and there are two roads before me, one to Gehenna and one to paradise and I know not to which one He will sentence me."

The founder of Rabbinic Judaism, the founder of Talmudic Judaism did not know if he was going to heaven or to hell. And, that is the Judaism of the synagogue today that rejects Yeshua.

His classmate, on the other hand, founded another expression of Judaism, Messianic Judaism and its Gentile form, Christianity. When he was on his deathbed he said:

> *"I know henceforth is stored up for me a crown of righteousness. I have run the good race. I have fought the good fight."*

Every Jew will follow one of these two rabbis.

Jesus deals with the national aspect. Paul writes about the salvation aspect of the time of the Gentiles coming to a close. It was not one day; it's the time of the Jews, the next day; it's the time of the Gentiles. There were a series of events; the ministry of Paul and Barnabas; the event with Cornelius in Acts 10, the destruction of the Temple; The *Birhat Ha Minim*, (circa 90 AD/CE) ultimately the expulsion of the Messianic Jews from the Jewish community by Rabbi Akiva. There were a series of events when God turned His grace from Israel to the nations. Well, Paul tells us a time will come when the reverse will happen. The time of the Gentiles will come to an end. You see, there have been many times in the history of the Church when believers thought these were the last days.

Our children were born in Israel. As little kids in Israel, they had no idea who Jesus Christ was. They never heard about Jesus Christ until they came to England. They heard about Yeshua HaMashiach but never about Jesus Christ. They didn't know what a church was. There was the *Kehilth Meshechet* (Messianic congregation). The unbelieving Jews went to the *Beit Knesset*, (their synagogue) and we went to ours. All they knew was that He was a Jew, they were Jews. He was from Galilee, they were from Galilee and He was the

Messiah who died for their sins and rose from the dead to give eternal life and He is coming again. That's all they new. I remember trying to explain to my then little daughter Batmiel "Abba, who is Jesus? Why do they call Him that? What's Christmas?" She knew about Hanukkah, Jesus talked about Hanukkah in John chapter 10. She knew about the nativity – *Hag Ha Molad*, but Christmas? She didn't know what that was. "What's Easter?" She new about Pesach, Passover. She had no idea what Easter was. All four Gospels say it happened at Passover, not Easter. That was the first Sunday after the equinox. It was a pagan day. He didn't die on Good Friday and didn't rise from the dead at Easter. The King James Version makes this mistake as well.

Many times, sincere Christians thought it was the last days. Now, if you have heard some of our teaching tapes you can understand how the Gentile Church makes this mistake, of understanding prophecy in terms of futurism, preterism, polemicism, or historicism, while to the Jewish minds, all the New Testament, all four are simultaneously true. Basically, it comes to this; many times sincere Christians thought it was the last days, while the Apostles allowed for the fact that Jesus might not come in their lifetime. They understood that He didn't have to come in their lifetime, many believers plainly thought so.

In 70 AD when the Temple was going to be destroyed and Jerusalem was surrounded, the Apostle James had been murdered, martyred, and the siege of Jerusalem by Titus, you read about it in Eusebius and Josephus, commenced at the same time when Jesus was rejected, Passover time. The believers saw this as a judgment for the martyrdom of James. But, remember what Jesus said, "When you see Jerusalem surrounded by an army of Gentiles, flee." And they did it. They fled to a place called Pella. Not Petra but Pella. They thought that was going to be the rapture, you understand. Now, in a way, it typifies the rapture. It's a foreshadowing of what the rapture will be. What happened to Jerusalem when the Jewish believers were taken out and when you read in Josephus how women were eating their babies and such things, that's a picture of the great Tribulation. What happened in Jerusalem after the believers were taken out is a picture of the great tribulation. The Jews who believed were taken out, this is a picture of the rapture.

Believers in England were convinced that Napoleon was the anti-Christ. Much the same as the economy of the west is largely dependant on oil from the Middle East, in the aftermath and during the crusades in the Renaissance, the economy of Europe was dependent on the spice trade. Finally, the popes ran the banking families of Italy; the Borgia families, the Medici families. They wanted to control the spice trade thus they had to control the trade routes to Israel, so they had to liberate the Holy Land. You understand, it is banking business. Saladin finally defeats them and the balance of power in the Middle East goes into the Muslim world. Napoleon comes to reverse this. He defeats the Marmalukes near Egypt, near the pyramids and he goes to the Jezreel Valley, the Valley of Armageddon and up Mt Tabor, the same place as the story of Deborah takes place, in the Book of Judges, and he says, "This is the perfect place of my ultimate military campaign." Then he returns to Europe and looks like he is trying to revive the Roman Empire and he puts the emperor's crown on his head. Evangelical Christians in England thought that he was the Antichrist. Now, in some way that does foreshadow the Antichrist.

In the 1930's was the final aliya before Israel became a nation. The holocaust was just beginning. Mussolini made a pact with the pope, the Lateran Treaty. The Catholic bishops of Bavaria, lead by Michael Schmauss of Munich in Bavaria, made an alliance with Hitler. The Plymouth Brethren saw the Jews going back and saw Mussolini making an alliance with the pope, and thought that they were the Antichrist and the false prophet. They thought that was going to be the end. Not all the Brethren but some of them thought that, particularly in England. There were many times.

In 70 AD the Temple was destroyed, Mt Vesuvius blew up, blowing volcanic ash into the upper atmosphere, the sun not giving its light. Rome burns under the Emperor Nero, fallen is Babylon they thought, just out of the book of Isaiah. It looked like the end to them. Reuniting the Roman Empire, Napoleon tried that and so did Charlemagne. This was not the first time people tried it. Others have tried it, in the 18th century, the 19th century, the Millerites. There have been at least seven major times, when sincere Christians interpreted world events as being the last days and thought Jesus was going to come in their lifetime. In the Doomsday Book in England they tried to number people. There are seven major times when Evangelical Christians thought that they were living in the last days.

What makes this time different? Why should I believe this time is different from the other times? Because the countries that were in the Roman Empire are reuniting? Charlemagne did that and Napoleon did that. Because the countries that were important in the Bible are important again at the centre of world events? Well, that was true during the crusades and it was true during the Napoleonic wars. It's not the first time that's happened. What makes this time different?

You see, what God said to Israel was this, *"Oh Israel, My people Israel, in a covenant relationship with Me, I pleaded with you."* And Paul quoted from the prophet Isaiah:

> *"I let Myself be found by those who did not seek Me. I became manifest to those who did not ask for Me...... Because of Israel, all day long I stretched out My hands to an obstinate and rebellious people."*
> -Isaiah 65:1-2

"Oh Israel, I've had enough. You went against My covenant so I sent you my messengers. I sent you Jeremiah, Israel, but you put him in prison. I sent you Isaiah, Israel, but you sawed him in half. I sent you prophets but you killed them, you persecuted them. I sent you leaders, preachers of righteousness who brought revival. I sent you King Josiah and King Hezekiah. I sent you righteous men who called you to repentance, to revival. I sent you John the Baptist but you rejected him and finally you have rejected My Son. That's it. I'm going to the Gentiles. You have had you chance."

Fortunately, that is temporary and partial. If they are being cut off for the salvation of the Gentiles, how much more will them being grafted in again be a blessing to everybody. God is going to bless the Church through the natural branches being grafted in, in the last days. Just look at it; the founder of Christians in Sport, Eddie Wax, a Jew, Christ to the communist nations, Richard Wurmbrand, a Jew. From the beginning, the only one to have the number one hit single in the secular pop charts, Norman Greenbaum, 'Going up to the Spirit to the Sky', a Jew.

The finest Bible teacher on the subject of evangelism that I know of, in the whole world, is Ray Comfort, a Jew from New Zealand, who now lives in Los Angeles. God is going to bless the Church through Jewish believers in the last days. But He tells the church to provoke them to Jealousy. How are you going to provoke Jews to jealousy? Do you know what Christianity is to my wife's parents? You know what the Gospel is to her family? It's Jewish children being kicked into an oven in the name of the Father, the Son and the Holy Spirit. It was the Russian Orthodox Church who machined gunned her grandfather; my wife's grandfather. That's what it is to them. How are you going to provoke Jews to jealousy; by people rolling on the floor in hysterics in Pensacola, Florida, imitating animals? That can provoke the Jews to jealousy? Those con artists and money preachers on TV, one after another, prostituting the Word of God, is that going to provoke the Jews to jealousy? What is the acid test? When will the bride be dressed and ready for the bridegroom to come? What is God's acid test when the church is going to be ready? When you can provoke the Jews; "we want what you have." And I'll tell you something; I know many people today, Jew and

Gentile are seeing the state of the Church, particularly televangelists and if, by the grace of God, I was not already a born again Christian, and I saw that stuff, I wouldn't want to become a Christian either. Provoke them to jealousy?

Now God says, "Don't' think I can't make My ancient people believe again. I've already done something more difficult than that. I've taken pagans. I've taken demon worshippers." (Other gods are called demons by both Moses and Paul. *Shedim* in Hebrew and *demonoi* in Greek. Hare Krishna is a demon. Ramah is a demon). "If I can take people whose ancestors, whose heritage was paganism, superstition, demonic religion and make them believe in the Gospel. How much easier it is for Me to take the natural branches and put them back into their own tree." Jesus was a Jew. Abraham promised the Messiah would come as his seed. Isaiah was a Jew. To them belong the oracles of God. "If I can make non-Jews believe in My Son how much easier can I make My own people believe in their own Messiah again. I've already done something harder than make Israel believe!"

So, I come back to the question. What makes this time different? Why is this time different from 70AD or 120AD? Why is it different from the 1930's? Why is it different from the year 1000? Why is it different from the Napoleonic wars? Why is it that we can be so confident that Jesus is coming soon? That it's not just another time when sincere but misguided evangelical Christians thought it was the last days, but He didn't come. What wasn't around a thousand years ago? I'll tell you what it was; the natural branches being grafted in again.

Twenty-five years ago the American College of Rabbis said that more Jews have turned to Jesus Christ in the last eighteen years than in the last eighteen centuries. I speak to congregations of Jews in South Africa, in Russia, in Israel, in America, everywhere. Not one here, one there! My little children witness to their grandparents who were in the holocaust; "why don't you believe in our Messiah Yeshua Saba?" They understand something. It is the generation of Jews whose parents and grandparents were in the holocaust, the most notorious Jewish bloodbath in history, in proportionate terms, the worst since Bar Kochba's rebellion that are returning to faith in Jesus as their messiah. The holocaust was a bloodbath, largely perpetrated in the name of Christendom. Yet it's their children and grandchildren who are turning to Jesus Christ as the Messiah. Don't tell me there is no God. Don't tell me this book is wrong. The Calvinists are wrong. The reconstructionists are wrong. The replacementists are wrong. The identity of movement is wrong. But the Bible is not wrong.

What was missing a thousand years ago, five hundred years ago, and one hundred years ago? I'll tell you what was missing; my daughter, my Israeli daughter Batmiel and my son Eli: "Abba, why do the Gentile Christians call our Messiah Jesus? Isn't His name Yeshua?" They weren't around a hundred years ago. Jews who believe weren't around in any conspicuous numbers five hundred years ago or a thousand years ago. You had the odd one like Benjamin Disraeli, the prime minister of England or Felix Mendelssohn, the composer.

You always had individual Jews. But families of them, congregations of them, tens of thousands of them? The number of Jews who believe in Jesus Christ has quadrupled in the last five years, in Israel, by conservative estimations, by immigration of Russian believers, and the spiritual vacuum in Israel that Rabbis can't meet, so the young people are turning to Christ. I've read an article in an Israeli newspaper recently. Approximately 465 Israeli conscripts, eighty three wanted to take the oath to Israel on the New Testament. That was not around a hundred years ago.

So, what does Paul say? This is what he says, *"I don't want you to be unaware of this mystery, my brethren, lest you be wise in your own estimation that a partial hardening has happened to Israel."* Then he continues, *"If God did not spare the natural branches,* (verse 21) *He won't spare you either. Behold the kindness but the severity of God."* You see, God loved Israel, God chose Israel. God desired Israel but God didn't need Israel. God loves me. I believe that. Does He choose me? I believe that. Does he need me? Not for one second. If He didn't need the natural branches why should He need alien ones that are grafted in, if they go the same way as Israel; unbelief! Major Protestant denominations are ordaining homosexuals and lesbians. The United Reformed Church, the Methodist Church, the Anglican Church, ordaining homosexuals. The time of the Gentiles will come to a close. No, the time of the Gentiles is coming to a close!

What did God tell Israel? "I pleaded with you for centuries. I gave you my covenant. I gave you My Truth, My Promise. When you rebelled I sent you Isaiah, but you sawed him in half. I sent you Jeremiah but you put him in prison. I sent you My prophets but you persecuted them. I sent you men who caused you to repentance. I sent you leaders who brought you revival, like Hezekiah and Josiah, but you forgot those revivals Israel. I'm turning My grace to the Gentiles."

Now that same God is saying this. "I sent you Charles Spurgeon. I sent you John Wesley, George Whitfield. For centuries I pleaded with you. I sent you preachers of righteousness Christian America, Christian Britain. I sent you DL Moody and Harry Ironside. I sent you AW Tozer and Jonathan Edwards. You forgot those revivals backslidden America now I'm turning My grace back to My ancient people Israel." Am I saying that that's going to happen? No friend. I'm telling you, by the Spirit of Jesus, that that is happening. The time of the Gentiles is coming to a close. Now is the time. This is the time, and the time is not coming again. Who is coming again is Jesus Christ - Yeshua HaMashiach.

Chapter 11

Book of Ruth

The book of Ruth is read in the Jewish Synagogue at the feast of Pentecost, which is the first day, as it were, of the Gentile church. The book of Ruth tells the story of a rich powerful Jewish man who takes a Gentile bride and exalts her, the way that Jesus, on the day of Pentecost, raised up the Gentile church, as the Bride of Christ.

> *Now it came about in the days when the judges governed, that there was a famine in the land. And a certain man of Bethlehem (meaning 'the house of bread') in Judah went to sojourn in the land of Moab with his wife and two sons. And the name of the man was Elimelech, (which means, 'my God is King') and the name of his wife Naomi; and the names of his two sons, Mahlon and Chilion, Ephrathites of Bethlehem in Judah. Now they entered the land of Moab and remained there. Then Elimelech, Naomi's husband, died; and she was left with her two sons. And they took for themselves Moabite women as wives; (the Moabites were particularly despised by the Jews because of the maltreatment of them during the Exodus period) the name of the one was Orpah and the name of the other Ruth. And they lived there about ten years.*
>
> *Then both Mahlon and Chilion also died; and the woman was bereft of her two children and her husband. Then she arose with her daughters-in-law that she might return from the land of Moab, for she had heard in the land of Moab that the Lord had visited His people in*

giving them food. So she departed from the place where she was, and her two daughters-in-law with her; and they went on the way to return to the land of Judah.

And Naomi said unto her two daughters-in-law, "Go, return each of you to her mother's house. May the Lord deal kindly with you, as you have dealt with the dead and with me. May the Lord grant that you may find rest, each in the house of her husband." Then she kissed them, and they lifted up their voices and wept. And they said to her, "No, but we will surely return with you to your people."

But Naomi said, "Return, my daughters. Why should you go with me? Have I yet sons in my womb, that they may be your husbands? Return, my daughters! Go, for I am too old to have a husband. If I said I have hope, if I should even have a husband tonight and also bear sons, would you therefore wait until they were grown? Would you refrain from marrying? No, my daughters; for it is harder for me than for you, for the hand of the Lord has gone forth against me."

-Ruth 1:1-13

Ruth's loyalty

And they lifted up their voices and wept again; and Orpah kissed her mother-in-law, but Ruth clung to her. Then she said, "Behold, your sister-in-law has gone back to her people and her gods; return after your sister-in-law." But Ruth said, "Do not urge me to leave you or turn back from following you; for where you go, I will go, and where you lodge, I will lodge. Your people shall be my people, and your God, my God. Where you die, I will die, and there I will be buried. Thus may the Lord do to me, and worse, if anything but death parts you and me."

When she saw that she was determined to go with her, she said no more to her. So they both went until they came to Bethlehem. And it came about when they had come to Bethlehem, that all the city was stirred because of them, and the women said, "Is this Naomi?" And she said unto them, "Do not call me not Naomi; call me Mara, for the Almighty has dealt very bitterly with me. I went out full, but the Lord has brought me back empty. Why do you call me Naomi, since the Lord has afflicted me?"

So Naomi returned, and with her Ruth the Moabitess, her daughter-in-law, who returned from the land of Moab. And they came to Bethlehem at the beginning of barley harvest.

-Ruth 1:14-22

This is read in the synagogues at the Feast of Weeks, when the barley harvest is underway in Israel.

Ruth gleans in the field of Boaz

Now Naomi had a kinsman of her husband, a man of great wealth, of the family of Elimelech, whose name was Boaz. (Boaz in Hebrew means 'in his strength.' It is also the name of one of the pillars in the temple) And Ruth the Moabitess said to Naomi, "Please let me go to the field and glean among the ears of grain after one in whose sight I might find favor." And she said to her, "Go, my daughter."

And she departed and went and gleaned in the field after the reapers; and she happened to come to the portion of the field belonging to Boaz, who was of the family of Elimelech. Now behold, Boaz came from Bethlehem and said to the reapers, "May the Lord be with you." And they said to him, "May the Lord bless you." Then Boaz said to his servant who was in charge of the reapers, "Whose young woman is this?"

And the servant in charge of the reapers answered and said, "She is the young Moabite woman who returned with Naomi from the land of Moab. And she said, 'Please let me glean and gather after the reapers among the sheaves.' Thus she came and has remained from the morning until now; she has been sitting in the house for a little while."

Then Boaz said to Ruth, "Listen carefully, my daughter. Do not go to glean in another field; furthermore, do not go on from this one, but stay here with my maids. Let your eyes be on the field which they reap, and go after them. Indeed, I have commanded the servants not to touch you. When you are thirsty, go to the water jars and drink from what the servants draw."

Then she fell on her face, bowing to the ground, and said to him, "Why have I found favor in your sight, that you should take notice of me, since I am a foreigner?" And Boaz answered and said to her, "All that you have done for your mother-in-law after the death of your husband has been fully reported to me, and how you left your father and your mother and the land of your birth, and came to a people that you did not previously know. May the Lord reward your work, and your wages be full from the Lord, the God of Israel, under whose wings you have come to seek refuge."

Then she said, "I have found favor in your sight, my lord, for you have comforted me and indeed have spoken kindly to your maidservant, though I am not like one of your maidservants." And at mealtime Boaz said to her, "Come here, that you may eat of the bread and dip your piece of bread in the vinegar." So she sat beside the reapers; and he served her roasted grain, and she ate and was satisfied and had some left. When she rose to glean, Boaz commanded his servants, saying, "Let her glean even among the sheaves, and do not insult her. And also you shall purposely pull out for her some grain from the bundles and leave it that she may glean, and do not rebuke her."

So she gleaned in the field until evening. Then she beat out what she had gleaned, and it was about an ephah of barley. And she took it up and went into the city, and her mother-in-law saw what she had gleaned. She also took it out and gave Naomi what she had left after she was satisfied. Her mother-in-law then said to her; "Where did you glean today and where did you work? May he who took notice of you be blessed."

So she told her mother-in-law with whom she worked and said, "The name of the man with whom I worked today is Boaz." And Naomi said to her daughter-in-law, "May he be blessed of the Lord who has not withdrawn his kindness to the living and to the dead." Again Naomi said to her, "The man is our relative, he is one of our closest relatives."

('Close' as in 'one of an extended family').

Then Ruth the Moabitess said, "Furthermore, he said unto me, 'You shall stay close to my servants until they have finished all my harvest.'" And Naomi said to Ruth her daughter-in- law, "It is good, my daughter, that you go out with his maids, lest others fall upon you in another field." So she stayed close by the maids of Boaz in order to glean until the end of the barley harvest and the wheat harvest. And she lived with her mother-in-law.   -Ruth 2:1-23

Boaz will redeem Ruth

Then Naomi her mother-in-law said to her, "My daughter, shall I not seek security for you, that it may be well with you? And now is not Boaz our kinsman, with whose maids you were? Behold, he winnows barley at the threshing floor tonight. Wash yourself therefore, and anoint yourself and put on your best clothes, and go down to the threshing floor; but do not make yourself known to the man until he is finished eating and drinking. And it shall be when he lies down, that you shall notice the place where he lies, and you shall go and uncover his feet and lie down; then he will tell you what you shall do." And she said to her, "All that you say I will do."

So she went down to the threshing floor and did according to all that her mother-in- law had commanded her. When Boaz had eaten and drunk and his heart was merry, he went to lie down at the end of the heap of grain; and she came secretly, and uncovered his feet and lay down. And it happened in the middle of the night that the man was startled and bent forward; and behold, a woman was lying at his feet.

And he said, "Who are you?" And she answered, "I am Ruth your maid. So spread your covering over your maid, for you are a close relative." Then he said, "May you be blessed of the Lord, my daughter. You have shown your last kindness to be better that the first by not going after young men, whether poor or rich. And now, my daughter, do not fear. I will do for you whatever you ask, for all my people in the city know that you are a woman of excellence. And now it is true I am a close relative; however, there is a relative closer than I. Remain this night, and when morning comes, if he will redeem you, good; let him redeem you. But if he does not *wish to redeem you, then I will redeem you, as the Lord lives. Lie down until morning."*

So she lay at his feet until morning and rose before one could recognize another; and he said, "Let it not be known that the woman came to the threshing floor." Again he said, "Give me the cloak that is on you and hold it." So she held it, and he measured six measures of barley and laid it on her. Then she went into the city. And when she came to her mother-in-law, she said, "How did it go, my daughter?" And she told her all that the man had done for her.

And she said, "These six measures of barley he gave to me, for he said, 'Do not go to your mother-in-law empty handed.'" Then she said, "Wait, my daughter, until you know how the matter turns out; for the man will not rest until he has settled it today."

-Ruth 3:1-18

The marriage of Ruth

Now Boaz went up to the gate and sat down there, and, behold, the close relative of whom Boaz spoke was passing by, so he said, "Turn aside, friend, sit down here." And he turned aside and he sat down. And he took ten men of the elders of the city and said, "Sit down here." So they sat down. Then he said to the closest relative, "Naomi, who has come back from the land of Moab, has to sell the piece of land which belonged to our brother Elimelech. So I thought to inform you, saying, 'Buy it before these who are sitting here, and before the elders of my people. If you will redeem it, redeem it; but if not, tell me that I may know; for there is no one but you to redeem it, and I am after you'" And he said, "I will redeem it."

Then Boaz said, "On the day you buy the field from the hand of Naomi, you must also acquire Ruth the Moabitess, the widow of the deceased, in order to raise up the name of the deceased on his inheritance." And the closest relative said, "I cannot redeem it for myself, lest I jeopardize my own inheritance. Redeem it for yourself; you may have my right of redemption, for I cannot redeem it." Now this was the custom in former times in Israel concerning the redemption and the exchange of land to confirm any matter: a man removed his sandal and gave it to another; and this was the matter of attestation in Israel. So the closest relative said to Boaz, "Buy it for yourself." And he removed his sandal.

And Boaz said to the elders and to all the people, "You are witnesses today that I have bought from the hand of Naomi all that belonged to Elimelech and all that belonged to Chilion and Mahlon. Moreover, I have acquired Ruth the Moabitess, the widow of Mahlon, to be my wife in order to raise up the name of the deceased on his inheritance, so that the name of the deceased may not be cut off from his brothers or from the court of his birth place; you are witnesses today."

And all the people who were in the court, and the elders, said, "We are witnesses. May the Lord make the woman who is coming into your home like Rachel and Leah, both of whom built the house of Israel; and may you achieve wealth in Ephrathah and become famous in Bethlehem. Moreover, may your house be like the house of Perez whom Tamar bore to Judah, through the offspring which the Lord shall give you by this young woman."

So Boaz took Ruth, and she became his wife; and he went in to her. And the Lord enabled her to conceive, *and she gave birth to a son. And the women said to Naomi, "Blessed is the Lord who has not left you without a redeemer today, and may his name become famous in Israel. May he also be to you a restorer of life and a sustainer of your old age; for your daughter-in-law who loves you and is better to you than seven sons, has given birth to him."*

-Ruth 4:1-15

The line of David began here

Then Naomi took the child and laid him in her lap, and became his nurse. And the neighbor women gave him a name saying, "A son has been born to Naomi!" So they named him Obed. He is the father of Jesse, the father of David. Now these are the generations of Perez: to Perez was born Hezron; and to Hezron was born Ram, and to Ram, Amminadab, and to Amminadab was born Nahshon, and to Nahshon, Salmon, and to Salmon was born Boaz, and to Boaz, Obed, and to Obed was born Jesse, and to Jesse, David.

-Ruth 4:16-22

The genealogy of Jesus does not begin in Matthew chapter one, it begins in Ruth chapter four. My family is a combination of Jew and Gentile. My wife and I have seen two false religions in our lives: nominal Christianity (which does not teach that salvation comes from the new birth) and Rabbinic Judaism (which rejects its own Messiah).

Why us?

The book of Ruth tells the story of an old woman who feels that God Himself is against her. She was forced out of her land for some time, her husband died, her sons died and she was left alone. She feels bereft, embittered, rejected. She feels that the hand of God is against her.

This is a picture of my wife's parents, Jews who were in the Holocaust, their families murdered by people who claimed to be Christians. Some of the Jewish writers after the Holocaust wrote, "One and one half million Jewish children kicked into ovens. God must hate us." Many Jews have asked, "Why us? Why the holocaust? Why the inquisition? Why the crusades? Why always us?"

Jews know they are different from other people, but they do not know why.

Something special...

There is nothing special about Jews. There is nothing unique about Jews. Jews are people who need to be saved, the same as anyone else but there is something very special about the God of the Jews. There is something very special about the covenant of the Jews. There is something very special about the book of the Jews. There is something very special about the Messiah of the Jews! But until they see Him, they will not understand the rest of it.

The Jewish people today are in the character of Naomi. They feel rejected, cursed by God. For nearly two thousand years the Jews were outcasts from their own land. They have regathered because they heard things were beginning to get better and out of desperation they are returning to Israel. They are coming back the same as Naomi did. They are coming back with the burden of rejection, of pain, of a sense of anguish and agony of their souls. If you talk to them about God, even religious Jews express the feeling that God is against the Jewish people.

Orpah

There are two Gentile women. Every Gentile Christian and Gentile church will come either in the character or Ruth or in the character of Orpah. Orpah seems to be quite polite and pleasant but once her own interests are at stake, she goes back to her people and to her gods.

Notice that: "to her gods" (Ruth 1:15). The post-Nicene Church, after Constantine 'christianized' the Roman Empire, the Church lost sight of its Jewish roots, some-thing that Paul warned should not happen (Romans 11:17-18).

> *I say then, God has not rejected His people, has He? May it never be! For I too am an Israelite, a descendant of Abraham, of the tribe of Benjamin. God has not rejected His people whom He foreknew. Or do you not know what the Scripture says in the passage about Elijah, how he pleads with God against Israel? "Lord, they have killed Thy prophets, they have torn down Thine altars, and I alone am left, and they are seeking my life." But what is the divine response to him? "I have kept for Myself seven thousand men who have not bowed the knee to Baal." In the same way then, there has also come to be at the present time a remnant according to God's gracious choice. But if it is by grace, it is no longer on the basis of works, otherwise grace is no longer grace. What then? That which Israel is seeking for, it has not obtained, but those who were chosen obtained it, and the rest were hardened; just as it is written, "God gave them a spirit of stupor, eyes to see not and ears to hear not, down to this very day."*
>
> -Romans 11:1-8

The Church lost sight of their Jewish roots. Then what happened? Paganism invaded Christendom - the emergence of Roman Catholicism and Eastern Orthodoxy, perverting the original Christianity of the New Testament, which was a Jewish Hebraic faith. They went back to their old gods once they lost sight of their Jewish roots!

Ruth

But then there is Ruth. *"Your people shall be my people, and your God, my God"* (Ruth 1:16). The New Testament speaks that kind of language:

> *Remember that you were at a time separate from Christ, excluded from the commonwealth of Israel, and strangers to the covenants of promise, having no hope and without God in the world. But now in Christ Jesus you who formerly were far off have been brought near by the blood of Christ.*
>
> -Ephesians 2:12-13

You (Gentiles) have been brought near *karov*, like a close relative - the Hebrew concept of a 'relative' is someone who is close to you. Romans chapter 11 speaks the language of *incorporation*, not of *replacementism*. Gentile Christians who repent and accept Jesus replace Jews who reject Him. But the tree stays the same! It is not a different tree; the church is not the 'New Israel.'

By a sovereign act of God's Grace, Gentile Christians are spiritually grafted in and become descendants of Abraham by faith. That is the meaning of the book of Ruth.

Levirite marriage

To go further, we need to understand certain things about the Torah. The Torah had geriatrical and legal provisions. Remember that the book of Ruth records the beginning of the lineage of David. However, the genealogy of Jesus in Matthew has certain discrepancies when compared with that in Luke.

There are two main ways to account for those discrepancies. One of the ways is called 'Levirate marriage':

> *When brothers live together and one of them dies and has no son, the wife of the deceased shall not be married outside the family to a strange man. Her husband's brother shall go in to her and take her to himself as wife and perform the duty of a husband's brother to her. And it shall be that the first born whom she bears shall assume the name of his dead brother, that his name may not be blotted out from Israel. But if the man does not desire to take his brother's wife, then his brother's wife shall go up to the gate of the elders and say, "My husband's brother refuses to establish a name for his brother in Israel; he is not willing to perform the duty of a husband's brother to me."*
>
> *Then the elders of his city shall summon him and speak to him. And if he persists and says, "I do not desire to take her," then his brother's wife shall come to him in sight of the elders* (there had to be ten of them, a 'minyan') *and pull his sandal off his foot and spit in his face; and she shall declare, "Thus it is done to the man who does not build up his brother's house." And in Israel his name shall be called, "The house of him whose sandal is removed.*
>
> -Deuteronomy 25:5-10

Let me explain this:

Importance of genealogy

Kings had to be descendants of David. Priests had to be descendants of Levi. High Priests had to be descendants of Aaron. The tribal inheritance allocated by Joshua had to be preserved according to Torah. So a legal descent had to be perpetuated. Otherwise, how would you know who the high priest was going to be? How would you know who the King was going to be? How would you know what was the inheritance of your family? And ultimately, how would we know the Messiah? The lineage had to be established and perpetuated. There is a biological bloodline, and a legal one. One of the genealogies in the New Testament gives a legal descent; the other gives the biological, or genetic descent. That is one of the ways you account for the discrepancies; there are other ways, but that is one of the two main ones.

Ex-vaginal ejaculation

There was only one form of birth control practised in ancient near east - ex-vaginal ejaculation. Today you will find Christians teaching against birth control for married people based on the verse that says there was a sentence of death if you practised ex-vaginal ejaculation. But the only situation where that was forbidden was in Levirate marriage. It was designed to prevent you from reducing your brother's widow to a concubine, a sex object. The reason for having sex with your brother's widow was to procreate offspring on his behalf for two reasons:

Social welfare provision

The first reason was financial provision for his widow. The Hebrew word for 'honor your parents' (it has to do with *honorarium*) does not mean you have to agree with every word of your parents, just because they are your parents.

It means it is something heavy for you, that you are expected to carry. The same thing as a mother is supposed to take care of the baby when it is little so, when she is old that baby is going to be responsible for her in God's economy. Having children was a form of welfare provision for the aged. The first reason for Levirate marriage was so the brother's widow would have provision for her old age.

Family inheritance

The second was the inheritance. The off-spring would perpetuate the family inheritance. If the land went out of the family line, due to debt, in the year of jubilee there would be a restoration of it to the family.

The Pharisees taught that you could legally deny giving help to your parents by dedicating your goods to God - rendering them 'corban.'(Mark 7:11-13) They invalidated the commandments of God by their teachings. Jesus attacked them for this.

Your responsibility to your parents was woven into Jewish thought. It is perpetuated in the New Testament, which says you will not have a long life in this world if you do not look after your parents in their old age. (Ephesians 6:2-3)

'Right of redemption'

We read in Ruth that the widow's brother would not raise up children on behalf of his brother in order to keep his brother's name from being cut off.

This is a typology of Jesus. The Jews who, under the Old Covenant, died faithful to God needed somebody to come after them to redeem them. When someone procreated children on behalf of their deceased brother and took his land, it was called a 'right of redemption.'

A Jew who died under the Old Covenant needed someone from among his kinsmen to come after him, someone who would redeem him, prevent his name from being cut off from his fathers, and prevent him from losing the inheritance of promise. It points to Jesus.

How were the Jews under the Old Covenant saved?

The same way we are. Hebrews tells us that the blood of animals could never take away sin. They could only cover the sin, if accompanied by faith and repentance, until the Messiah came and He would take them away. Under the Old Covenant the Jews were dependent on someone to come after them, to bring their redemption. It all points to Jesus.

Gleaning

Another form of social provision was gleaning. We need to understand this. Narrow pathways would separate the fields of the different farmers or families. The Jews were forbidden from harvesting the corners of their fields.

Why? As form of social welfare provision, the poor, the widows, the orphans, the socially disenfranchised, even sojourners (foreigners traveling through the land) had the right to glean.

This is what we see in the book of Ruth. Ruth arrives with her mother-in-law who says, *"Don't call me Naomi, call me Mara; for the Lord has dealt bitterly with me."* When Jewish people today come back to their own land after the holocaust and after what happened with the Communists, they have a feeling of "God did this to us."

Orthodox Jews will look at Leviticus 26 and Deuteronomy 28 and admit that their experiences reflect the curse of the law as recorded in those passages. What happened to them was somehow God's hand. Not all Jews make this admission, but the ultra-Orthodox certainly will.

I will bless them that bless thee

Boaz, a Jewish man, said to Ruth, a Gentile woman:

> *"Let your eyes be on the field that they reap, and go after them. Indeed, I have commanded the servants not to touch you. When you are thirsty, go to the water jars and drink from what the servants draw."* *Then she fell on her face, bowing to the ground and said to him, "Why have I found favor in your sight that you should take notice of me, since I am a foreigner?" And Boaz answered and said to her, "All you have done for your mother-in-law after the death of your husband has been fully reported to me"*
>
> -Ruth 2:9-11

I will bless them that bless thee, and I will curse them that curse thee. Not because the Jews are special, but because the God of the Jews and his covenant with their fathers is special. God will honor his covenant, and it does not depend upon the faithfulness or unfaithfulness of man. His covenant depends on the faithfulness of God.

This is illustrated to us in the story of Abraham, who is the father of all those who believe, both Jew and Christian:

232

> *And it came about when the sun had set, that it was very dark, and behold, there appeared a smoking oven and a flaming torch that passed between these pieces.*
>
> -Genesis 15:17

That flame is the same as the pillar of fire called the *Shekinah* of God, the Holy Spirit.

God is faithful

The term for making a covenant in Hebrew is "to cut a covenant." The corpse of an animal is cut in half. Both parties making the covenant would pass through the two halves of the carcass.

When God made His covenant with Abraham, only the flame passed through, not Abraham.

Why? Because God knew from the beginning, that His people would be unfaithful in keeping the covenant, but He would not. Praise the Lord that His covenants do not depend on the faithfulness or unfaithfulness of Israel or the church, but they depend on the faithfulness of God Himself.

If God is finished with Israel because they broke the covenant, give me one good reason why God should not be finished with the church also? Anything that the Jews have done wrong, I can say the same about the church, or worse. What has the church done? The same thing Israel did, gone after other gods. Look at New Age in the Church.

Sacrificing babies to demons

What did Israel do before the captivity? Sacrificed their babies to demons. Yes they did that, and that is when the judgment fell. God said, "No more. I will put up with idolatry. I will put up with immorality. I will put up with social injustice. But I will not put up with you sacrificing babies to other gods, to demons."

If you take all the medical considerations warranting abortions into account, they would account for less than 1% of all abortions performed. More than 99% of all abortions are performed for non-therapeutic reasons. They are not carried out for any clinical or medical reason. They are carried out for social and economic reasons, what Jesus called the "worship of Mammon."

Make no mistake about it, non-therapeutic abortion, theologically and spiritually, is a form of demon worship. If God did not spare the natural branches, He will not spare you either. If Israel and the Jews did not get away with that abomination, neither will the Western Christianized world.

Learning from Israel's mistakes

> *Now these things happened as examples for us...*   -1 Corinthians 10:6

The mistakes of Israel were recorded so that the church would not make the same mistakes. The church should learn from their errors. But have we? No! We have everything they had, and much more. They only had the Old Testament, but we have the New also. They only looked forward to the coming of the Messiah; the Church already has the Messiah. Under the old covenant the Holy Spirit was only for certain people at certain times: High Priests, Kings, and Prophets. Now the Holy Spirit is for all who believe.

On top of that, we have their example to learn from, but we do not learn. If God is finished with the Jews because they broke the covenant, how much more should He be finished with the church. Praise God that His faithfulness is what determines the validity of the covenant, not our unfaithfulness. Otherwise we would be as finished as the Jews ever were. But God is not finished with the Jews. The judgment of God would have fallen on the United States a long time ago, except for two things.

One, salt preserves. The USA still has more evangelical Christians and churches than any other Western country. Three out of four dollars spent on missions, Christian charity and evangelism comes from North America, while three out of five full time missionaries to poor countries come from America.

The other reason is that America has treated the Jews better than any other nation in history. Otherwise God's judgment would have come on them long ago. Amsterdam is the most wicked city in the developed world. I have seen depravity in a lot of cities. In Bangkok they are selling the kids into sexual slavery. Amsterdam is just as bad. If you were to walk through Amsterdam and Holland you would not believe the moral depravity. It is unspeakable, an absolute disgrace. However that country protected the Jews during the Holocaust and I am convinced that God's judgment would have prevailed, but they blessed the Jews. "I will bless them that bless thee, and curse them that curse thee."

That does not mean that God's judgment is not going to come. It just means that it has been delayed by grace. "Why are you showing me favor?" asked Ruth. Because you blessed my people! God will bless those Christians, churches and nations who bless His people. Not for their sake, but for the sake of His own name. And, by extension, God will even bless unsaved people who bless Christians.

Second class Christians

"I have commanded my servants not to touch you," says Boaz. "Where they eat, you eat. What they drink, you drink."

The Hebrew word to 'bow down' and 'to worship' is the same word. When you see a Roman Catholic bowing down before a statue and praying, that is idolatry in the Hebrew language. That is why the Roman Catholic church took the second commandment out of their catechism for so many centuries.

> *"You shall not make for yourself an idol, or any likeness of what is in heaven above or on the earth beneath or in the water under the earth. You shall not worship them or serve them...."*
>
> -Deuteronomy 5:8-9

I lived on Mt. Carmel in Galilee. At Mount Carmel they have apparitions of Mary, the same as in Fatima and many other places - demonic apparitions. The people there carry a statue of Mary from her summer home to her winter home. Why? Mary does not like the cold weather!

Twice a year they carry the statue down the mountain and put it in the church in the middle of Haifa. They bow to it, pray to it, burn incense to it, and sing to it. I had a friend who was a Charismatic Catholic monk. He would come to our meetings, waving his hands, and be one of us, Hallelujah! Then, when they carried the statue down, he would be there with the rest of the idolaters, singing, burning incense, bowing down and worshipping the statue!

When the Jews and Moslems saw this idolatry, they thought that was Christianity. The born again Christians, the Messianic Jews, had to explain to them that it was not.

Satan's first tool for getting Jews into hell is false Christianity - Roman Catholicism, Eastern Orthodoxy, idolatry.

A woman of excellence

Which countries protected the Jews in the Holocaust? The ones with high evangelical Protestant populations: Denmark, Holland. Which ones betrayed the Jews? The Roman Catholic and Eastern Orthodox countries, Latvia, France, Romania. If you go to Israel today, you will see the young volunteers working on the kibbutzes. Some are from Canada, Japan, Argentina, Holland.

"What country are you from?" "Oh, Holland," they will say. "Maybe you would want to come for tea tonight? We know it was Christians in Holland who saved my Grandmother during the Holocaust.

"Where are you from?" "Denmark," they would say, and the people would tell how the Nazis occupied Denmark and ordered all the Jews to wear yellow stars. The Danish King, who was a Christian, came out wearing a yellow star and said Jesus Christ was a Jew. Anyone who believed in him had to identify with the Jews. Everyone in Denmark had to put on a yellow star.

A woman of excellence. The Jews teach about it in the high schools in Israel. If you love the Jews, get out of false churches. Get out of anti-Semitic churches. Get out of Jew-hating churches. Get out of idolatrous churches. Get out of Roman Catholic, Eastern Orthodox, and so-called evangelical Jew-hating churches.

Not going after young men

> *Then he said, "May you be blessed of the Lord, my daughter. You have shown your last kindness to be*

better than the first by not going after young men, whether poor or rich."

-Ruth 3:10

What does it say about Jesus, in the fourth Servant Song of Isaiah?:

He has no stately form or majesty that we should look upon Him, nor appearance that we should be attracted to Him. He was despised and forsaken of men, a man of sorrows, and acquainted with grief; and one from whom men hide their face, He was despised and we did not esteem him.

-Isaiah 53:2-3

The key to their redemption

"And now it is true I am a close relative; however, there is a relative closer than I."

-Ruth 3:12

"I am next in line, but he is first in line. He has the right of redemption from Elimelech - to buy the land, to get the inheritance, to take you, to procreate children for his deceased brother."

At first this man - whoever he is, he is not named for some reason, only being referred to in Scripture as *He whose sandal was removed* - says, "Yes, give me the inheritance. I want it."

But when Boaz tells him that he also has to take the Gentile woman (Ruth 4:5) he changes his mind.

"I cannot redeem it for myself, lest I jeopardize my own inheritance" (Ruth 4:6). The inheritance I want. The promise of my fathers I want. The right of redemption I want. The blessing I want. But I do not

want anything to do with that *shixa* (derogatory Yiddish slang, meaning 'a Gentile woman'). Yet it was that *shixa* who was the key to him getting his promise, his blessing, his redemption.

He whose sandal was removed is not named. Those Jews who will not come to the body of Christ to receive their inheritance will not be named. Their names will be blotted out. Only those who come to the body of Christ will receive their redemption. That Gentile woman is the key.

Take the grain to my people

Boaz gave Ruth six measures of barley (Ruth 3:15).

> *And she said, "These six measures of barley he gave to me, for he said, 'Do not go to your mother-in-law empty-handed'"*
>
> -Ruth 3:17

What did Jesus tell the Gentile church? "Take the grain, and give it to my people Israel." Be very careful of organizations that want to bless the Jews without giving them the Gospel.

In the same way that God used the Jews to give the Gospel to the Gentiles in the first century, God is using the Gentiles to give the Gospel to the Jews in the last century.

> *For if their rejection be the reconciliation of the world, what will their restoration be but life from the dead?*
>
> -Romans 11:15

Make no mistake about it, God is going to bless the Church through Jewish people again before Jesus returns. The first Christians were

Jews; the last Christians are going to be Jews. Give them the grain! The challenge is to bring the Good News back home again.

This particular man refused the right of redemption. So they went through the ritual prescribed in Deuteronomy 25. Then the marriage took place and, eventually, a baby boy was born.

Who built the house of Israel?

At the wedding they said to Boaz:

> *"May the Lord make the woman who is coming into your home like Rachel and Leah, both of whom built the house of Israel."*
>
> -Ruth 4:11

The typology here comes from Genesis. Jacob came for a bride from his own people. He desired Rachel, but he did not get Rachel at first, but Leah. After he learned to love Leah as much as he did Rachel, he got Rachel as well. In the beginning Leah had all the babies, her womb was most fruitful. But then Rachel conceives.

Israel shall be a fruitful vine. Jesus came for Israel. He wanted to marry Israel, but He did not get Israel. He ends up with the bride He did not desire at first, the Gentile church.

After He learns to love the Gentile church, then He gets Israel. In the beginning, the church has all the babies. But in the end, Israel becomes a fruitful vine. "Both of whom built the House of Israel."

Don't let Rick Godwin or any of these other lying heretics tell you different. *Both* of whom built the House of Israel. The church is Jew and Gentile, one bride.

A redeemer in Israel

> *Then the women said to Naomi, "Blessed is the Lord who has not left you without a redeemer today, and may his name become famous in Israel. May he also be to you a restorer of life and a sustainer of your old age; for your daughter-in-law, who loves you and is better to you than seven sons, has given birth to him."*　　　　　　　　　　-Ruth 4:14-15

The baby who was born from this union between Boaz and Ruth was called the redeemer from Bethlehem. "May His name become famous in Israel." Who came from Bethlehem? Who is a Redeemer? Who is famous? The lineage of David stems from a union between Jew and Gentile because the salvation that would come from it would be for both Jew and Gentile.

Better than seven sons

> *"May He also be to you a restorer of life and a sustainer of your old age; for your daughter-in-law...is better to you than seven sons."*　　　　-Ruth 4:15

The Gentile woman who gave birth to this baby called Redeemer is better to her than seven sons. There are Gentile Christians who treat the Jews better than their own kind. More than that, this baby who is called "the Redeemer from Bethlehem" becomes a restorer of life to the Jewish woman.

A restorer of life

> *Then Naomi took the child and laid him in her lap, and became his nurse. And the neighbor women*

gave him a name, saying, "A son has been born to Naomi."

-Ruth 4:16-17

He is a Jewish baby. And so begins the line of David from whom Jesus would come.

A woman of excellence can take a Jewish baby, born in Bethlehem, called the Redeemer, a restorer of life to the Jewish people, and present Him to this Jewish woman, who was bereft, who was grieving, who was scorned, who was embittered, and felt that God Himself had set His hand against her.

But when the Jewish woman receives the child, she says, "This is really *my* baby here. He is really my Messiah. This baby is the restorer of my life." Then all of her grief, all her anguish, all her pain, all her bereavement and rejection is taken away by that baby.

The Bride of Christ

All of these brides, these good women in the Bible, teach about the Bride of Christ from different aspects.

Ruth teaches us about the Bride of Christ as the one who would give the Redeemer back to the Jewish people.

That Bride is you!

> *"And I say to you, everyone who confesses Me before men, the Son of Man shall confess him also before the angels of God."*

-Luke 12:8

242

Chapter 12

Seduction of the
Hebrew Root Movement

Moriel has long urged the Body of Christ to rediscover the Hebrew root of its faith for four reasons:

The **first** is that the destiny of the church is bound up with God's prophetic plan for the future of Israel and the Jews.

The **second** is that Christians need to evangelize the Jewish people, in recognition of the fact they remain the eternal people of God by covenant relationship, and that the plan of God for the salvation of the nations is bound up with His plan for the salvation of Israel.

The **third** is that we need to understand the Scriptures in their original Judaic context. We advocate that Christians familiarize themselves with the works of those who have understood this, from Alfred Edersheim to Arnold Fruchtenbaum. We have also tried to reacquaint the church with the lost art of Jewish hermeneutics in terms of New Testament uses of Midrash, and the illustrative Hebraic models of typology and allegory.

Fourth, the church needs to learn from Israel's history and not repeat the same kind of mistakes as Israel. Israel's history was written for our instruction. The church has instead of learning from them, replayed those mistakes and they have sometimes been worse than those of Israel.

Blinding the Church

Satan seeks to blind the church to the prophetic purposes of God for Israel in order to deceive the church about its own future. The exegesis of biblical prophecy that states that the Olivet Discourse and the Book of Revelation is only about God's rejection and judgment on the apostate nation of Israel and not about the Last Days, is demonic in origin and dangerous to the church.

Satan also knows that the eschatological mysteries surrounding the return of Christ are sealed up, and a key to this unsealing will be in understanding a Judaic approach to biblical interpretation. Where Satan is unable to blind Christians to the need to return to its Hebraic root, his alternative strategy is to corrupt that trend.

True and false Philo-Semitism

There are various areas in which Satan is attempting these seductions of the trend back towards the Hebrew Root.

The Christian Zionist Movement is not a monolith. There are good factions, ones that do some good but no harm, and others that are simply dead wrong.

Some are "over the top" about Israel and the Jews, often focusing on everything except the Messiah of the Jews or His command that we bring His message of salvation to His ancient people. Such Christian Zionist groups are as unbalanced and unscriptural on one extreme as are the replacementists, denying the prophetic plan of God for Israel and the Jews, on the other.

In order to justify not witnessing to Jewish people, these groups tend to pervert biblical passages such as Romans 10:14 and Isaiah 40:1-9. They falsely claim that they can fulfill the church's mission to Israel and the Jews with immigration programs, political and social programs, and inter-faith dialogue. This is not to suggest all of those involved in these organizations are intentional deceivers. On the contrary, while some of their leaders are plainly money grabbing heretics, many sincere people are misled into joining and supporting these deceptions. Neither is it to suggest that all of what they do is wrong. The problem is that in trying to communicate Christian love to Israel to undo the damage done by Christian anti-Semitism, they leave out Christ and the whole purpose of God - they preach a Christless social gospel.

The church must both proclaim God's purpose in returning the Jews to their ancient land and the way of salvation. Some ministries indeed do both. Moriel endorses Church's Ministry Among the Jews, Jews For Jesus, the Messianic Testimony, Chosen People Ministries, Ariel, the Lausanne Consultation On Jewish Evangelism, the Danish and Norwegian Missions To Israel, and Christian Witness To Israel, but warn against such deceptions as Bridges For Peace, Wings Of Eagles, the Ebenezer Fund, Christian Action For Israel, and above all the International Christian Embassy. Once examined biblically such agencies are deceptions and not of God.

The Messianic Movement, the true and the false

Messianic Judaism also has multiple trends within it, some scriptural, others not. Another aspect of Satan's attempted seduction of the trend back to our Hebrew root has been the lunatic fringe of the Messianic Movement.

This is characterized by so called 'rabbis' who are not, an emphasis that lifts up Judaism and Judaica, but rarely the King of the Jews, and seems good for little other than rebuilding the wall of partition that Yeshua died to break down.

To the detriment of seeing Jews saved, this unfortunate axis of Messianic Judaism has discredited Jewish belief in Jesus as being unJewish. Its make-believe rabbis have been debunked as charlatans by the orthodox (as happened in the case of Chuck Snow, an ex-messianic rabbi who renounced Yeshua after his ignorance of Judaism was demonstrated to him by a real rabbi), and in debates between real rabbis and the messianic fake ones.

Yeshua commanded believers not to use the term "rabbi" as a title. (Matthew 23) This axis also ignores the fact that for all of the academic and apologetic value in studying it, the Rabbinic Judaism it imitates is a corruption of biblical Judaism that points people away from their own Messiah.

The Lord wants a Messianic Movement capable of pointing the Gentile Church back to a solid, biblical expression of what it is supposed to be, but instead many of the hyper-messianic extremists are into Toronto, Pensacola and the seductions destroying the Gentile Church.

Most Jews are skeptical of anything to do with Yeshua to begin with, and seeing the sick depravity of Toronto and Pensacola does not help.

While Moriel has sympathy for the more balanced and more biblical Hebrew Christian-Messianic Jewish Alliance, we must distance ourselves from the extreme lunatic fringe factions.

Women in leadership

What is perhaps most absurd is the fact that, contrary to both New Testament Christianity and Orthodox Judaism, the extreme axis of the Messianic Movement has women teaching mixed groups and in positions of senior leadership.

Both faiths allow women to teach other women, but to have women in leadership and teaching roles violates the teaching of the New Testament.

It also discredits the presentation of the gospel and offends the very orthodox Jewish community the messianic extremists supposedly try to imitate in order to reach with the gospel.

Moriel supports a biblical Messianic Judaism which is both Judaic and Christian. However, the issue of women in what observant Jews can only see as rabbinic roles, and, so functioning in these roles in rejection of the plain New Testament instruction, makes one question to what degree such extreme factions of the Messianic Movement can claim to be either Judaic or Christian.

There is hype, trappings, and trimmings but little substance.

Second class believers

The other thing that the extreme axis of the Messianic Movement appears good at is making non-Jewish believers feel like Second Class believers on the basis of race – as if Jewish birth, instead of New Birth, was a spiritual qualification.

In actual fact there are totally non-Jewish messianic writers, like Walter Riggins and Dwight Pryor, who are not only quite scholarly and adept in Hebrew rabbinics, but could very easily run rings round 90% of the Messianic Rabbis in terms of what they know about Hebraics and Judaism, not to mention the Word of God.

Judeo-Christian scholarship, the true and the false

The problems of Messianic extremism and non-evangelistic Christian Zionism are not new problems. What is new is Satan's attempted corruption of Jewish hermeneutics and the use of the return to the Hebrew Root trend to undermine the Authority of God's Word.
Liberal scholars are citing Jewish Midrash to justify dismissal of the

historicity and doctrinal authority of Scripture, claiming midrash employed in the New Testament provides an alternative basis for establishing doctrine other than what is literally stated.

In no place does the Bible use allegory, typology, symbolism, or any midrashic material as the basis of doctrine. It is rather a mode of illustration of doctrinal truth.

In the Judaic midrashim we never see a denial of the historical authenticity of biblical accounts.

For decades the liberal theological establishment tried to dismiss the historicity of the Gospels and the authenticity of Apostolic doctrine on the basis that it was a creation of a later Gentile church. With the Dead Sea Scrolls supporting the compatibility of the gospels with First Century Jewish thought, and both conservative and Jewish scholars having demonstrated the familiarity of the gospel writers with the *sitz im leben* (cultural and life situation) of Second Temple Period Palestinian Judaism, the old liberal presuppositions are discredited. Since the newly demonstrated Jewishness of the gospels wreaks havoc with their old arguments, they must now invent seemingly Jewish (bogus) arguments to continue to argue against the historical and doctrinal truth of the Scriptures. The lie is the same, but the method of telling it has changed.

The Jerusalem School of Synoptic Research

A further threat to the authority of Scripture coming up through the Hebrew Root Movement is found within the Jerusalem School of Synoptic Research.

This facility has expanded into a broader network of individuals looking for a better grasp of understanding of the Scriptures from a Judaic perspective. I would not be prepared to dismiss all of the

Jerusalem School as Satanic. I agree with the need for a scholarly investigation into the Hebraic nature of New Testament literature. There are things in the Jerusalem School with which I would agree. There are other aspects of it however that I can only regard as false and dangerous.

Bivin and Blizzard, in essence, argue that Jesus' words, even affecting the meaning of His doctrinal pronouncements, can have a very different meaning from the way they are conventionally understood, because - they maintain - the original gospel documents are in Hebrew, and the Greek translations are less than reliable translations in relating the actual meanings.

Indeed there is credence in uncovering the underlying Hebraic thought patterns of the Greek texts, and this has as much to do with linguistics as it does *sitz im leben*.

However to suggest the reliability of Christian doctrine drawn from the Greek manuscripts must be brought into question is baseless.

No one reading the Greek text can determine linguistically if the manuscripts are translations from orally transmitted accounts of Jesus and His words from Aramaic or from Hebrew; both are similar semitic languages.

No one can tell an Aramism from a Hebraism by reading translations in a third language.

Only odd episodes record Hebrew being employed for vernacular purposes during the Second Temple Period. Most of the Qumran literature (apart from biblical manuscripts) are Aramaic, few are Hebrew and one Nabatean. The existing biblical manuscripts (with the possible exception of Matthew) tend to follow the Septuagint, and nothing akin to the Masoretic Hebrew.

The volume of codexes, manuscripts, and fragments of the gospels are astronomical in number. There are literally thousands, having no parallel in any of the Greek or Latin Classics. Yet not one is in Hebrew.

We do have an argument in Eusebius, which he traced back to the time of Heggisipus, that Matthew was originally Hebrew and there are source critical arguments for a Hebrew Matthew original.

But to suggest that the fundamental doctrinal meaning is therefore misunderstood, is absurd.

We have at least two good Hebrew translations of the New Testament. Neither determines a need to question again traditional Christian understanding of the gospels in a fundamental way based on linguistics.

We also have the Epistles, written to both Hebrew and Greek believers and communities of believers, which are inspired apostolic commentary on the gospels.

Traditional Christian understandings of doctrine in the gospels have never rested on the gospels alone, but how the Apostles understood, interpreted and applied them.

It is ludicrous how much time and effort has been wasted on the conjectures of the Jerusalem School. It is profitable for nothing other than casting unnecessary doubt on the credibility of an orthodox Evangelical understanding of the doctrinal content of the gospels.

The Jerusalem School trumpets the endorsement it receives from Rabbi David Flusser, admittedly a major scholar. Yet they fail to mention that his American counterpart, Rabbi Jacob Neusner dismisses their theory.

They also fail to note that David Flusser has an interest in giving a different meaning to the Words of Jesus. Flusser argues that Paul taught a different Christianity from Jesus, and seeks to establish a discontinuity between Pauline and Early Apostolic Christianity.

Lance Lambert

Another way in which Satan is attempting to corrupt the Hebrew Root Movement into a vehicle for undermining the authority of Scripture is through Lance Lambert's claims that New Testament doctrine no longer always means for today what it meant when it was written. In a tape rubbishing Jewish evangelism, Lambert argues that the history of anti-Semitism means that we do not need to preach the gospel to the Jews.

The Bible states that God's Word is the same yesterday, today, and forever. He also suggests that the biblical teaching that there is no other Name under heaven by which someone may be saved than the Name of Jesus may not apply to Jews who perished in the holocaust while rejecting Him. This is heretical!

Direct revelation?

Mr. Lambert falsely claims that most Jews being saved are being saved by direct revelation and not witnessing. This is of course manifestly untrue.

Moriel [in the UK] distributes four books with the testimonies of Jews who believe in Yeshua, and while there are rare cases where Jews are saved by direct revelation alone, not one of the testimonies in any of these four books has a Jew being saved through a vision or appearance of Jesus or anything of the sort. If what Lambert said was true, the majority of these Messianic Jews would have been saved by direct revelation and not witnessing or preaching or evangelism.

In fact, their testimonies instead show that they were all saved in exact accordance with what the Word of God says about preaching the gospel to the Jews "how will they hear without a preacher?" (Romans 10:14).

Lambert's tape was first put out 15 years ago, at the time that brave young Israelis first began taking to the streets of Jerusalem and Tel Aviv, tracts in hand. I recall the first evangelistic campaign in 1985 in Tel Aviv. Prayer, wisdom, and sensitivity are required in witnessing to Jews and we may debate method and questions as to "how", but not "if".

"We Jews"?

More strikingly, Lambert, speaking against this Jewish evangelism to mainly non-Jews, says "We Jews!"

One only wonders who issued Mr. Lambert the credentials, to deride what young Jewish Israeli believers in Yeshua were doing to see Yeshua become an issue among His own people in His own land. In fact, Lance Lambert did not even grow up in the Jewish faith, but is the product of assimilation. As far as anyone knows he does not attend a local indigenous Israeli Hebrew language fellowship, and for all the time he has lived in Israel has never apparently even learned the Hebrew language.

Yet he sets himself up the spokesman to the Gentile Church on the subject of Jewish Evangelism by saying "We Jews!" What about the other Jews who fight in Israel's wars, and the ex-refuseniks (like my wife), who grew up as Orthodox Jews and who disagree with him?

I knew a Jewish holocaust survivor named Gershom in Haifa. His wife and five children were all murdered in the holocaust. For forty years he carried a pain in his soul that even time itself could not heal.

The only thing that took that ceaseless tormenting grief away was a saving knowledge of his Messiah Yeshua, who was also a Man of sorrows acquainted with grief. I can only thank the Lord that the Gentile evangelists who witnessed to Gershom and led him to His Messiah before he died were not discouraged from Jewish evangelism by Lance Lambert.

Lance Lambert's exegesis of Romans 11 was the most preposterous exposition of that text I have ever heard. It was pure eisegesis.

Yet, until this tape resurfaced, I had never once had an occasion to criticize him if others were blessed by his ministry. At least he opposed anti-Semitism and replacement theology. But once Mr. Lambert propounded heretical views, attacking the evangelizing of Jews, we have no choice but to take a stand.

Altering eternal truth

The real problem is not that Lambert discourages Jewish evangelism, nor his suggestion that because of Christian anti-Semitism, Jews who died without Jesus might escape eternal damnation without faith in Him.

The real problem is Lance Lambert's argument that Scripture no longer doctrinally means what it says in every context. The idea that history and the cultural changes it evokes, alters eternal truth, is a lie of the devil.

This is the same argument of homosexual clergy, Christian feminists, liberal theologians, and also Lance Lambert. God's Word is the same, yesterday, today, and forever. He does not change, and neither does His Word.

Lance Lambert plays the same card, saying we must sacrifice some of the Bible's original meaning to accommodate those not wishing to evangelize Jews. It is all the same tactic, the same devil, and the same lie.

GOOD MEN, BAD THEOLOGY

It is not my intention to imply that Lance Lambert is not a true believer or that he is insincere in his motives. This becomes part of the problem. I believe him to be true brother in faith and I have no doubt of the nobility of his intentions. Nor do I discount the positive contributions made by Lance Lambert in educating the church about the biblical importance of Israel in eschatological prophecy. To his credit, Mr. Lambert has stood, at times nearly alone as an almost solitary voice opposing the rampant replacement theological error so prevalent among British Evangelicals. In this, I can only commend him and express my appreciation to him, and my gratitude to some of the doctrinally better Christian Zionist organizations such 'Prayer For Israel' and 'Christian Friends of Israel' for giving Lance Lambert a platform to redress these errors.

Far from being a bad man, he is in actual fact quite a good man who has made a very bad mistake in his doctrine. In correcting one error, he has fallen into a no less serious one.

JOHN HAGEE - THESSALONIKA REVISITED

Texas Pastor John Hagee is also by no means a nefarious figure, but rather a positive one who has rigidly withstood the growing tide of anti-Semitism and anti-Zionism from the pulpit and in the media. He is in a broad sense the American version of Britain's Lance Lambert, and creates the same dilemma: right about Israel, wrong about the Israelites.

As the Mother country, Great Britain does it first; Texas always does it bigger. Mr. Hagee skates very close to the edge of dual covenant theology, even erroneously arguing that Jews cannot be held responsible for not recognizing Jesus as the Messiah, on the badly conceived and utterly unbiblical notion that Jesus never claimed to be the Messiah. The complication that emerges is that John Hagee, at least officially, appears to deny that he adheres to dual covenant theology and he seems to accept the basic tenets of the New Testament faith.

In his book, In Defense of Israel, Hagee is way out of his league as he plainly does not comprehend the Jewish Messianic expectations of the time of Jesus; Ha Moshiach Ben Yosef (Messiah Son of Joseph, aka Ben Ephraim, the suffering servant of Isaiah 52 and 53 prefigured by Joseph in the book of Genesis), and Ha Moshiach Ben David, Messiah Son of David, the conquering King prefigured by David.

In a promotional ad Hagee produced to sell his book, he made some outrageous claims. "In Defense of Israel will shape Christian theology," Hagee boasted. "Jesus did not come to the earth to be the Messiah. Since Jesus refused by word and deed to claim to be the Messiah, how could the Jews be blamed for rejecting what was never offered?"*

He plainly does not understand the Jewish background of John 10, among other passages.

1. There were miracles of healing blindness that only the Messiah would be able to do, according to Jewish thought of the Second Temple period. They also believed that Messiah would reveal Himself at Chanukah (the Feast of Dedication) in the 5th and 10th chapters of the book of John. Contrary to the assertions of John Hagee, Jesus did publicly complain about disbelief in Him after effecting Messianic miracles, even though these are not the key to faith in Him, but rather hearing the Word of God.

At some points Jesus did play down the miracles, but during the Jewish Feast of Miracles Jesus pointed to them openly and publicly as evidence of His Messiahship (John 10: 22-26).

John Hagee is dead wrong. At Chanukah, the Jews were expecting a warrior-priest Messiah in the character of the Maccabees to rid them of the Romans as the Maccabees did the Seleucids. As seen on Palm Sunday/Pesach the people anticipated a kingly Messiah like David to depose the Romans at the triumphal entry by making a right turn inside the East Gate and kicking the Roman legion out of the Fortress Antonio. Instead, He made a left turn and got rid of the Kenneth Copelands and Benny Hinns of the day.

It is His purpose as the Son of David at His Second Coming to set up the Kingdom/Dominion. His first coming was to atone for sin.

2. John Hagee is additionally wrong about most Jews not rejecting Him as Messiah (Mark 8:31, Luke 9:22, Luke 17:25, John 1:12, Matthew 21:42, Acts 2:31& 36 in Peter's kerygma; Christ = Messiah). To claim that Jesus never openly proclaimed Himself as Messiah is dishonest. He did it both privately (John 4), and when the time was correct, publicly (Matthew 23:10).

Hagee does not understand the Jewish Festival background in the Gospels and how Jesus fulfilled them. He could only openly reveal His Messiahship by the prophetic agenda in the Hebrew Holy Days of Leviticus 23 & 24, specifically at the high Pilgrim Feasts. The times when Jesus (Yeshua) played down His Messianic identity is because it was not the appropriate time or place. The Jews rightly believed Messiah would reveal Himself at Chanukka and Passover in Jerusalem, not at another time elsewhere such as in Galilee.

Again, the level of ignorance exhibited by Hagee is astounding. It is not his obvious ignorance of the Jewish background of the Gospels that is the main problem, but rather that in writing his book he misrepresents himself as having an expertise where he has none.

He is a doctrinally confused man who is misleading others and such an irresponsible book does more to harm the cause of opposing the error of replacement theology and of enlightening the church about the prophetic purposes of God for Israel and the Jews than it does to assist it. I am sad that a good friend of Israel, with what I believe is a sincere love for the Jews, has frankly made himself look like a theological charlatan in the eyes of any serious conservative Evangelical scholar.

Having said that, the definition of a heretic from the Greek 'heraseis' or Hebrew 'kopher' is one who forms a schism based on a serious false doctrine.

There are avid supporters of Israel who indeed are proven heretics such as Malcolm Hedding (leader of International Christian Embassy), and there are certainly heretics within the Messianic Movement (e.g. Mark Kinser), and we openly say so.

The problem with John Hagee appears to be rather ignorance, and a misguided zeal that has rendered him doctrinally delusional. He is not in denial of any basic tenet of biblical Christianity and because he claims not to be 'dual covenant', I would not define him as a heretic. I do not think he has gone quite that far. But once again, he is skating dangerously close to the edge and there is a need for a clear caveat. What we have in Lance Lambert and John Hagee is what we had in the apostle Paul's epistles to the ancient Thessalonians (that likewise was a church in some eschatological confusion) – simply stated, we have some otherwise Good Men With Some Bad Doctrine.

The true and the false festal prophetic paradigm
A further area of Satanic corruption of the Hebrew Root Movement is the contextual corruption and replacementist approach to the Hebrew Feasts.

Such corruption of valid Hebrew root material causes others to dismiss all Hebrew Root material. The proverbial baby is thrown out with the bath water, forgetting that Satan only counterfeits things that are real and only corrupts things worth corrupting. Reacting to one error by falling into another is unwise.

Among the first to corrupt the eschatological illustrations of the Hebrew Festal material was 'Manifest Sons' preacher George Warnock, whose distortion of the Feast of Tabernacles accounts set a precedent.

In ancient Israel, Tabernacles (which speaks of the giving of the Holy Spirit in the first instance, and the establishment of the millennium, as in Zechariah 14, in the second instance) occurred during the Year of Jubilee.

In this avenue of Satan's seductions of the Hebrew Root Movement, such ideas become linked to the Year 2000 celebrations, and the Ecumenical objectives of Pope John Paul II for the year 2000.

Pope Peter?
This could have become particularly problematic if the recently deceased Cardinal of Paris, Jean-Marie Lustiger, an ethnic Jew, had become pope as some predicted. The papacy, by biblical definition, is an anti-Christ institution claiming doctrinal infallibility when the pontiff speaks 'ex cathedra' and that the authority of Christ is vicariously imputed to a man. Additionally, there are arguments that one of the two Beasts of Revelation 13 will be an ethnic Jew in the conclusions of some.

Romans 11 and Revelation 7 indicate that Jews will again come into prominence and leadership as believers in Jesus in the Last Days. Satan of course, will attempt to have a counterfeit.

We never said that Lustiger is the ultimate Antichrist or false prophet, (although had he become pope, he would have automatically become both a false christ and a false prophet). But the trend he embodied made him, and others akin to him, a man to watch closely.

If Lustiger (or another Jewish cleric at some future point) had become pope, we would not have been surprised if he took the name 'Peter'. The issue was not Lustiger or the pope as such, but what they represent. Satan knows that God will raise up Jewish believers in Jesus to guide the true church in the Last Days, and Satan therefore knows he must infiltrate and corrupt the Messianic Movement with both aberrational doctrine, and those prepared to compromise with it – some even stating that belief in the deity of the Messiah is not mandatory.

Embracing a Jewish 'Pope'

Without doubt, the lunatic fringe of the Messianic Movement and the lunatic fringe of Christian Zionism would be enthralled that the Pope were (in their warped mentality) a Jewish 'believer,' without any consideration of the heretical essence, false gospel, and anti-Semitic nature of the Roman system.

And why wouldn't they? People already paired with the likes of Morris Cerullo are capable of anything. They have already demonstrated that they have very little, if any, discernment or doctrinal grounding in Scripture, and even less in the way of scruples.

Pat Robinson (who once held up the distorted International Christian Embassy's Feast of Tabernacles as a model of Jubilee and who signed Chuck Colson's acceptance of Roman Catholicism and has adopted dominionist ideas) is a similar proponent of this 'Man Child/Latter Day Rain' corruption of Jubilee.

It is not surprising that the International Christian Embassy leaders, such as Jim Schutz, went to Toronto on a pilgrimage and into Toronto Experience, just as the Christian Embassy are involved with the neo-Gnostic hyper faith prosperity money preachers like Ulf Eckmann and Morris Cerullo (who was a featured speaker at the Feast of Tabernacles).

The Second Coming?

The papacy proclaims the year 2000 as a 'Second Advent of Christ' type. While Manifest Sons advocates like Jay Gary see it as a manifestation of 'the Corporate Christ' event.

We do not suggest that all of these men are willful deceivers, (though some certainly are) but many are undiscerning and doctrinally ignorant who are deceived themselves.

This hotchpotch of Pat Robertson, the Vatican, the Manifest Sons crowd and the International Christian Embassy, is paving the way for the great *apostasia* (falling away) of Thessalonians.

The antichrist implications of this network of deception are clear. The underlying deception of Kingdom Now theology is not only the wrong view that the church will triumphantly establish dominion over the world for Christ prior to His return, but that "Christ returns to the church through the birth of the Manifest Sons/Manchild of the Latter Rain" before He returns for the church. It was precisely of this that Jesus warned us to beware. (Matthew 24:23-27)

Yet the linchpin of the trap is becoming Satan's corruption of the Hebrew Root Movement, in this instance through an attempt to malign the eschatological and prophetic meaning of the Feast of Tabernacles and Jubilee.

Satan knows the centrality of Israel and the Jews to the return of Christ, and he is aware of the need for the church to grasp these concepts in order to be properly pre-pared for the Last Days.

So it is, predictably, here that he injects his subtle toxins of seduction. Probably few of the people involved have any clue that the typology of the Feast of Tabernacles has no relation to the kind of Manifest Sons rubbish being popularly trumpeted.

Charismatic Anglican clergy were mainly educated in literary criticism and not doctrine. Like most charismatics they have had little Biblical teaching, so they accept words by proven false prophets like Paul Cain as the 'Word of the Lord.' Most people caught up in the errors of the Restoration Movement, the March For Jesus, Alpha Course, Ecumenism, Promise Keepers or other Manifest Sons related deceptions have no idea that the basis of such things is unscriptural.

Last days' deception

Those not knowing their Bibles in the Last Days really do not know their Lord. They will be deceived. The same is true of the extreme axis of the Messianic Movement.

We are distraught over the manner in which Satan has infiltrated the Hebrew Root Movement. Yet, when God moves, we must expect the Wicked One to react. When heretics tried to seduce the early Jewish Church, Rabbi Shaul of Tarsus (Paul the Apostle) rose up and defended the unchanging truth of God's Word. When hyper-Messianic extremists arose in Galatia, Paul called it "witchcraft." When charismaniacs ran wild in Corinth, Paul did not use his Jewish identity to give them credibility.

The doctrinal authority God gave through Paul still exists in Paul's writings. Paul's understanding of the future prophetic relationship between Israel and the Church still exists. We can still use Paul's writings to sort out the true from the false.

There seem to be few today with the courage and integrity of Paul, people who refuse to be man pleasers when the authority of the Word of God is at stake in these last days.

Chapter 13

Christian Zionism - Is It Biblical?

> *Now when they had come together, they were asking Him, saying, "Lord is it as this time that you are restoring the kingdom to Israel?" He said to them, "It is not for you to know the times or epochs which the Father has fixed by His own authority; but you shall receive power when the Holy Spirit is come upon you; and you shall be My witnesses, both in Jerusalem, and in all Judea and Samaria, and even to the remotest parts of the earth."*
>
> -Acts 1:6-8

Those were the final words of Jesus!

Biographical Notes

I have two first names - James and Jacob. When I was a baby they called me James. It was Anglicised from my father's grandfather's name, Ya'akov - Jacob. It is good that I have two first names because my family is a combination of two backgrounds – Irish Catholic and Jewish.

My wife is a Romanian Jew. She was a refusenik under the Communists. She immigrated to Israel as a kid. Her parents are holocaust survivors; the rest of the family was killed by the Nazis. My wife suffered under the Communists as a child. Her parents knew nothing but anti-Semitism the whole of their lives.

Our children were born in Galilee, in Israel. I understand both sides. I understand things from the Jewish perspective, to a degree, I think, more than most other Christians, and I understand the way Gentile Christians who love Israel feel. I can see things from both perspectives because of my background.

We know the last question Jesus was asked and the answer He gave to it. It helps to understand why they asked Him that question. In Judaism there are two pictures of the Messiah, and the rabbis later define it: HaMashiach ben David (the Messiah the Son of David) and HaMashiach ben Yosef (the Messiah the Son of Joseph).

The son of Joseph is the suffering servant Messiah of Isaiah 52 and 53. The son of David is the conquering King Messiah, who sets up the Kingdom.

HaMashiach ben Yosef

The rabbis in the Talmud understood that the Messiah was to be both in the character of David and in the character of Joseph.

Joseph was betrayed by his Jewish brothers into the hands of Gentiles. God took that betrayal, turned it around, and made it a way for all of Israel and all the world to be saved. Jesus, the son of Joseph, was betrayed by His Jewish brothers into the hands of Gentiles. God took that betrayal and turned it around and made it a way for all Israel and all the world to be saved.

Joseph was the beloved son of his father. Jesus, the son of Joseph, was the beloved son of His Father.

Joseph knew the wickedness of his brothers. Jesus, the son of Joseph knew the wickedness of His brothers.

Joseph was condemned with two criminals, and as he prophesied, one lived, and one died. Jesus, the son of Joseph, was condemned with two criminals, and as He prophesied, one lived and one died.

They brought Joseph's tunic to prove he was not in the pit. They brought Jesus' shroud to prove He was not in the tomb.

Joseph went from a place of condemnation to a place of exaltation in a single day. Jesus, the son of Joseph, went from a place of condemnation to a place of exaltation in a single day.

When Joseph was exalted every knee had to bow to him, and when Jesus is exalted, every knee shall bow to Him.

Joseph was betrayed by his brother Judah (Judas) for twenty pieces of silver. After inflation, the Lord Jesus, the son of Joseph, was betrayed by His brother Judas for thirty pieces of silver.

> *"And I will pour out upon the house of David and on the inhabitants of Jerusalem, the Spirit of grace and of supplication, so that they will look upon Me whom they have pierced; and they will mourn for Him, as one mourns for an only son, and they will weep bitterly over Him, like the bitter weeping over a first born."*
>
> -Zechariah 12:10

Joseph's brothers did not recognize him as his first coming. They recognized him at the second and wept bitterly. Jesus' brothers, the Jews, did not recognize Him at the first coming. They are going to recognize Him at the second, and weep bitterly.

The one they rejected and betrayed is the one who is going to save us in the Great Tribulation – the son of Joseph.

Jewish Objections To Jesus

Most Jews reject Jesus for two reasons. The first reason – and the one that intimidates Gentiles the most – is the easiest to deal with, the unfortunate history of Christian anti-Semitism. It sounds intimidating, yet it is the easiest objection to deal with.

An orthodox Jew murdered Yitzak Rabin in the name of the Torah. Do you reject Moses and the Torah because of what somebody did in his name? Well, don't expect me to blame Jesus for what somebody did in His name! The murderer of Rabin perverted the teachings of Moses and the Torah. And Nazi anti-Semites perverted the teachings of Jesus to do the same thing to the Jews. More than that, Jews murdered their own prophets in the name of the Torah.

HaMashiach ben David

The second objection is more difficult. If He is the Messiah, how come He did not set up the Messianic Kingdom and bring in worldwide pace? The Messiah is supposed to be "the Prince of Peace."

The answer is found in Daniel chapter nine. The Messiah had to come and die before the second temple was destroyed. Wars and desolation are determined to the end. To set up His Kingdom and bring in worldwide peace is the purpose of His second coming. The purpose of His first coming was to bring peace to the hearts of those who repent and accept Him as their Messiah.

Fulfilling Prophecy

From a Jewish perspective, the Messiah must fulfill all the Old Testament Messianic prophecies – both the Son of David ones and the Son of Joseph ones.

266

The Son of David prophecies have only been fulfilled in a spiritual sense. Jesus did not bring in worldwide peace and fulfill those prophecies historically.

In other words, if He is not going to come back and set up the millennial Kingdom, He is not the Messiah of the Jews. And if He is not the Messiah of the Jews, neither is He the Christ of the church.

Forget all this amillennial, post-millennial hogwash. It is an invention of Roman Catholicism, with no biblical basis.

All of the pre-Nicean fathers held to pre-millennial eschatology, and also said that the Apostles held pre-millennial views.

It was only after Constantine 'Christianized' the Roman Empire and made it the religion of the state, that they began saying Israel was spiritualized in the church. And the Kingdom Now, Dominionist rubbish you see today is part of the same post-millennialist error that has been around since Constantine's day.

It needs to be repeated - If there is no millennium, Jesus is not the Messiah of the Jews. And if He is not the Messiah of the Jews, neither is He the Christ of the church. A Jewish understanding of eschatology can allow for nothing but pre-millennialism.

So what the Apostles are saying here is, *"When are you going to set up the Kingdom?"*

The Kingdom Restored To Israel

The last thing Jesus said is, *'That's God's worry. You let God worry about restoring the Kingdom!"*

The Bible never says the Kingdom will be restored to the church. It says the Kingdom will be restored to Israel. Replacement theology (which says that the church has replaced Israel in God's plan) is false!

The Jews going back to Israel is the fulfillment of what Jesus said:

> *"Jerusalem will be trampled under foot by the Gentiles until the time of the Gentiles be fulfilled."*
> - Luke 21:24

It is one of many signs that Jesus gave to let us know that the end is near. If the devil cannot blind people to pre-millennialism and the prophetic purposes of God for Israel and the Jews, he is going to blind them the other way. Instead of worrying about what Jesus said to worry about, they worry about things He said not to worry about!

Jesus' Command To Us

Suppose your husband was in the Navy and he was going away and you were not going to see him for a year. He kisses you goodbye and walks out the door. The last thing he tells you should be the thing you remember the most.

Jesus is the Bridegroom - He is the Husband. The last thing He said is the thing the church is forgetting the most. On the one hand we have people forgetting that the Kingdom must be restored to Israel – that is the post-millennial Kingdom Now, Replacement Theology types – but on the other hand we have Christian Zionism. "Lord when are you restoring the Kingdom?" That is God's worry! What is your worry? Evangelism!

"Be My witnesses both in Jerusalem, and in all Judea and Samaria, and even to the remotest parts of the earth."

-Acts 1:8

"You let God worry about bringing the Jews back to Israel and restoring the Kingdom, you worry about giving them the Gospel." Today, we have sincere, honest people, many of whom have a genuine love for Israel, that are doing the opposite.

The International Christian Embassy Jerusalem (ICEJ)

One of the most difficult questions I get asked around the world is this: "How come Dr. Arnold Fruchtenbaum, the leading Jewish Christian scholar in the world is so much against the International Christian Embassy?" "How come Jews for Jesus are so much against the International Christian Embassy?" "How come so many Israeli pastors are against the International Christian Embassy?" "How come so many of the leading Jewish Christians in the world have written articles against it?" (Just read issue 12 of Mishkan, the Messianic theological Journal)

Why? Because they are doing the opposite of what Jesus said! They are signing agreements to not give the Gospel to the Jews, in order to obtain government cooperation in bringing Jews back to Israel.

The International Christian Embassy people took Morris Cerullo and "Toronto" to Israel. I do not question the love or sincerity of these people but they are caught up in a big deception. They say that, by denying the Gospel to the Jews that they rescue, they are able to get the cooperation of the rabbis, the Jewish Agency, and the Israeli government.

There are many people involved in bringing Jews back to Israel and still preaching the Gospel. The biggest ones are Jonathan and David and Prayer for Israel. Two others are Sister Alice and Beryl Hunter. The people who bring the most Jews out do not look for the cooperation of the rabbis or the Israeli government, because they are not willing to compromise giving the Gospel to the Jews.

I believe in getting the Jews out of Russia, but I also believe in getting them out of hell!

Yitzak Rabin knew many Christian Zionists. They shook his hand, applauded him, and ingratiated themselves. If Yitzak Rabin could come back for five or ten seconds, do you know what he would say? "You people said you loved me, my nation, and my people. But you let me enter eternity and stand before the judgment seat of my Messiah without having His blood to atone for my sins! If you loved me, why did you let me die without my Messiah?"

Jewish Evangelism

What did Paul say about Jewish evangelism in Acts?

> *"I am innocent of the blood of all men. For I did not shrink from declaring to you the whole purpose of God."*
>
> -Acts 20:26-27

> *"When I say to the wicked, 'You shall surely die' and you do not warn him or speak out to warn the wicked from his wicked way that he may live, that wicked man shall die in his iniquity, but his blood I will require at your hand."*
>
> -Ezekiel 3:18

In context, God is speaking to Ezekiel about Israel. If you don't warn them, I will require their blood from your hands!

Withholding the Gospel is not a form of love. Paul had a biblical definition of love for the Jews - *"My heart's desire ... is for their salvation!"* (Romans 10:1)

Comfort My People
The ICEJ say they can justify trying to bless Israel and the Jews without giving them the Gospel.

> *"Comfort, O comfort My people," says your God. "Speak kindly to Jerusalem. Call out to her, that her warfare has ended, that her iniquity has been removed, that she has received of the Lord's hand double for all her sins."*
>
> -Isaiah 40:1-2

"Comfort My people ... her iniquity has been removed ...she has received double for her sins." Isaiah goes on to explain how to comfort His people.

"Get yourself up on a high mountain, O Zion, bearer of good news ..."   -Isaiah 40:9

The Hebrew word for "good news" is *bisorah* – good news, the Gospel!

> *"Lift up your voice mightily, O Jerusalem, bearer of good news; lift it up, do not fear. Say to the cities of Judah, 'Here is your God!'"*
>
> -Isaiah 40:9

He says it twice. How do you comfort His people? Tell them the Gospel. You say: "Here is the Gospel; here is the *bisorah*; here is your God the Messiah."

That is the biblical method for comforting God's people. Do you think that Israel's iniquity can be removed by anything other than the blood of the Messiah? There is no other name under heaven by which men can be saved.

> *"The gospel is the power of God for salvation to everyone who believes, to the Jew first and also to the Greek."*
>
> -Romans 1:16
>
> *How lovely on the mountains are the feet of him who brings good news (bisorah) who announces peace and brings good news (bisorah) of happiness, who announces salvation.*
>
> -Isaiah 52:7

Jesus – Yeshua – is salvation! How do you comfort God's people? Tell them about Jesus!

No Gift Of Evangelism?

Not every Christian has the gift of preaching or the gift of teaching. But would you refuse to read the Bible because you do not have the gift of teaching? Not every Christian is a pastor. Would you refuse to act as the spiritual head and shepherd of your family because you are not called as a pastor?

It is just as wrong to refuse to witness because you do not have the gift of evangelism. It is true that we cannot all stand on a podium and preach to a large group and see numbers saved, but there is nobody who cannot witness one on one. Nobody! *"Let the redeemed of the Lord say so!"* (Psalm 107:2)

Regathered For Judgment

Romans 9-11 is the heart of God's purpose for Israel and the Jews, and the relationship between Israel and the church. Read Romans

9-11! There is no emphasis on national restoration in it. None! National restoration is subordinate to Israel's salvation.

The Jews are being regathered to Israel, not for a blessing, but for the "time of Jacob's trouble," the Great Tribulation. They are being regathered for a holocaust. They are going to be deceived by the Antichrist.

Jesus said:

> *"I have come in My Father's name, and you do not receive Me; if another shall come in his own name, you will receive him"*   -John 5:43

The only way the Jews will have the peace they long for is by turning to the Prince of Peace. Jews who accept Jesus will have that peace. There is no peace outside of Jesus.

The regathering of Israel is a sign of the last days. So are famines, wars, and earthquakes.

Don't thank Jesus for the earthquake that just wiped out Guatemala or for those starving little children in Ethiopia. In the same way, do not praise God for Israel, praise God that your name is written in the Lamb's Book of Life!

Social Gospels

Give Israel the Gospel! They are going to be deceived by the Antichrist and face the Great Tribulation. The seventieth week of Daniel is a reality. They need the gospel now more than ever, and thank God, they are getting it – but not from the Christian Zionists.

> *How shall they believe in Him whom they have not heard? And how shall they hear without a preacher?*

>   -Romans 10:14

This idea that all we have to do is show love, bless them socially, and then God will save the Jews, is not biblical.

Do you know what dragged the Salvation Army down? They turned away from preaching the Gospel as William Booth its founder had done, to social programs.

Dr. Bernardo was a man of God, if there ever was one. Several years ago Bernardo's in England abrogated the Evangelical statement of Faith. They don't preach the gospel to the kids any more.

I believe in social programs as a way of giving the Gospel, but not in place of it. Social gospels are not the Gospel of Jesus; they are only a trick!

Yes, bless the poor, help the Jews, but to give them the Gospel! "If they have no preacher, how shall they hear?" The idea that we only need to bless them and bring them back and God will save them is unbiblical.

The Curse Of The Law

> *"But it shall come about if you will not obey the Lord your God, to observe to do all His commandments and His statutes with which I charge you today, that all these curses shall come upon you and overtake you. Cursed shall you be in the city, and cursed shall you be in the country ......"*
>
> -Deuteronomy 28:15-68

And terrible things have happened to the Jews in the fulfillment of those curses: the scattering to the nations following the Bar Kochba rebellion (70 AD), the Spanish Inquisition, the Holocaust, the pogroms – these are the curse of the Law described in Lev 26 and Deut 28.

According to Romans, chapters one and two, because the gospel was first available to the Jews, the consequences for rejecting it are manifested against them first.

The Law is either a blessing that points the people to the Messiah, or it is a curse that will judge them for rejecting Him. (Deuteronomy 18:18-19)

The Jews are under the curse of the Law. Only Jesus can break that curse, because He became a curse on the cross. Every Jew is under one covenant or another – either the Torah will point them to the Messiah, who fulfilled the Law, or they are under its curse.

Restoration Promised

> "So it shall be when all of these things have come upon you, the blessing and the curse which I have set before you, and you call them to mind in all nations where the Lord your God has banished you, and you return to the Lord your God and obey Him with all your heart and soul according to all I command you today, you and your sons, then the Lord your God will restore you from captivity ......"
>
> -Deuteronomy 30 :1-3

The idea that we just bring the Jews back and then God will bring them to repentance is ridiculous. The opposite is true! More Jews get saved in the Diaspora. How many Jews got saved under the Communists in Russia? How many Jews are saved in North America? By some estimates there are over 100,000 Jewish born again believers in Jesus in North America. And more than 90% of them have been saved in the last fifteen to eighteen years. According to the American College of Rabbis, more Jews have embraced Christ in the last eighteen years, than in the last eighteen centuries. As the

Torah said, the revival among the Jews would not begin in Israel; it would begin outside of it.

That is not to demean Jewish evangelism in Israel. I was an evangelist in Israel for years. I have been beaten up on the streets of Haifa. But I am telling you the truth. What the ICEJ are saying is just not biblical. Those whom the devil cannot blind with error (like Replacement Theology and Cessationism) he will try to blind with Christian Zionism.

Those who bring the most Jews back to Israel also bring them back to their Messiah! A 'love for the Jews' that does not tell them about Jesus is not the love of Jesus. A burden for Jews that is not a burden for their salvation is not the burden of Christ!

Read what the Word of God says. Romans 9 through 11 is the reason why Arnold Fruchtenbaum and Jews for Jesus are so against the ICEJ; why the Lausanne Consultation on Jewish Evangelism said, "Withholding the Gospel from the Jews is a form of anti-Semitism;" and why Dr. Harold Sevner, former President of the American Board of Missions to the Jews called the International Christian Embassy 'heretical' in the Jerusalem Post.

I would not go that far because I know most of the people who are in the ICEJ are sincere, but what they are doing is not biblical. The ICEJ diverts millions of dollars away from the indigenous congregations in Israel and from Jewish evangelism to social programs in order to impress the rabbis and Israeli politicians.

Yiddishkeit

These people are infatuated with Diaspora Jewish culture. They are lifting up Yiddishkeit, (Western European, Ashkenazi Jewish culture) not biblical Jewish culture.

If they want to say there is something special about the fact that these Jews are growing up believing in their Messiah, despite the fact that their parents came through the holocaust, this would be one thing. But they do not marvel over my Jewish children accepting their Messiah, and the God of their fathers, they lift up Yiddishkeit.

They have become fascinated by Jewish schools and Jewish music. Let me tell you something, a lot of Jewish believers laugh at this stuff. They cannot help it. Some pro-Jewish believers are trying to be more Jewish than the Jews! Read Acts 15 - you have your own culture! Don't be so ridiculous.

Blessing and Cursing the Jews

Now I can accept that people have done this out of ignorance, but once you have been told, it is no longer ignorance. God says, "I will require their blood at your hands."

It is the Jewish missions who preach Yeshua that need your prayers. It is those who bring the Jews out of Russia and also share the Gospel, like Beryl Hunter and Sister Alice, who deserve your support.

If you come across people who say "We don't evangelize, we just love," they do not have the love of Jesus.

> *"I will bless those who bless you, and the one who curses you I will curse."*   -Genesis 12:3

The best way you can bless a Jew, is to give them the Gospel! Pray for their salvation and support those who witness to them. The worst way a born again Christian can curse a Jew is to withhold the Gospel.

If Yitzak Rabin could stand here right now in front of the ICEF people, he would say, "You loved me? You loved me? Do you know where I am going to spend eternity because of your 'love'? Jesus was my Messiah. He died for me. He was one of my people, and you did not want to tell me about Him, because you 'loved' me?" Friends, that is not love!

The Jews Need Jesus

When the *mo'el* (person specially trained to perform circumcision) came to circumcise my son, I said the Hebrew prayers. The *mo'el* put some wine on cotton to give my son, and I asked him what the wine was for. He said, "To deaden the pain."

Then he took out the circumcision knife, and I said, "If that kid could see the knife, he'd say, 'Keep the wine, give me some Jack Daniels!'"

There is nothing special about Jews. There is something very special about the book of the Jews. There is something very special about the covenant with the Jews. There is something very special about the God of the Jews. There is something very special about the Messiah of the Jews.

But the Jews are people who need their Messiah, just as much as Gentiles. I love Israel. I love the Jewish people but I stand with Rabbi Sha'ul of Tarsus:

> *"My heart's desire and my prayer to God for them is for their salvation."*   -Romans 10:1

Dear friends, please do not participate in or support organizations that withhold the gospel from Jewish people. If you love the Jews tell them about the King of the Jews!

Chapter 14

Romans 11 - Replacement Theology

> *And the Lord said to Abram "go forth from your country, from your relatives, from your father's house to the land which I will show you. I will make you a great nation and will bless you, I will make your name great and so you will be a blessing. I will bless those who bless you and the one who curses you I will curse and in you all the families* (or tribes or peoples) *of the earth shall be blessed."*
>
> -Genesis 12:1-3

Right from the beginning God tells Abraham "I'm going to make you a nation," but he didn't say "I'll make you a great nation to make you a great nation." He said "I'll make you a great nation that through you all of the peoples, all of the tribes of the earth shall be blessed." We have to make a distinction between the universalism of the liberals, liberal theologians and the universalism of Scripture.

The universalism of the liberals is the kind of lies that we see today - that all religions including Islam, Hinduism, Sikhism and Buddhism lead to God. The reality is that the only place it leads to is deception that hides the truth that Jesus is the way to the truth and the life. What they hold to is universalism of the world, which doesn't lead to salvation and I'm sorry to say that, now in the ecumenical movement, more and more traditional evangelicals are joining forces with inter-faith theology. A major Christian writer in this country, Colin

Chapman, wrote a book where he has basically said that he's not sure that people of the Islamic faith and the Hindu faith, cannot go to heaven without faith in Jesus. This is quite disturbing!

But there is another universalism which is Biblical, which says that God's redemption is for all nations and peoples, and Israel was to be His mechanism for giving His truth and His Messiah. That's the kind of universalism I agree with and this is connected to the promises to Abraham about making him a great name, the father of all who believe He is.

Arabs call him *Ibrahim*, Jews call him *Abba Abraham*, that's true. "I will bless them that bless thee and curse them that curse thee." I'm convinced that's true. I have no doubt in my mind that one of the reasons that the judgment of God has not already fallen on the United States of America is because of the way it has treated the Jews. America is a country which is blood guilty before God, because of the amount of Christian influence in its social fabric and its history. One of the reasons God's judgment has not already come on America, why it has not declined as a world power the way that Russia and Britain has, is because it has treated the Jews better than other nations. I believe that's a factor. I also believe that's a factor why God's judgment has not come on Holland. Look at Amsterdam. The wickedness in that city, yet they protect the Jews. I believe that that is a factor. It's not the only reason but it is a factor. It's a wicked city. It's got to be the most wicked city in the developed world. If God didn't destroy that place, as people say, he would have to owe Sodom and Gomorrah an apology.

"I'll curse them that curse thee." Historically that has always been born out. Right after the Spanish Inquisition, after the bad treatment of Jews, Francis Drake sinks the Armada, then Britannia ruled the waves. As shown in *Schindler's List*, they built a wall around the *shtettle,* around the ghetto and any Jew trying to climb the wall would get machine gunned. What happens? A wall was built around the great German capital Berlin and any German that tried to climb over the wall would get machine gunned, until that entire generation responsible for the holocaust, or the blitz was dead. It is amazing that not until the last person, the last of the Nazi leaders responsible for what happened, Rudolph Hess, died in Spandau Prison, the Berlin Wall didn't come down.

I believe in the historical outworking of these promises, but they all lead up to the final one. God didn't chose Abraham or raise him up to be a great nation because he wants to bless one nation. He did it that through the Jews, through Israel, so that salvation would come to all nations and for all peoples. It is in this light that we need to understand Romans 11.

Romans Chapters 1-8 deals with subjects such as the purpose of the law. How it teaches how all were fallen. That's what it deals with. How Yeshua fulfills it. But then the question remains, if He fulfils the law (it never says that He is the end of the law, the Greek word is *Teleos* but the aim of the Torah, the target, the purpose of it) what of Israel and the Jews?

Has God finished with them? What happens to Jews? Chapters 9, 10 and 11, and into chapter 12 deals with this. Some people say its parenthetical, you could say that in a way but it answers questions like "well if Jesus fulfills the Torah then what's the purpose of the Torah" and the answer is - the Jews, then it goes back to the issues in chapter 12 that it was dealing with in the earlier chapters.

The Torah reveals the law, Romans has its counterpart in Galatians, Romans deals with the purpose of the law – proactively that is "here's what it means" and in Galatians deals with it reactively, reacting against the legalists, the Judaizers, and today again we see people caught up in things like the Seven Day Adventists movement and the extremes of the Messianic movement or basically going in the same direction as the foolish Galatians. But then in chapters 9,

10, 11 and into chapter 12, we have the counter part in 1 Corinthians. In chapter 12 of Romans, Paul begins to talk about things like spiritual gifts, right after he talks about Gods purpose for the Jews. (We have no chapter divisions in the Greek texts - it's a letter, people divided them later.) This is very similar to 1 Corinthians - it began speaking about the gifts, right after the Jews, and that's just as Paul does in 1 Corinthians 1. Paul writes in 1:22 "Jews seek a sign," referring to the *nessim v'niflaot* "miracles as Greeks seek wisdom."

"Jews seek a sign as Greeks seek wisdom." For the patristic writers, the early church fathers, some of them like Justin Martyr believed that what was best about Greek philosophy, not all of it but what was best about it, the monotheism of Socrates specifically, helped prepare the Greek world for the coming of the gospel, much the same as Torah helped prepare the Jewish world. They believe that and maybe they have a point. Others like Tertullian disagreed. But here Paul is talking about Jews seeking a sign *nessim v'niflaot* and we see this in the gospels. "When the Messiah comes will he do more signs than this? Will he do more signs then Yeshua?"

Of course Jesus handled things very differently than we see people handling it today. In Israel there was a rabbi who they said could do miracles (Sali Baba) and has a large following. If you understand the Hassidic movement, (the Hassidic Jews have the earcurls) you will know that they are into Cabala, Zohar, very much into manifestations, signs, wonders - it's a charismatic movement within Judaism. I wish more Jewish people as well as Christians understood what the Hassidic Movement was about. If they had read Zohar and they understood it they would realize that it is not Biblical Judaism at all, much of it is actual occult.

Nonetheless, we have Jews "seeking a sign" and Jewish history has been permeated by people like the galactic people (Bar Shem Tov and Jacob Frank) and all kinds of acrobats. You see Rabbi Gamaliel looking for a sign in the book of Acts 4. Judah of Galilee and Simon

Magnas and so on, and we've seen since early church history Jews having an attraction to this, while the Greeks although they have that element, were more into philosophical debating like Paul in Athens with the Epicureans and Stoics.

"Jews seeking a sign." Now not only was Jesus different from the other miracle workers, that he was not a fraud, but he was also different to some of the miracle workers today, so-called, also frauds. When Jesus did miracles he usually said "don't tell anybody!" When he got the response "but I was blind and now I can see!" Jesus would say "Yeah praise God you can see, now repent, sin no more, go your way!"

When he healed somebody he usually played it down. These signs bear witness to Him, never to a man, and He never allowed signs, wonders and manifestations to eclipse His message. Never! Yeshua would never allow these things to become essential to His ministry but they do bear witness to Him - He says it in John "believe for the sake of the works." It says this in Hebrews. It is predominantly a Gentile church with some Jews mixed in Corinth. In Romans it is the same.

Now in Corinthians he warns about excesses of signs and wonders, of people entering and saying "are you mad?" We see that today. We have the case of a young woman, she's Jewish her parents are Jews, they have become more observant since she became a believer in Yeshua. They saw these Toronto meetings on TV and they say to her "that's what you left Judaism for? – to bark like a dog!" People being shown these things would say they are mad, particularly Jewish people because they're skeptical of Christianity anyway.

Nonetheless "Jews seek a sign." That's why something curious happens. Why is it in Roman 11 that he talks about Gods purpose for the Jews in 9, 10 and 11 but in verse 29 he goes back to the theme of Corinthians? - where the gifts and calling of God are irrevocable. He writes about gifts and calling when he's talking about the Jews. That's the same thing Paul does in 1 Corinthians 12. In 1 Corinthians 12 he says there are a great variety of gifts, in verse 4, but in verse 5 - a variety of ministries. There has always been the relationship between somebody's ministry and their gifts - someone's calling and their gifts. Your ministry will in some way determine what spiritual gifts you have. You see this in Romans and you see it in Corinthians - the linkage between gifts and calling. Strange that he puts it right there when he's talking about the Jews.

Something I had always known, but never fully grasped, was in what happens when we erase the chapter divisions. For instance: a pastor is called to know the condition of his flocks. So a pastor will frequently have things like words of knowledge because that helps him to be a pastor. Elders, pastors are called to pray for the sick and healing will be more frequently found in people with pastoral ministry. Evangelists and people who do mission work in countries where they are up against the occult in a hard pressed way in certain places like I've seen in Africa and Asia, (It's like Elijah and the priests of Baal), there's definitely more of the need for miraculous dealings in signs and wonders in certain environments than there are in others. I am simply saying you have an appropriate parity the true power has to outshine the first one. The truest power will always be the power of the Holy Spirit to bring conviction from the word of God to the hearts of the lost. That will always be the truest power. The signs again always follow but never the ingredient.

So he puts this in Romans 11:29, about the gifts and calling, and then in the next chapter once again he begins talking about gifts as a natural flow, bearing in mind there is no chapter division in the original Greek text. Verse 29 makes a natural flow with the things we read in chapter 12:

> *"just as we have many members of one body*
> *and all the members do not have the same function, so*

> *we who are many are one body in Christ individually*
> *members one of another and since we have gifts that*
> *differ according to the grace given to us, let each*
> *exercise them accordingly. If prophecy according to*
> *the proportion of his faith."*

Paul also says *"despise not prophetic utterance."* He goes further:

> *"If service in his serving, he who teaches in his*
> *teaching. He who exhorts in his exhortation, he who*
> *gives with liberality."*

This is a much broader perspective of spiritual gifts than we see in
Corinthians. In Corinthians most people are thinking of the 9
charismatic gifts. Here he talks about the gift of philanthropy, people
with the gifts of health service, people with gifts of mercy. A medical
missionary will frequently have the gift of mercy. But in what
context? One is to have a Body in Christ that will provoke the Jews
to jealousy.

Now when we have *meshuganas*, when we see crazy people doing
crazy things, like when we see people barking like dogs and laughing
hysterically, like some of the things I saw in Toronto, no Jewish
person or anybody else in their right mind is going to think that they
are seeing something that they want to consider. In fact they want to
see the real thing.

On the other hand the gifts and calling are there - Roman's 11 is a
polemic against replacement theology. Replacement theology says
that the prophetic purposes and calling of God of the Jews ended in
the 1st century - that God ceased to be the God of Israel, Israel has
now been replaced by the church. That is one form of
cessationalism, that Israel has ceased to be the people of God. As
we've been looking at, Romans 11 says that this isn't true. The other
form of cessationism says the same kind of thing, the gifts of the

spirit ended in the 1st century. So you have the linkage in Romans between that which says Gods purposes for Israel ceased then His calling or His gifts ceased then.

I don't believe in replacement theology any more than I believe in having a faith focused on Israel instead of the Messiah of Israel, and I don't believe in cessation theology any more than I believe in the Toronto Deception, the Emergent Church, or other such extremism and experiential pseudo theology - there is a balance. There is a direct linkage in Romans between replacement theology and cessationalism, the gifts and calling of God go forth for repentance. Chapter 11 leads directly into chapter 12 where you have this issue, this subject of the gifts being discussed in the body, the kind of Body of Christ that will provoke the Jews to jealousy.

Now let's begin to look at this olive tree - what Paul was saying here is not all that complicated. First he says *"God has not rejected his people I too am an Israelite,"* then he goes on to say *"they killed thy prophets and torn down thine alters."* He compares the situation of Jewish believer's in the church from the 1st century and even now to what happened in the days of Elijah. Our way of thinking about this has been distorted by our western year of history instead of a biblical view of history. If you went back the last 2000 years of the history of the church remember the history of Israel from the time of Abraham to the time of Jesus was just as long. Amazing isn't it? And now their duel history went something like this.

Only a percentage of Jewish people accept Jesus as the Messiah now, but in the first century it was substantial. In the 2nd century, even according to the Talmudic literature and Jewish historians it was very substantial. For example, published on an academic level the books of Max Dimont are historically accurate and easy to read. In his book - *Jews God and history* he talks about the very high percentage of Jews in the 2nd century at the time of Bar Kochba's rebellion who believed that Jesus was the Messiah. So Jewish historians estimate it as 25% of the population of Jerusalem - that's very high. And we see Talmudic references and things like the *Avodah Zara* and *Birkhat Ha Minim*, where we read rabbis getting very nervous about the large numbers of Jews believing in Jesus as the Messiah.

Throughout history there's always been the odd individual, in Britain and Europe there has been a number. Benjamin Disraeli former English Prime Minister, was a Jew who believed in Jesus as the Messiah. Felix Mendelssohn the composer - a German Jew who believed that Jesus was the Messiah. Alfred Edersheim a historian, a Jew who believed that Jesus was the Messiah. It's amazing you see a lot more messianic work and research and scholarly things written now but Edersheim's book is still foundational. It is still the book that anybody interested in this subject should read, even though it is from the last century.

Once again the number is increasing! We're told that the size of the Israeli, the Hebrew, Jewish body of Christ in Israel has quadrupled in the last 5 years. Some have been because of the Russians immigrating who had started underground Pentecostal Baptist churches in the old Soviet Empire, and because of the numbers of people getting saved within Israel. There were 15 congregations when I was living there, now there are about 40. There are a lot of little ones that nobody knows about, being in apartments today that people don't even know about. Nobody knows how many Jews believe, nobody knows how many Jewish believers there are in Russia, but there are a lot and a lot getting saved all the time. In the United States it is absolutely incredible. There are tens of thousands of Jews in North America who believe. More than that I would say more than 90% of them have been saved in the last 15-18 years.

A couple of years ago I was in New York at a picnic. (I'm from New York originally and my family currently lives in England, my wife and children are Israeli but I'm originally from New York.) I was at a picnic of two churches together and they weren't messianic fellowships they were just ordinary evangelical churches and both of them happened to have Jewish pastors. I know of fewer than five churches that I know of, probably more now that have pastors who are Jews, not Messianic fellowships just churches run by Jews. You see this happening, and more Jewish people coming to Jesus - Helen Shapiro, Romanian Jews like my wife, Founder of "Christians in sport" Eddie Wax is Jewish. The only person to have a number one top single in the U.S. secular pop charts that was Christian Norman Greenbaum, known for "Spirit in the Sky" - he's Jewish. You see this happening with more Jews believing all the time, but at the moment it is still a minority. Isn't it a pity how Jewish people reject their own Messiah, but this is nothing new Paul is saying in Romans.

In the days of Elijah, there were only seven thousand who didn't bow their knee to Baal. How many did not participate in Korah's rebellion in the Sinai. As a matter of fact when we look at the typology of the exodus, only Joshua and Caleb, a Jew and a Gentile from the generation that came out made it into the promised land. There will always be a remnant that will be saved. Look at 1 Kings, look at 2 Kings, 1 Chronicles, 2 Chronicles. So only a minority of the Jews accept Jesus - so what else is new? There's never been anything more than a minority of Jews who have accepted the truth of their own faith. There's nothing new. We just have a warped perspective of it, never, nothing new, it's always been like that.

They all put Jeremiah in prison, they all sawed Isaiah in half. They all said stone Zechariah in the temple - they all said that! Look at the history of the church of all the so called Christians in the world, and all the so called Christian denominations in the world, how many do you think throughout history have been truly born again and known Jesus and believed the Bible? Is the average person in the world who says he's a Christian a Christian? Of course not!

Born Again Christians have always been a minority throughout most of history, except for the very beginning. Long before Luther,

Calvin, Zwingli, for 1200 years you have these groups in England, it was the Lollards, founded by John Wycliffe. Remember there were only 7000 who didn't bow the knee to Baal. In 15th Century Europe you had the Bohemian Brethren following John Huss, those were the 7000 Christians not bowing their knee to Baal. In Western Europe, the Waldenseans, those were the 7000 Christian not bowing their knee to Baal. It's the same truth. There's one difference, they point a finger at the Jews, there's three coming back at the church. Why? The Jews are looking forward to the coming of the Messiah. The so called church has the Messiah.

In the old covenant, the Jews couldn't have the Holy Spirit, it was only for kings, high priests and prophets. The Jews only had the Tenach, the Old Testament, we have the Tenach and the New Testament. On top of all that we have their example to learn from. If God is finished with them, show me one reason why he shouldn't be finished with Christianity? As a matter of fact he has more reasons to give them a chance then he does us now. *"The name of God is blasphemed among the Gentiles because of the you"* he says and in the early church this was true. Now the opposite is true. Now the name of Jesus is blasphemed among the Jews because of Christianity! Not only because of Roman Catholicism and nominal Christianity, even Protestantism. Luther said that "every Jew should be forced into a corral and forced to profess Christ at the point of a knife?" That was 500 years ago, today is the same with people like Rick Godwin saying the Jews have no right to be in the land and that it is just wasted money. He is an evangelical charismatic supposedly in the know.

There is only a minority who believe but there has never been any more than a minority who truly believe. Always remember what Jesus said: *"If you believe Moses, you will believe me also."* In other words the average Jewish person who is observant, their problem is not that they reject Jesus as the Messiah. The problem with the Jewish people is not that they reject their Messiah, the rejection of their Messiah is the result of their problem. Their problem is they don't believe the Torah. They don't believe Moses – *"if you believe Moses you'd believe me also."* Jesus spoke of the Torah, not the end, the target, the purpose, the fulfillment of it. That's the problem - they don't believe the Torah. Every Jew is either under one or the other covenant.

In the same way there has come at the present time a remnant according to Gods gracious choice, yes, a remnant of Jews who believe. Thank God, there is a growing community of Jewish believers who do follow their true King! That is good, Praise the Lord, these are part of the remnant. It is no different than the mainstream church, evangelicals are a minority and many of the minority today are apostatized and compromising.

To continue with what Paul is saying - he goes and he talks about grace. Now it's interesting that here the word forgive is also grace - *charism.* With the wrong mentality, people go around saying "this one has the gift of this, and the gift of that, the gift of tongues, the gift of healing the gift of miracles! etc etc" This is absolutely ridiculous in two ways. Its not that "I have the gift of tongues" or "I have the gift of prophesy" it's that "I have the grace to prophesy, I have the grace to pray in tongues, I have the grace!" So it is not your gift it is your grace - an undeserved favor - a gift! More than that what else does it say in chapter 12 of Romans - *"it's not for you - it's through you to the body!"* People often have the wrong perspective. Nobody has any gift - the gift of the Spirit is the Holy Spirit Himself. The pledge of our salvation! The gift of God is eternal life thought Jesus Christ the Lord. That's the gift that you and I have, but the gifts of the spirit are never to individuals. They are to the body through individuals, and they are gifts, not in the wrong perspective but as the Greek word is - grace.

What then? That which Israel is searching for,
it has not obtained, but those who were chosen

obtained it and the rest were hardened; just as it is written, "God gave them the spirit of stupor....."
-Romans 11:7

There are other quotes from various texts in the Old Testament like Deuteronomy 24 and so on. In other words Israel's rejection was prophesied. So it was consistent to what always happened, there was never anything more than a remnant - a minority.

So too the incorporation of Gentiles was prophesied. Verse 11:

> *"I say then they did not stumble so much to fall did they? May it never be! But by their transgression salvation has come to the Gentiles to make them jealous."*

Now the Greek word for Gentiles is *ethnon* - "these peoples." The Hebrew word is *goyim* - "the nations" and in Isaiah Israel is called the *goyim*.

> *"Now if their transgression be riches for the world and their failure be riches for the Gentiles, how much more will their fulfillment be! I am speaking to you who are Gentiles. Inasmuch then as I am an apostle of Gentiles, I magnify my ministry, if somehow I might move to jealously my fellow countrymen and save some of them. For is their rejection be the reconciliation of the world, what will their acceptance be but life from the dead?"*
-Romans 11:12-15

Jesus is coming for a spotless bride. What is the acid test of a spotless bride? The acid test of a spotless bride is a church that can provoke the parents of my wife to jealousy - who are holocaust survivors. That's a spotless bride! It's going to take one spotless bride to make them want what we have. Its part of Gods thermometer of what the church should be.

But lets look further; *"if their rejection be the reconciliation of the world what will their reconciliation be but like from the dead?"* Make no mistake about it - God is going to bless the church through Jewish people before Jesus comes again!

Now moving on - the same as God used the Jews to give the gospel to the Gentiles in the 1st century church, God is going to use the Gentiles to bring the good news back home to the Jews in the last century church. Undoubtedly the overwhelming majority of Jewish people who get saved come to faith though the witness, testimony and prayers of Gentile people. This is with good reason as so much of the damage of anti-Semitism was done by people claiming to be Christians, so now there is a chance for this to be undone by true Christians.

Not only that but the overwhelming mass of financial support for Jewish missions and Jewish evangelism comes from Gentile churches. This is the same as when the church in Antioch sent out Paul and Barnabas to the Gentiles, when Jewish believers gave financial support. Jewish missions in the modern sense were born here in Britain. See the evangelists to the Jews people like William Wilberforce and the Earl of Shaftsbury who started Churches Ministry to the Jews as they realized the prophetic purposes of God for Israel. Other societies such as the British Jewish society and the Presbyterian believers in Scotland and Northern Ireland who saw and understood this.

"If their rejection be the reconciliation of the world what will their reconciliation be but like from the dead?" Let's go on. Romans 11:16:

> *"And if the first piece of dough be holy, the lump is also and if the root be holy, the branches are too."*

In the Bible, the New Testament explains this here by an olive tree, other places like in Corinthians and in Peter Biblical typology uses a building - the temple. Using variant Greek words for temple such as *oikos, naos,* and *hieron,* seven times the New Testament calls the church the temple.

Before we look at this - think of a skyscraper! When I look at a skyscraper a 60, 70, 80 story building I am flabbergasted. I'm not an engineer or an architect but even an engineer or an architect is amazed because they know to get something that high to stay there has to be something pretty remarkable underneath that is holding it up.

He knows that even though the foundation isn't normally seen it is there, because if that foundation was not there, the building would not be there. You are aware of this so much in New York as there are hundreds and hundreds of skyscrapers, there are 1200 just in Manhattan, buildings over 50, 60 stories, some over 100 stories.

When they build a skyscraper - they dig and dig and dig, and they have the boards around them with pictures of what it's going to look like, the architect's drawing, but they just keep digging and digging and digging. "When are these guys going to stop digging? Every time I come by they're digging! 6 months later they're still digging!" But when the time is right!.... What we are talking about in Romans is the same! God spends 2000 years getting the foundation right before he builds the church. The history of the Jews from Abraham to the time of Jesus is as long as the time from Jesus as to now. It is the same principle.

So it is with the tree, when you plant a new cedar tree you know it has roots. And you know if it didn't have roots or if those roots were dead, the tree would be dead. What does Paul say about the roots? In Greek the word is *reza.* *"If the roots be holy"* so in verse 16 the branches are too. The holy branches blossom from *'ha shoresh ha kodesh'* (the holy root). If the root is not there the tree isn't either! If God is finished with the Jews, He's finished with the church. What had the Jews done that God was angry with them at the Babylonian captivity - what had they done? Idolatry – do you think our society is not idolatrous? Is the Christian world idolatrous? Is the Roman Catholicism "Christianity" idolatrous? It is idolatry – *hishtachvya* it bows down to worship. The Hebrew infinitive for to bow down is the same as the word for worship *L'hishtachavot*, it is idolatry.

What else did the Jews do? They sacrificed their babies to Molek? As you've heard me say non-theraputical abortion is just sacrificing babies for Mammon, these babies are executed for economic reasons. Anything the Jews did, the church did and more so. And the church had much more than the Jews ever did, they had Jesus. Yet if He's finished with them, the tree is finished!

Listen to what he says about the tree - everything underneath the surface is the Old Testament - the old covenant, everything above it is the new covenant. Does that make one tree or two? One! In the old covenant the branches of the churches were being bonded, most of the roots were Jews, however in the old covenant you still have a remnant of Gentiles. Abraham, Isaac and Jacob, Isaiah, Nahum, Samuel – but wait a minute there is Ruth, Ziporrah, Uriah and there is Caleb the Kennite. Most of the branches of the roots were Jews, but even in the old covenant God had a faithful remnant of Gentiles grafted into it. There's nothing new!

Up to this point, I would agree with covenant theology, the Calvinists have this part at least partly right. Above the surface it's the New Testament. The lower branches are all Jews. Peter, Andrew, James, John, Philip, Bartholomew, Matthew, Simon, Timothy, Paul: right! Mary, Lydia were all Jewish! Then it's Gentiles. Pay attention! It is true to say that Gentile Christians replace Jews who reject Jesus. It is true - Jews who reject their Messiah are cut off from their own tree and Gentiles who accept them replace them. But the tree remains the same tree!

> *"The days are coming" declares the Lord*
> *"when I will make a new covenant with Israel and the*
> *house of Judah, not like the covenant I made with their*
> *fathers (ani achtok Brit Hadasha Lo Kmo Ha Brit Sha*
> *Ani Tochti Im Avotchem)."*
>
> -Jeremiah 31:31

Covenant and testament are the same word - *brit*.

I will make a new covenant with the house of Israel and the house of Judah. I will give the new covenant to the Baptists, I will give the new covenant to the Pentecostals, I will give the new covenant to the Pope? No!! The new covenant is given to the Jews. God never made a covenant with the Gentiles, never!

In the Old Testament any Gentile who wanted to be part of the covenant had to join themselves to the Jewish people the way Ruth did. And it is the same thing now. Any non Jews who want to be part of God's covenant have to join themselves to Israel and the Jews. Spiritually, not by circumcision, but by circumcision of the heart - faith in the Messiah. Yes, Gentiles replace Jews who reject Him but it's the same tree, there's no new tree. They're taken from a wild tree he says and grafted into the cultivated one. If what is underneath is dead, so is what is above the surface.

But then he goes on and says something else, "I'm going to tell you a mystery" the mystery is this:

"There was a time when the Jews for centuries killed their prophets and broke the covenant and finally rejected their Messiah, so I carry my grace to the Gentiles but the reverse is gonna happen. The same as I got fed up with them, I'm going to get fed up with Christianity, in its popular sense. For centuries I sent Jeremiah and I sent Isaiah and Zechariah and John the Baptist, *Yochanon Ha Matbeel*, and they rejected their prophets - so did the church! So did the church!"

Did the Methodists follow the teaching of Wesley? No! The Baptists - did they follow the teaching of Spurgeon and John Bunyan? No! Did the Anglicans follow the doctrines of Thomas Cranmer or John Hooper? No! He got fed up with the Jews and turned his face to the Gentiles, keeping a faithful remnant of Jews. But the time will come when the reverse will happen. Jesus spoke of this *Tekufa HaGoyim* the time of the Gentiles, He spoke of it in a prophetic sense in Luke 2, this verse about Jerusalem being trampled down. Here Paul deals with it salvifically, to deal with salvation, but it is the same idea, the time of the Gentiles comes to a close and what begins to happen? The top branches are Jews.

The first Christian were Jews, and the last Christian are going to be Jews. Whether John Piper, John Stott, and Rick Godwin like it or not. The first believers were Jews and the last are gonna be Jews. Some people of the premillennial persuasion would see that in revelation the reference to 144,000 is along this line. A view which I have a considerable amount of sympathy about, though I am not professing to totally understand it.

> *"If they do not continue in their unbelief... if you were cut off and were by nature a wild olive tree and grafted contrary to nature into a cultivated olive tree, how much more shall these who are natural branches be grafted into their own olive tree?"*
> -Romans 11:23-24

It reminds me of when I was witnessing to my wife (before she was my wife) in Jerusalem. I was showing her the 22nd Psalm - the Messiah being crucified and where they gambled for his clothes. She said that's very interesting, but now show it to me in the Tanach - in the Jewish Testament. She thought I was reading from the New Testament. I said "but Pavia, this is the Tanach, it's the book of Psalms, it's the Psalm of David." If you were a Jew that came to believe in Jesus, do think you would get more Jewish or less? More

Jewish! Practically everyone. I can find very few Jewish believers who will tell you that they're Jewishness and Jewish identity become less significant after they got saved. Almost everyone will tell you it became more significant but you'll find very few who say the opposite.

Now let's look. It's a mystery - He got fed up with the Jews but a time will come when he will get fed up with the Gentiles – *"and thus all Israel will be saved."* This does not mean every Jew will be saved - that is the error of dual covenant theology. What it does mean in its context is when the deliverer comes to Zion - those Jews will accept Him as Messiah when he comes back. This is highlighted in the prophecy of Zechariah chapter 12, where the Jews who see Him and accept Him as Messiah in the Last Days and some of these will survive the Last Days, the Tribulation – the remnant, and they'll recognize him as Messiah.

Now we have to be careful, Galatians talks about the Israel of God. The Israel of God is the faithful remnant of Old Testament Israel who are faithful under the law. The faithful remnant of New Testament Israel are the Jews who accept Jesus. Together with the Gentiles grafted in. The faithful remnant of Gentiles of the old covenant and the faithful remnant of Gentiles grafted in from the new. Most of the branches in the Old were Jews with some Gentiles, most of the branches in the New were Gentiles, with some Jews.

The Israel of God. In heaven everybody's name will be Cohen. Seriously it will be Cohen – a kingdom of priests! Some Jewish people have names like Cohen and Levi - those are priestly names! From the stand point of the gospel they are enemies for your sake, that is for that sake of the good news, the salvation of non Jews, the Jews are enemies. However from the stand point of Gods choice they remain beloved for the sake of their fathers. They are beloved for the sake of their fathers!

Lets look at Genesis 15:17 where a covenant is formalized with Abraham the father:

> *And it came about when the sun had set and it was very dark and behold there appeared a smoking oven and a flaming torch passed between these pieces and on that day God made a covenant with Abraham.*

The way you make a covenant, in Hebrew - *Laktok brit* you need to cut a covenant. You sacrifice an animal ritually and cut it in half and both parts in ancient Near Eastern Suzerainty rituals and others like this were where both parties would pass between the dissected carcass of the sacrificed animal. Notice only the flames goes through. We call this flame in Hebrew *'Shalhevit Ya'* the flame of Yahweh. It's the same as the pillar of fire – the *Shekinah*.

Only God went through, Abraham didn't. Why? – because right from the beginning God knew that He would keep the covenant that Abraham's descendants wouldn't. The validity of a covenant does not depend on the unfaithfulness of man but rather on the faithfulness of God. They remain beloved for the sake of their fathers. He made a promise to Abraham and that is it! God cannot lie! It does not depend on us being faithful. Now the individuals rejecting Him are one thing but the corporate covenant with Israel cannot be broken. Anymore than it can be broken with the church, because it is two covenants with one nation. For the sake of their fathers.

Now this is the key! Verse 29: *"for the gifts and calling or God are irrevocable."* Just like in Corinthians it links gifts and calling. This introduces what we built up to in the following chapter 12, when he begins talking about gifts. Notice it's the same mentality, the same mentality that gave us the errors of replacement theology. It is the same mentality that gave us the errors of cessation theology – the same roots. It dates back to when Constantine Christianized the Roman Empire and the Pope became 'Pontificus Maximus' and this kind of thing that saw the hellenization and then the paganization of Christendom.

There is a story about when Thomas Aquinas, went to Rome and the Pope showed him the Papal Treasury and he said to Thomas Aquinas "You see, the church can no longer say 'gold and silver have I none'" and he begins laughing to Aquinas and Aquinas said "yes you are correct but neither can the church say 'in the name of Jesus Christ get up and walk.'" I'm no fan of Aquinas but on that point he was right.

The reformists said and did a lot of good things, but they only went back to part of the Biblical truth. The authority of the Scripture they got right, justification by faith they got right, the corruption and idolatry of medieval Rome, they got right, but they didn't break the unscriptural marriage between church and state and end Erastianism (the church as a political organ of the state). They didn't restore a Biblical view of mission. They also did not see God's end time purpose for Israel and the Jews. They did not go back to the apostolic faith of the New Testament in its totality either theologically or spiritually. This is the big issue!

Protestantism and Roman Catholicism both go back to Augustine, instead of back to the Bible. They go back to what the post-Nicean fathers, particularly what Augustine said about the Bible, instead of back to God's Word alone. That was and is their problem, they are all inmates in the same prison. Catholicism and Protestantism both derive form Augustine. That is their problem.

Other groups like the nonconformists, the Baptists and the Brethren, are not Augustine influenced. If you are a Pentecostal or Baptist or a Brethren, never consider yourself a Protestant. You may have heard me say this. During the Reformation, you would have been called an Anabaptist. If you don't believe in sprinkling babies, infant baptism, pedobaptism, if you don't believe in state church (Erastianism), you would not have been considered a Protestant during any part of the

Reformation. You would have been called an Anabaptist and have been terribly persecuted by both Protestants and Catholics alike. It's only later that these other nonconformist churches became socially identified with Protestants, but during the Reformation they would have been seen as Anabaptist sects and were usually persecuted as badly by the reformers and their followers as they were by the Pope. Particularly Zwingli's people - they would drown them in the ice and other terrible things.

Nonetheless, let's continue. The same root, the same mentality! This idea that God has finished with the Jews directly connects here to Romans where God has finished with the church. It is just two different expressions of cessationism! Two different expressions of replacementism! Were the gifts and calling of God irrevocable? *"Despise not prophetic utterance"* – *"Jews seek a sign."*

What about all the craziness that went on in Toronto? Charismania (the actual theological term is 'neo-montanism'). That is the other extreme! Cessationism is one extreme, *meshugana* hyper charismatic extremism based on experiential theology, emotionalism, and mysticism is the other extreme. The balance is the Bible.

> *"For just as you once were disobedient to God, but now have been shown mercy because of their disobedience..."*
>
> Romans 11:30

It is amazing how they have replaced replacementism with cessationism. There is a reason that the Holy Spirit put that verse in that place.

> *"For just as you once were disobedient to God, but now have been shown mercy because of their disobedience, so these now have been disobedient in*

order that because of the mercy shown to you they also
may now be shown mercy. For God has shut up all in
disobedience that he might show mercy to all."
                                            - Romans 11:30-32

He shows he favors the Jews. He drives out the Amorites, the Jebuzites, the Perezites and the Gentiles saw what the Jews had and wanted it but most Jews blew it. Then He blessed and profited the church, so the Jews will see it and want it. But then Christendom blows it. Except in both cases there's a remnant! Jews are no better or no worse than anybody. Were all corrupt and we all need Gods mercy – this is what Paul is saying here. That's what the gospel of Yeshua means:

> *"Oh the depth of the riches both of the wisdom*
> *and knowledge of God! How unsearchable are His*
> *judgments and how unfathomable His ways. For who*
> *has known the mind of the Lord, or who became His*
> *counselor? Or who has first given to Him that it*
> *might be paid back to Him again? For from Him and*
> *through Him and to Him are all things. To Him be the*
> *glory forever. Amen."*
>
>   -Romans 11:33-36

None of it is new! In seven places Isaiah says the Messiah would make the Gentiles believe in the Jewish God. Turn to Isaiah 11: We call it *Shoresh Yshai*, the root of Jesse in verse 1 and in verse 10:

> *"Then it will come about in that day that the*
> *Gentiles (the goyim) will resort to the root of Jesse who*
> *will stand as a signal for the peoples."*

The Gentiles will come to believe in the Jewish God of the Messiah. Rambam, Maimonides, the most important Rabbi to Rabbinic Judaism, said that Christianity came to make the Gentiles believe in the Jewish God. He actually said that in his most important book *Guide For The Perplexed*; at least he had half of it right. Higher critics try to argue Isaiah is written by two or three people - I say it is two or three books written by the same person, at least the core of it certainly because they all have the same themes.

> *"For thou art our Father, though Abraham does not know us and Israel does not recognize us."*
> - Isaiah 63:16

You see that? Isaiah 63:16 - *"For thou art our Father, though Abraham does not know us and Israel does not recognize us."* You don't need a drop of Jewish blood in your veins or a Jewish gene in your genetic pool or a Jewish ancestor. You don't need any of it! If you have faith in the Messiah, if you have faith in the Jewish Messiah, God is your Father and you are descended from Abraham by faith. Even though, what does it say? - "Israel does not recognize us!"

You are grafted in - it was never in the basis of race per se:

> "Then Abraham took Ishmael his son, (not only Isaac would be circumcised) *and all the servants who were born in his house, and all who were bought with his money, every male among the men of Abraham's household, and circumcised the flesh of their foreskin in that very same day..."*
> -Genesis 17:23

It was slaves, people he bought he circumcised them and brought them under the covenant as well. Jewish identity was never based on race - it was based on faith.

Here's where the reformers really got it wrong.

> "...I will make new covenant with Israel and
> the house of Judah, not like the covenant I made with
> their fathers."
>
> -Jeremiah 31:31

The old covenant had this problem Jeremiah faced. Because people were born into the Jewish culture and circumcised as babies, they thought they were in a covenant relationship with God and that made them right. God tells Jeremiah "when the Messiah comes its not going to be like that – I will write my law on their heart - it wont be like the covenant that I gave to your fathers, you will have to make the individual choice."

In fact Jesus comes against the family culture of the Middle Eastern accents - father turned against children, children against parents. He realized it will have to be a difficult choice. So what happens is Constantine comes and puts it back! Augustine come with the sprinkling of the babies and puts it back. Before Satan paganised the church he tried to Judaize it! In Galatians - before he paganised it he tried to Judaize it. Sprinkling babies and all this stuff that's what it is – it's a form of Judaization - going back under that law. It is essentially the same as the Roman Catholics having a separate priesthood, apart from the priesthood of all believers, akin to the Old Testament Levitical priesthood - that is Judaization. The tabernacle and mass or the anglo-catholic mass and the priests in the box - that's Judaization – same as the old covenant.

So people are born into a "Christian" culture, in the so called "Christian" family, get sprinkled as kids and they think that they are part of the covenant. You understand - it is the same mentality and the reformers failed to address that. When you understand it then you understand all this nonsense like where replacement theology comes from, and this nonsense like where cessation theology comes from -

it comes from the same thing! A fundamental misunderstanding of covenant. They got it partly right!

But then we get to the end. Things begin to change Paul says, God can graft them in again because they are the natural branches, and its amazing, it is the generation of Jews that came out of the holocaust and their families, who are the ones who have turned back to their Messiah. The same century that has seen the worst episode in anti-semitism, is the same century that sees the rebirth of Jewish Christianity. That has got to be the hand of God - it defies any kind of logical or historical precedent - it has to be the hand of God. I have no doubt, I'm absolutely positive, I've never been so sure of anything - the numbers of Jewish people that we see coming to faith in Jesus today, are a sign of the Last Days and Jesus returning.

We even see Orthodox Jews open! When I was in South Africa, Rabbi Graham Finklestein, a major Rabbi, came to hear me speak, in Johannesburg. Nobody got saved in Cape Town, I was discouraged, because in an evangelistic meeting, in a big Jewish area of Cape Town, nobody got saved, no Jews got saved. But a lot of Jews came to the meeting, including the leading expert in nuclear medicine, a radiologist and her husband in South Africa. She is one of the five top radiologists in the world published in medical journals - Nuclear medicine and for some reason there are many medical professionals who read our newsletter in South Africa. I think I am an adopted son to them. They received the tape of "A Prophet Like Moses" and she kept relistening to it. So she came to our office in Johannesburg to visit the Moriel office and asked our administrator for more of my tapes and he asked if she was a believer, she said that she wasn't and he said "I cant give you anymore tapes, we only sell them to people that believe, but we can give you some." (Moriel uses the proceeds of what we sell to subsidize those that we give away to the unsaved.) So she came and he said "I will give you some." So he gave her a whole lot of tapes and she and her husband listened to them for about a week to 10 days and came back and prayed to receive Yeshua as the Messiah. They also made a contribution to Moriel South Africa.

This is happening all over the world. In Australia, it is happening! South Africa, Great Britain, especially Israel, American and Russia. It's happening! 10 years ago, 12 years ago, "What? He believes in Jesus and he's Jewish?" now it's "Yeh my nephew is one too!"

The first Christians were Jews - the last Christians are going to be Jews. There has never been anything more than a faithful remnant under the Old Covenant and there's nothing more than a faithful remnant under the New Covenant, but that is reality. They are being grafted in again! Our task is to make them jealous. They have to want what we have! That's quite a task - but we are living in exciting times. God bless you!

Chapter 15

The New Galatians

Jeremiah 31:31 and the Epistle to the Galatians
You Foolish Galatians, Who Bewitched You?
A Crisis in Messianic Judaism?

> *"A time will come when I will make a new Covenant with the House of Israel and the House of Judah, not like the Covenant I made with their fathers.."*
>
> -Jeremiah 31:31

We see the stage being set with current Middle East events for the prophetic fulfillment of Zechariah 12 and 13, for the Great Tribulation, (The "Time of Jacob's Trouble" in Jeremiah 30) the dawn of the Anti Christ, and the Return of Jesus. At the same time we see the fulfillment of the prophetic predictions of Paul in Romans 11, with the increase in Jews being saved and a rediscovery by many Evangelicals of the Hebrew origins of the Christian Faith.

Concerning this rediscovery, non Jewish Christians are warned by God's Word in Romans 11 not to boast against Israel, the natural branches, just as Jewish believers are warned not to berate non Jews who believe (Ruth 2:15, Acts 15:13-19). In the Messiah we are "one new man" where cultural differences between the natural Jewish and in-grafted non-Jewish branches, like the socio-economic differences between bond servant and free, or the biological and emotional differences between male and female, constitute no spiritual difference; we all have one salvation, One Savior, one promise, one Bible, One Spirit, and one eternal destiny (Galatians 3:28). So now bond servants are free in the Lord and the free are now the Lord's bond servants. The wife in Christ is now co-heir with the husband (1 Peter 3:7) and believing Gentiles are co heirs with Israel (Ephesians 2:11-14).

As we always note, according to Jeremiah 31:31, the New Covenant was made with Israel and the Jews, not the church. The church is the spiritual continuation of Israel of the faithful remnant of Israel into which believing non Jews are in-grafted, but not the replacement of literal Israel. Believing non Jews are grafted in while unbelieving Jews rejecting Yeshua as their Messiah have been cut off from their own Olive Tree, but are grafted in again by receiving Him (Romans 11: 17-24).

But as we see the prophecies of Zechariah, Jeremiah, The Olivet Discourse, Daniel and Revelation and the eschatological (end times) prophetic material in the Epistles, coming into fulfillment, we see a confusion and a deception of which God is not author.

In the past we have published articles warning against the errors of replacement theology, and of Calvinistic covenant theology (which denigrates the New Covenant by falsely teaching that God only made one covenant with Adam and one with Abraham, and further states that Israel is now the church). We have warned about Post Millennialism (if Satan is bound, when did the 1,000 years begin and more importantly who keeps letting him go?) which when mixed with the charismania of latter day reign/Joel's Army-Manifest Sons hyper Pentecostalism yields the deceptions of the Vineyard Movement and the over realized eschatology of Kingdom Now Theology.

We have also warned of the Christian anti Semitism of the Identity Movement, and the Christian anti Zionism of Rick Godwin, Bryn

Jones, and the pro-Arafat Anglican Bishop of Jerusalem* who preached against Israel recently in the late David Watson's St. Michael Le Belfry in York (now predictably a swamp of Alpha course ecumenical deception, Toronto lunacy etc.). We have warned against the de-Jewishisation of Jesus by the Elim Movement in its "Jesus Christ had no Jewish blood" article by George Canty published in Elim's tabloid (like St. Michael Bat in Le Belfry, Elim from bogus gold teeth to promotions of apostate money preachers remains a quagmire of deception, still trying to revive the failed Toronto Experience at its conference featuring John Arnott). Our readers, and other biblically knowledgeable and discerning Christians know these things.

On the other extreme, we have joined David Brickner, Tuvya Zaretsky and Jews For Jesus, John Ross and Christian Witness to Israel, Dr Arnold Fruchtenbaum and Ariel, and others involved in seeing Jewish souls saved in warning against ministries to the Jews that with hold Christ. We appreciate Arnold Fruchtembaum's recent letter stating that the actions of Ebenezer Fund are not biblical or of God, and a scandal yet again haunts the International Christian Embassy in Jerusalem, after its new leader, Malcolm Hedding produced a tape teaching that Jesus never came to die but that Israel would simply be Born Again without Him going to the cross.

Jesus on the contrary Himself said concerning His death and resurrection *"For This Purpose I Have Come"* (in order to fulfill Isaiah 53, Daniel 9 etc. to make salvation possible), and Romans 6 makes it clear that regeneration unto salvation is impossible without His death. Malcolm Hedding, (like the ICEJ founder Jan Willem Van der Hoven) is a complete and unmitigated heretic. As Jeremiah 31:31 states, the New Covenant was made with Israel, and dual covenant beliefs claiming Jews can be saved apart from the New Covenant are a lie of Satan. Those not bringing Israel the New Covenant have a mere social and political gospel which from the view point of Scripture is no gospel at all.

The New Dilemma

Now however, we have a new threat to the purposes of God for Israel and the Jews. Replacementists, anti-Zionists, and anti-Semites and the Identity Movement inspired Ruckmanites (Aho, Dillen, Howard and Buester) have a new weapon against Jewish believers retaining their God given identity as Jews - and ironically, that weapon is provided by a combination of certain Jewish believers and judaized Gentiles from the extreme axis of the messianic movement.

The nomianism (soft legalism) of hyper messianic extremists we have warned against in articles such as "The Seduction Of The Hebrew Roots Movement," and "Why I Do Not Accept The Jerusalem School of Synoptic Research." The latter was written as a compliment to Andrew Gould's article addressing the precarious and unsubstantiated claims of Messrs Bevin and Blizzard of the gospels being originally in Hebrew, (which were supported by the late Rabbinic scholar David Flusser and Roman Catholic writer Joseph Francovic). No manuscript evidence exists for these speculations, the linguistic arguments are convoluted and faulty, and the one historic reference from the time of Hegisippus in the post apostolic/early patristic era of Matthew's gospel being originally in Hebrew, if true, could simply have been the Hebrew dialect of Aramaic.

There is a misguided element in the Gentile church, who are understandably disgusted with what they see as the distorted Christianity of the contemporary church in the age of ecumenism, Toronto, money preachers and higher criticism. In reaction these people desire to return to the source of the Christian faith, which is biblically and historically a primordial Jewish faith. Unfortunately, they arrive at the abrupt conclusion that anything Messianic must be right, when in fact there is as much lunacy of every description in the various strands of the Messianic Movement as there are in any other component of the Body of Christ.

One popular expression we have witnessed of this is the use of David Stern's "Jewish New Testament" and his "Complete Jewish Bible" (as if there were any other kind). While at one time we did recommend Mr Stern's book "Restoring The Jewishness of The Gospel," Mr Stern's book "Messianic Manifesto" calling for a "Messianic Sanhedrin to issue chalakik (legal rabbinic Jewish) decisions for Jewish believers is too ludicrous a proposition to deserve serious comment. While fine as a reference book , Mr Stern's Jewish New Testament is one of the worst paraphrases from the original Greek I have ever seen. His mistranslation of Ephesians 5 is so absurd that the Jehovahs Witnesses wouldn't go that far in their highly distorted so called "New World Translation." Yet too many sincere, yet naïve Christians assume "Oh, if it is the Jewish New Testament it must be the uncorrupted original one," not knowing the translation is badly corrupted.

There are similar reactions among many Southern Baptist and other groups, who in reaction to the avalanche of error in the church revert to Reformed theology, complete with its errors of cessationism and hyper Calvinism, (and sometimes replacementism) because they see it as the diametric opposite of ecumenism and charismania. Thus instead of correcting an error with truth, one error is redressed by another one of the opposite extreme. This same warped and unbiblical reasoning happens when people react against the errors of supercessionism (Replacement theology) with hyper Messianic extremism.

In the last few years, hyper Messianic extremism has reached new heights of erroneous belief with the deity of Yeshua even being rejected in some cases. There are crazy conferences lifting up "Jewishness" instead of "Jesus-ness" and misplaces and displaces the proper emphasis Scripture says we are to have. Jewish believers do not need conferences, (usually run by biblically ignorant kooks) telling them how to be Jewish. Jews know how to be Jewish just as Mexicans know how to be Mexican or Koreans know how to be

Korean. They need discipleship and biblical exposition telling them how to be followers of their Messiah Yeshua, the same as any other believer.

No one argues with voluntary Jewish observances. They are optional as a matter of personal choice and culture (Roman 14: 4-5, Colossians 2:16-18). There can be an advantage in observance of Jewish customs as an evangelistic strategy in reaching Jews (1 Corinthians 9: 20) and no place are people called to abandon their culture upon becoming believers in Jesus, in fact on the contrary are told not to forfeit their identity (1 Corinthians 7:18). Moreover, Jewish ritual fulfilled in Christ is used repeatedly in the New Testament as an illustration of doctrine (1 Corinthians 5:7-8, Hebrews 9:1-22) and in accordance with biblical and apostolic tradition these observances remain a biblical way to reinforce and illustrate our understanding of New Testament doctrine. It was the post apostolic and post biblical patristic tradition of the Church Fathers such as the anti-semitic John Chrysostom who first opposed such things. The New Testament however never does.

Indeed, as Paul wrote, "all things are lawful, but not all things are helpful." A Jewish believer eating pork, while lawful, may not be helpful to his or her testimony in reaching Jews being told by rabbis that believing Jews have abandoned being Jewish. Pork or shellfish are now 'kosher' but may hinder one's testimony, just as taking the Lord's Supper with wine could damage one's testimony - for instance a Celtic culture where alcohol abuse is so prolific a problem. But when these observances become compulsory, (eg. for membership in a Messianic Congregation) or are seen as a means of sanctification in and of themselves, one goes back under the law Christ came to free us from. Those finding something inherently wrong in non kosher foods the Bible tells us are "weak in faith."

If it is folly to hold conferences telling Jews how to be Jews, it is even more ridiculous telling non Jews how to be Jews. Yet, now we see Gentiles being brought under the law. There is a messianic group in South Africa urging Gentile adult males to undergo ritual Jewish circumcision. Some judaized Gentiles such as Israel Hawkes dress like ultra orthodox rabbis, and have begun a highly schismatic belief of cultic proportions believing that it is wrong to call Yeshua Jesus or God anything other than YHWH.

Indeed, what our translations usually call LORD is actually YHWH in the original Hebrew Text, but the New Testament manuscripts translating the spoken Aramaic term *Mar*, (which would have been used by Jesus) and employed the term *kurios* (Lord) repeatedly. If the New Testament has no problem calling YHWH Lord, why should we?

Satan's first efforts to seduce the church were not to paganize it, (that came later with some of the Church Fathers and after Constantine with the papacy) as we see in the New Testament, his first efforts to seduce the Church were to Judaize it. The Roman Catholic priesthood, Calvinistic Covenant theology, Amillennial Calvinistic Reconstructionism, the Roman Catholic Mass, and the Seventh Day Adventists are all examples of a Judaized Christendom. So now are the hyper Messianic Extremists.

This error, a virtual throw back to the Book of Galatians, is being used to fuel the anti messianic rhetoric of the replacementists we have warned against in our article "Watchmen Who Are Not Watchmen" (still available on our web site).

In the past it has been easy to refute replacementists, especially the Ruckmanites. Ruckmanites are people who follow the beliefs of Peter Ruckman, combining debunked Gail Riplinger in support of the extreme King James Version Only position with White Supremacist Identity Movement beliefs. Some of these are often willing to lie to achieve their ends in spreading anti Jewish neo nazi propaganda within the church (things about "Jews having different DNA than other people." and "Jewish conspiracies to take over the Christian church," and outlandishly "Jews believing only they can interpret the bible, because of having different DNA.")

As Rick Godwin and Bryn Jones (both advocates of the Toronto deception) launched a tide of Christian anti zionism among Restorationists extreme charismatics, Ruckmanites like Aho, Buester, Howard and Dillen influenced by the racist and anti Semitic 'Balaam's Ass' web site, where Identity Movement beliefs are repackaged as supposedly "Christian discernment" wage a relentless tirade against Messianic Jews. The bigoted source of their propaganda and their general biblical ignorance means that they have never been a very serious challenge to God's purposes for the Church in relation to Israel. When biblically and logically refuted, they take bible passages out of context (as Satan did in Matthew 4) and turn them into clichés to hide under. When anyone points to New Testament teachings about believing Jews as the natural branches and the practical advantages of being the people of the covenants and having the oracles of God (Romans 3:1) they respond against the existence of Messianic Jews in the same way as Christian feminists arguing for the ordination of women pastors twisting the same verse out of context. That verse is inevitable Galatians 3:28 *"There is neither Jew nor Greek, slave nor free, neither male nor female."*

Do men have babies? Did the institution of slavery not exist in the age of the first century church? The temporal differences all remain, the text in its context is talking about spiritual differences disappearing in Christ. To say Jews no longer exist within the Body of Christ is to say that women don't either, or that Paul was wrong in giving instructions to Christian slaves (1 Corinthians 7:21-22) because there weren't any!

Unfortunately, the new tide of heresy among hyper messianic extremists encompassing everything from denial of the deity of Yeshua to financial scandal is providing the Israeli Press and anti

Messianic Orthodox Jewish Activists in the Jewish community, and radical replacementists and Christian anti semites, (if that is not a contradiction in terms) in the Christian community with new ammunition that is easy to exploit in the discrediting of the doctrinally sound mainstream of Jewish belief, Jewish evangelism, and a biblical understanding of the prophetic purposes of God concerning Israel and the Jews.

A recent article in the November issue of ISRAEL TODAY featured an article about Messianic Jews debating the deity of Yeshua. It is unfortunate this reached the secular media, but it has. A subsequent article in KIVUN, a Hebrew language messianic periodical carried an article by Udi Tzofef quoting various Israeli messianic leaders saying they do not view Yeshua as God in the same way as traditional Christian theology but as "The Son of God" and as the Messianic Redeemer. Some espoused what amounts to the ancient heresy of "Ebionism" held by the Ebionites - calling Jesus a uniquely inspired man but not God Himself. This caused a backlash with ISRAEL TODAY carrying a follow up piece suggesting that those messianic leaders now backtracking are doing so because they are threatened economically with withdrawal of financial support from abroad.

For some time one congregation in Jerusalem has tolerated Ebionites as members and while its leader in Israel uses abusive language such as "the smell of the Gentiles"(an odor he cannot find awfully foul given that the wife and mother of his children is one of them) and has made statements about "the whole Gentile church going to hell." It is for sure he does not speak that way in his fundraising trips to churches in the USA. This congregation combines the influences of the late Moishe Ben Meir, (a graduate of Moody Bible Institute who effectively rejected some of the writings of Paul) and influences from the Church of Christ, a sect holding to baptismal regeneration in a form of sacramentalism usually known as "Campbellite".

Among those quoted as rejecting the deity of Yeshua are Uri Markus of the Nehemiah Trust, which helps needy Israeli believers. While the aim of Nehemiah Fund is itself noble, Moriel sadly and regrettably cannot any longer sanction the support of any ministry under the direction of one no longer upholding the fundamental biblical truth of the deity of Yeshua.

Others quoted as rejecting the deity of Yeshua are Joseph Shulam, Hannah Weiss and Dodo Tel Tsur (Mr Shulam was quoted as saying "those believing Jesus is God have lost their search for faith"). Hanna Weiss and Joseph Shulam claim that their views were misconstrued and misreported out of context and that they do not reject the deity of the Lord, but merely do not express it in accordance with the terminology of the Councils or Creeds of the Gentile Church. There is nothing in Scripture mandating that one must accept the creeds of the church or define biblical truths in language and terms alien to the New Testament itself and to the original First Century Jewish Church. If Mr Shulam and Hanna Weiss do indeed uphold the deity of Yeshua, but simply reject hellenistic explanations of it, Mr Shulam and Hanna Weiss stand vindicated and publications misrepresenting their beliefs should apologetically retract these damaging misquotations and contextual distortions.

Others such as Mr Markus unfortunately defended and reiterate their rejection of the Lord's deity. It is clear however that while most Israeli Messianic Jews believe in the deity of Yeshua , there does exist a neo-Ebionite minority who do not.

Even more bizarre has been judaized Gentiles such as Joseph B. Good rejecting the trinity. Peter Michas (whose nonsense was dismissed by eminent apologeticist Dr Ron Rhodes) not only denies the eternal person-hood of Jesus within the Triune Godhead, but has concocted outlandish teachings such as Jesus and the two thieves being nailed to a tree growing out of the ground, and the Garden of Eden not being in Mesopotamia as Genesis says, but in Jerusalem apparently borrowed from a weird Cabalistic oddity in mystical Judaism.

Predictably, the most extreme elements of the Messianic Movement have been among my fellow Charismatics and Pentecostals. Dan Juster, leader of the Union of Messianic Jewish Congregations (UMJC) sadly endorsed the ecumenical Promise Keepers fad and has himself become the victim of hyper charismatic chicanery of the cruelest kind following the tragic death of his son in a terrible fire. The young boy's remains were kept on artificial life support as Mr Juster was receiving phone calls on his mobile telephone telling him that God was going to raise the boy from the dead. After the life support was shut down he was urged not to bury the corpse. Indeed God will raise his son on the Last Day and indeed God could have raised him at this death if God so willed, but it was not God's purpose. What Brother Juster mistook to be prophetic words from the Lord was the mere clairvoyance of hyper charismatic false prophets and deceivers who played on the emotional vulnerability of a bereaved family. Once leaders of a movement have no discernment, there is little prospect for the movement attaining the better purposes of God. We have been warning for some time that if Cardinal Jean Marie Lustigere of Paris (an ethnic Jew) becomes a future pope, hyper messianic extremists will rejoice that the individual in that anti-christ papal office is "a Jewish believer".

Conclusion

It is absolutely amazing to see the same Ebionite heresy with which Satan attempted to destroy the first Messianic Movement in the early centuries of the church making a come back today as God once again turns His grace back towards His ancient people Israel.

It is also amazing to see the same nomianism and legalism with which Satan tried to use hyper messianic extremists in Galatia to

316

subvert the gospel in the first century Church now resurfacing to subvert it in the twenty first century Church. Once the domain of Seventh Day Adventists, this unworkable striving to live under two covenants has now permeated most of the charismatic branch of the Messianic Movement. While representing only a minority of Jewish believers, these highly vocal neo Galatians have appointed themselves spokesmen for all Jewish believers and in peddling their nonsense have forgotten the message of Romans 3:17-23.

It is furthermore amazing to see Satan raising up the same anti-messianic arrogance warned against in Romans 11:18 in the early church, appearing again today. It is additionally amazing to see the vitriolic anti Semitic rhetoric masquerading as Christian doctrine which abounded in the early church in the malicious pulpit propaganda of John Chrysostom (and reiterated through the centuries by popes and Luther alike) now coming from the mouths of Satan's latter day messengers the Ruckmanites.

Last of all, just as Jewish believers like Paul withstood this confusion of the deception of Messianic extremism on one hand and Christian anti Semitism and Replacementism on the other in the Early Church, the Lord has once more raised up Jewish believers from Arnold Fruchtenbaum to Stan Telchin to Louis Goldberg - providing a scriptural and balanced response to these twin errors Satan has retrieved from early church history and stirred up again. Of one thing we may rest assure - God did not allow Satan to succeed back then in Ancient Galatia and the same God will not allow him to succeed now!